Confederate Hospitals on the Move

CONFEDERATE HOSPITALS ON THE MOVE

SAMUEL H. STOUT AND THE ARMY OF TENNESSEE

by

GLENNA R. SCHROEDER-LEIN

University of South Carolina Press

to

W. A. and Ruth Schroeder

and

Ronald D. Rietveld

CONTENTS

ILLUSTRATIONS

PHOTOGRAPHS
Following page 110

Samuel H. Stout
Andrew Jackson Foard
Samuel P. Moore
Dudley D. Saunders
The Crutchfield House hotel, Chattanooga
The Academy Hospital, Chattanooga
Edward A. Flewellen
Samuel M. Bemiss
Kate Cumming
Ferdinand E. Daniel
Samuel H. Stout at 80 souvenir

MAPS

ACKNOWLEDGMENTS

This book could not have been written without the help of a great many persons: the hoarding habits of the late Samuel H. Stout and his daughters, Margaret J. Stout and Katherine Stout Moore, preserved the documents; Lester N. Fitzhugh willingly shared his Stout materials with a perfect stranger; various reference librarians and archivists provided aid at Emory University, the Tennessee State Library and Archives, the Museum of the Confederacy, the National Archives, and the Eugene C. Barker Texas History Center (especially Ralph L. Elder); the interlibrary loan staff at the University of Georgia library procured obscure sources; Kay Lovingood provided companionship; David Pelletier extended hospitality; Richard G. Sellers and Darleen Powars answered medical questions; Rob Scott shared his computer skills; Paul H. Bergeron, John C. Inscoe, and W. A. Schroeder made helpful suggestions; James S. Burns prepared the maps; Emory M. Thomas advised and aided in procuring documents; F. N. Boney spoke encouraging words; Jean E. Friedman, Lester Stephens, and William McFeely served on my dissertation committee; Warren Slesinger made my interactions with the University of South Carolina Press pleasant; W. A. and Ruth Schroeder provided financial aid, encouragement, and a computer; Carroll Hart, Jan Powell, Rhonda Schroeder, and various Bible study members also encouraged; and Lonnie Lein cheerfully walked into the middle of all of this and helped me to survive. This book is dedicated to my parents, and to Ronald D. Rietveld who by his example as a historian, teacher, and friend encouraged me to become a historian.

11

EDITORIAL METHODS
AND ABBREVIATIONS

All abbreviations in quotations were abbreviated in the original. Only two types of editorial changes have been made silently as necessary. Some of the doctors and their clerks used commas indiscriminately for periods as well as commas. Periods have been substituted where appropriate. In quotations from the *Southern Practitioner* obvious typographical errors have been corrected to avoid unnecessary distraction.

All works that appear in the bibliography have been short titled in the footnotes with the exception of a few potentially confusing articles and obituaries from the *Southern Practitioner* and the *Confederate Veteran*.

ABBREVIATIONS USED

A&IGO	Adjutant and Inspector General's Office
Atlanta Hist. Soc.	Atlanta Historical Society, Atlanta, Georgia, Stout Papers
Duke	William R. Perkins Library, Duke University, Durham, North Carolina, Stout Papers
Emory	Special Collections, Robert W. Woodruff Library, Emory University, Atlanta, Georgia, Stout Papers unless otherwise noted
Ga. Hist. Soc.	Georgia Historical Society, Savannah, Georgia, Stout Papers
Mus. Confed.	Eleanor S. Brockenbrough Library, Museum of the Confederacy, Richmond, Virginia, Stout Papers

N A National Archives, Washington, D.C., Record Group 109, War Department Collection of Confederate Records unless otherwise noted

NCAB *National Cyclopedia of American Biography*

OR *The War of the Rebellion: A Compilation of the Official Records of the Union and Confederate Armies*

SHC-UNC Southern Historical Collection, University of North Carolina, Chapel Hill, North Carolina, Stout microfilm

So. Pract. *Southern Practitioner*

TSLA Tennessee State Library and Archives, Nashville, Tennessee, Stout Papers

Tulane Howard-Tilton Memorial Library, Tulane University, New Orleans, Louisiana, Joseph Jones Papers

UTX Eugene C. Barker Texas History Center, University of Texas, Austin, Texas, Stout Papers

Va. Hist. Soc. Virginia Historical Society, Richmond, Virginia, Stout Papers

Confederate Hospitals on the Move

PROLOGUE:

WAGING A BATTLE
BEHIND THE LINES

Shortly after Mrs. Katherine Stout Moore died at the age of eighty-nine in the Terrell State Hospital for the Insane (Texas) in 1955, Lester Fitzhugh, a lawyer and former pupil of "Miss Katie," decided to call on Herman Moore, husband of the deceased. Based on information he had received from Miss Katie herself, Fitzhugh, an avid student of the Civil War, had high hopes as he gained permission from Moore to investigate his wife's papers. Scattered around among a number of trunks in the small house in Lancaster, Texas, was the wreckage of one of the largest collections of Confederate medical records to survive the Civil War.[1]

Miss Katie's father, Samuel Hollingsworth Stout, was a gentleman farmer and medical doctor with a fairly lucrative practice near Pulaski, Tennessee, in the 1850s. When the Civil War broke out, Stout promptly joined the Confederates as surgeon for the Third Tennessee Regiment. In November 1861 Stout assumed charge of the Gordon Hospital in Nashville, where he remained until that city fell in February 1862. Stout next commanded two small hospitals in Chattanooga. In this capacity, Stout's administrative capability so impressed General Braxton Bragg, commander of the Army of Tennessee, that Bragg placed Stout in charge of all the Army of Tennessee hospitals in the Chattanooga area, a post with increasing responsibilities as a result of army movements. In mid-1863, Stout became medical director of hospitals for the Army of Tennessee, an enormously responsible position which he held until the end of the war. He assigned doctors, stewards, and matrons to hospitals, mediated their quarrels, and disciplined or transferred them as necessary. Stout selected hospital sites, designed structures, prodded medical purveyors, commissaries, and quartermasters who were often slow to supply hospitals, oversaw general obedience to Richmond's orders, and made

---

1. Lester N. Fitzhugh to Seale Johnson, August 28, 1955, Emory, box 3, folder 6. Unidentified newspaper clipping attached to letter from Katherine Stout Moore to W. E. Thomas, March 30, 1949, Emory, Stout microfilm.

sure that his subordinates completed paperwork properly. Overseeing these and many other facets of administration for more than fifty hospitals was no mean feat, especially when military movements forced hospital movements as well. As a result of these activities, many of his fellow medical officers considered Stout a gifted administrator and innovator.

During his hospital service Stout, of necessity and by design, accumulated many hospital records. Stout later claimed that he "was, from the very beginning of the war, profoundly impressed with a conviction that the Confederate war would be a long and bloody one, replete with many events and facts unique and stupendous in importance to humanity. Hence, I resolved to preserve duplicates of all my official papers," including reports and correspondence that most other medical officers disposed of when their initial purpose had been served.[2] At the close of the war, when Stout fled Columbus, Georgia, before Union General James Wilson's raiders, he boxed the papers, addressed them to himself in Tennessee, and left them on a railroad siding as he had no way to transport the records. He assumed that they would be lost. Several months later, much to Stout's surprise, he heard that the records were in a freight depot in Macon, Georgia. Stout claimed them and had them shipped to Pulaski, Tennessee—all 1,500 pounds of them.[3]

As Stout later described this massive collection, it consisted of:

> the original morning, weekly, and monthly reports of sick and wounded in hospital, from which I consolidated my reports to the Surgeon General, and to the General Commanding the Army of Tennessee; copies of all the special and general orders sent to me from the Head-Quarters of the Army of Tenn., and from the War Department, and my own circulars and reports of medical officers, hospital stewards, detailed men and matrons, and a vast amount of official and confidential private correspondence relating to the medical service of the department.
>
> In addition to the above, I also have documents relating to the construction and location of hospitals and the transportation of the sick and wounded, which are of great value and

---

2. Stout, "Some Facts," pt. 20, 25 (June 1903): 353; see also Stout, "Reminiscences," 228.
3. Ibid. Stout mentions the size of his collection in Stout to Officers and Members of Tennessee Historical Society, January 11, 1895, and Stout to Joseph Jones, July 24, 1890, both in TSLA, box 1, folder 12.

when published will prove to be of interest to those engaged in military medical service.

Stout's description does not even do justice to the tremendous variety of material found in the papers: lists of medical officers on duty, steward's lists of hospital property on hand and lost, reports of examining boards for furloughing soldiers, examination papers of doctors desiring promotion, hospital registers of patients and their diets or prescriptions, and numerous reports.[4]

With the arrival of these materials, Stout assumed a 1,500-pound burden which he bore for the rest of his life and bequeathed to his two daughters. At the time, however, Stout was pleased to have his papers and made plans for their use. But Stout had other problems and commitments after the war which prevented the writing he wished to do. By the late 1860s Stout had lost his property in Tennessee and moved to Atlanta where he practiced medicine and tried to raise enough money to support his wife and five children, the youngest of whom was born in 1866. Apparently never able to do more than scrape by, perhaps because his patients were also impoverished, Stout had neither time to write nor money to publish anything based on his war records.

A move to Cisco, Texas, a frontier railroad town, in 1882 failed to bring Stout the time and money required for his project. But he did not give up hope for he still intended to write a three-volume history of the Army of Tennessee medical department. Nevertheless, it was not until after he retired from active medical practice around 1900 that Stout was able to undertake a major writing project. Even then he did not write his proposed three volumes, but rather a number of articles for the *Southern Practitioner,* a monthly medical journal edited and published in Nashville, which, in 1900, had begun printing recollections of Confederate medical officers. By the time of his death in September 1903 Stout had completed only twenty-three installments, in the process using very few of the papers in his huge collection.[5]

After Stout's death his two daughters, Margaret (Maggie) and Katherine (Katie), both unmarried schoolteachers, inherited the papers. At

---

4. Stout to Jones, July 24, 1890, ibid. The wide variety of Stout's papers is especially evident in the Stout Collection at UTX, which, with more than twenty-two feet of materials probably has about two-thirds of the papers Stout collected. Stout also described his sixty-eight bundles of material in "Some Facts," pt. 20, 25 (June 1903): 350–52.

5. For a more detailed account of Stout's postwar career see chap. 7.

first they tried to persuade several of their father's former Civil War medical colleagues to undertake the project of editing and publishing the documents, but all declined the daunting task. In 1916 the sisters sold about two-thirds of the collection to the University of Texas at Austin, having carefully weeded the papers, removing much of the more personal or potentially controversial correspondence. Miss Katie began to sell these letters piecemeal to a variety of collectors after her sister died in 1942. Thus by the time Miss Katie herself died in 1955 only fragments of the once enormous collection remained in her possession.

Over the course of the 1950s, and occasionally later, the collectors donated or sold their Stout papers to various libraries across the eastern United States. Thus, in addition to the material at the University of Texas, Stout manuscripts can be found at Emory University in Atlanta, the Tennessee State Library and Archives, the Museum of the Confederacy in Richmond, Duke University, the Southern Historical Collection at the University of North Carolina at Chapel Hill, and several other repositories.[6] It seems to be because of the fragmentation of his collection that Stout has remained virtually unknown and information on the Army of Tennessee hospitals is limited. While some of his papers have been used in several studies, little attention has been paid to the man himself.[7]

Naturally the question then arises, why should one study Samuel Hollingsworth Stout? Clearly, his importance to the Civil War does not lie in the performance of heroics on the battlefield, the usual criterion for Civil War renown, for Stout was hardly ever on a battlefield. In fact, he said that he was within bullet range only twice.[8] Lack of battlefield experience does not mean that Stout was not fighting, however. In fact, he was waging a war behind the lines—a war where the enemies were disease, painful wounds, lack of sanitation, inadequate facilities, deficient supplies, and wretched transportation. Victory over these foes meant sick and wounded soldiers restored to health and service in the

---

6. See appendix A for a description of the dispersion and present whereabouts of Stout's papers.

7. Horace H. Cunningham, for example, used some Stout material in *Doctors in Gray*, which is still the standard source on the Confederate medical corps. More recently, Clarence L. Mohr used the Stout papers for information on the use of slaves in Georgia hospitals in *On the Threshold of Freedom*. The only known study of Stout specifically is a two-part article that resulted from an Emory University seminar paper. Julia Emmons, "The Medical Career of Samuel H. Stout."

8. Stout, "Some Facts," pt. 18, 25 (April 1903): 219.

army. Like any battlefield general seeking a conquest, Stout had to deploy his troops—from doctors to laundresses—to the best advantage in combat. Despite his valiant efforts some battles were lost. Some soldiers died, became permanently incapacitated, or deserted from the hospital. But, obviously, many hospital battles were won, since soldiers returned to the ranks to keep the Army of Tennessee fighting. Unquestionably, much credit for these victories belongs to Stout who, with his superior administrative skills, was the right man in the right place.

Stout had to perform a very complex administrative task as supervisor and coordinator for the hospitals of the Army of Tennessee during a crucial period in their existence. It took a great deal of skill to manage the personnel affairs of several hundred doctors and their several thousand subordinates; to coordinate the requirements of the medical department with the resources of their often recalcitrant suppliers; to select, supervise, and sometimes design more than fifty hospital sites; and to keep the system functioning even while the Confederacy collapsed. As a competent administrator (a rarity in the Confederacy) and organizer of hospitals, Stout, who like most nineteenth-century physicians had had no previous experience with hospital administration, made an important contribution to the war effort.

Stout's administrative competence takes on added significance because he occupied a unique position. The Union army did not have medical directors of hospitals. Union army medical directors only supervised the field hospitals and regimental surgeons of their particular army. Surgeons in charge of hospitals behind the lines were subject to the surgeon general, the local commanding general, and perhaps a post surgeon, but no individual coordinated the hospitals at the various posts.[9] Thus, the Confederate decision to establish the position of medical director of hospitals in 1863 was a departure from the federal army system on which the Confederates had based their organization. Stout was not the only medical director, of course. In fact, the Confederates had eight such positions. However, most of the military districts had few hospitals. In September/October 1864, the three largest districts were North Carolina with twenty-one hospitals, Virginia with thirty-nine, and Georgia/Alabama, Stout's district, with more than sixty facilities.[10] In July 1864, the Virginia hospitals dealt with an aggregate of 36,678

9. Adams, *Doctors in Blue*, 159.
10. Cunningham, *Doctors in Gray*, 285–90.

patients, while Stout's hospitals saw 49,091 sick and wounded men and were compelled, in many cases, to move their facilities out of the path of Gen. William T. Sherman's Union forces.[11] Clearly Stout was supervising a mammoth undertaking.

What makes Stout even more important is the fact that he kept his records. Thanks to this penchant, the historian has the opportunity to observe the work of Stout and his subordinates in some detail as they strove to make the hospital system work amid the realities of supply, transportation, and facility shortages, troop movements, and the collapse of the Confederacy. Since the papers were Stout's, it is therefore appropriate to focus on him as the lens through which to examine the hospitals in the region.

Yet another reason to study Stout's career is his involvement with the western theater of the war. Much more attention has always been paid to the eastern theater—to the activities of Robert E. Lee, and the battle of Gettysburg, for example—than to any events in the west. While Thomas L. Connelly, James Lee McDonough, and Richard McMurry have made attempts to remedy that neglect from the military standpoint, and Larry J. Daniel has examined the life of the ordinary Army of Tennessee soldiers, much remains to be done on other aspects of the war.[12] Stout's papers provide the opportunity to investigate the western hospitals, which are less well known than such eastern institutions as Richmond's enormous Chimborazo. The western hospitals, with their frequent movements, had some problems not experienced by their eastern counterparts. While differing in this important regard, the western hospitals were nonetheless representative of military medicine of the period in general and Confederate medicine in particular. The point of this study, then, is not to rewrite or replace Horace H. Cunningham's overview of Confederate medicine, *Doctors in Gray*, but to focus sharply on one section of the Confederate medical system.

Since Stout's superb management of facilities for healing the sick and wounded soldiers of the Army of Tennessee is the key to his importance

---

11. Ibid., 277–78. "General Summary of the Hospitals of the Army of Tennessee for the month ending July 30/64," UTX, box 2G379.

12. Connelly, *Army of the Heartland*, and *Autumn of Glory*. McDonough, *Chattanooga—A Death Grip on the Confederacy*, *Stones River—Bloody Winter in Tennessee*, and others. McMurry's *Two Great Rebel Armies* compares the experiences of the Army of Tennessee and the Army of Northern Virginia. Daniel, *Soldiering in the Army of Tennessee*.

during the Civil War, each chapter of this book focuses on the development and display of these necessary administrative skills. Chapter 1 acquaints the reader with Stout's youth and early manhood, which laid the foundation for his Civil War administration. In chapter 2 Stout begins his army career, developing and displaying his skills, and earning commendation. Two subjects are treated in chapter 3: how Stout finally achieves his position as medical director of hospitals for the Army of Tennessee and how Stout and his hospitals fit into the overall Confederate medical system. Chapter 4 discusses Stout's handling of personnel responsibilities while chapter 5 examines his administration of hospital sites with the manifold problems of site selection and maintenance. Chapter 6 explores Stout's attempt to cope with the administrative problems caused by the collapse of the Confederacy, especially the need to move hospitals frequently. Finally, chapter 7 shows how Stout, deprived of his administrative position by Confederate defeat, struggled to find a fulfilling niche for himself in the postwar world.

Even before the Civil War ended, Stout realized the importance of his wartime contributions, as well as those of his subordinates. He spent the remaining thirty-eight years of his life seeking to relieve the physical and emotional burden of the 1,500 pounds of hospital records he retained by telling the story of the Army of Tennessee hospital department and the battles it waged behind the lines. Tragically, circumstances, usually pecuniary, prevented Stout from ever presenting more than the most sketchy account of his experiences. To the extent to which a historian can write it, more than 125 years after the close of the conflict, this is the story Stout wanted to tell.

CHAPTER 1

ONE OF THE BEST MEDICAL
EDUCATIONS AVAILABLE

A brief biography of Samuel Hollingsworth Stout, published in the *Southern Practitioner* in 1902, mentions that Stout's children could trace their ancestors in America through two centuries. Richard Stout, son of John Stout of Nottinghamshire, England, was apparently the family member who immigrated to the colonies some time before he married Penelope Van Princes of New Amsterdam in 1648. Jonathan Stout, a minister and one of their ten children, was a founder of Hopewell, New Jersey. Jonathan's son Samuel (born 1709), great-great grandfather of the Civil War doctor, seems to have been the first of a long line of Samuels in the family, including his own only son (1732–1803) who married Ann Van Dyke about 1753. Abraham Stout (1754–1821), the oldest of Samuel and Ann's twelve children, enlisted in the Continental army from New Jersey in February 1776. Promoted several times, from his first rank as sergeant to his final rank as captain, Abraham spent two-and-a-half years as a prisoner of war, but was released in time to take part in the Virginia campaign of 1781 and be present at the surrender of Cornwallis. His descendants were proud that he had been an original member of the Society of the Cincinnati, the elite organization of Revolutionary War officers.[1]

After the Revolution, Abraham Stout married, moved to Pennsylvania, and had three sons. The oldest, born April 13, 1786, was named Samuel for Abraham's father, and given his grandmother's maiden name, Van Dyke, as a middle name. Although he was born in Pennsylvania, Samuel Van Dyke Stout may have lived in Kentucky before he moved to Nashville, Tennessee, about 1811. S. V. D. Stout established a carriage

---

1. "Samuel Hollingsworth Stout, A.M., M.D., LL.D.," 212. Genealogical information on Stout's family, some of it assembled by Stout himself, can be found in TSLA, box 2, folder 11. Abraham Stout's Revolutionary War record was listed by William Stryker, adjutant general, state of New Jersey, May 9, 1896, ibid., and in Ira A. Stout to Samuel H. Stout, November 25, 1894, ibid., box 1, folder 10.

factory on Clark Street and, about 1812, built a large house on the corner of the public square facing First Avenue. On October 12, 1813, at the home of Wilkins Tannehill, brother of the bride, twenty-seven-year-old S. V. D. Stout married Catherine Tannehill.[2]

Information on the ancestry of Catherine Tannehill Stout is much less complete than that available for her husband and goes back only two generations, to her grandfather John Wilkins. John Wilkins had at least three children: William, a judge and secretary of war under John Tyler; a daughter who married a man named John Hollingsworth; and a daughter Margaret, who married Josiah Tannehill, a veteran of the Continental army during the Revolution. Josiah acquired a good deal of land through speculation including, family tradition says, the original site of Detroit, Michigan. Little is known of his activities because Josiah's papers were burned in a fire in Kentucky. He evidently died in Baton Rouge, Louisiana, leaving his wife and two children, Catherine and Wilkins, dependent on Margaret's wealthy siblings, who apparently had little love for Josiah and made no effort to save his land acquisitions.[3]

Samuel Hollingsworth Stout was born to Samuel Van Dyke and Catherine Tannehill Stout in the large family home in Nashville on Sunday, March 3, 1822. The fourth son and fifth child of the couple, he was named for his father and his maternal great uncle, John Hollingsworth.[4] As Stout did not often refer to his childhood in his later writings, very little is known about this period of his life.[5] The Stout family was

---

2. 1880 Census, Georgia, Cobb County, Roswell, roll 9, p. 128, lists S. H. Stout's parents as born in Pennsylvania. The several sources do not clearly reveal exactly when or under what circumstances Samuel Van Dyke Stout came to Nashville. The biographical sketch of Samuel H. Stout in Evans, ed., *Confederate Military History* 11: 638, notes that Stout's parents moved to Nashville from Lexington, Kentucky, "in the first decade of the nineteenth century." Katherine Tannehill Stout ("Miss Katie"), in a sketch of "Samuel Van Dyke Stout," her grandfather, said that he came to Nashville as a boy, beginning work as an apprentice in the carriage factory and eventually owning it. TSLA, box 2, folder 13. The other information is found in TSLA, box 2, folder 11.

3. Genealogical fragment, TSLA, box 2, folder 9, and other material in folder 11.

4. There were seven Stout children in all: Margaret Jane (1815–85), Ira Abraham (1817–99), Josiah Wilkins (born 1818), Charles Crague or Craig (1820–83), Samuel Hollingsworth (1822–1903), Catherine Tannehill (1823–1900), and Augustine Francis (1825–29). TSLA, box 2, folder 11.

5. This dearth of information is probably the result of the later weeding activities of Stout's daughters Maggie and Katie. There is hardly any family correspondence in the Stout papers, but what remains suggests that Stout did correspond fairly frequently with family members, including sisters, cousins, and nephews. For example, a series of

fortunate that all the children survived to adulthood but the youngest child, Augustine Francis, who died when he was only three-and-a-half years of age. Thus, young Samuel had plenty of siblings with whom to play. He apparently was known in his Samuel-ridden family as "Holl," an abbreviation of his middle name. The family attended the Presbyterian church in Nashville, and many years later Stout recalled that during one morning service in 1829 or 1830 he sat in the pew in front of Davy Crockett who was on his way to Congress in Washington. With admiration and curiosity, the boy turned to stare at his hero until Crockett nodded and smiled. Stout also later recalled medical events of his childhood and youth—cholera epidemics in Nashville in 1833 and 1835. Whether these epidemics influenced his decision to become a doctor, he never said.[6]

The period of Stout's childhood and youth was also a time of increasing success in the carriage business, as well as prosperity and political influence for his father, S. V. D. Stout. The senior Stout was at one time the city jail commissioner, and served on the Nashville city council for sixteen of the years beginning in 1824 and ending with his death in 1850. In addition, he was mayor of the city in 1841. According to family tradition, Stout and his carriage works made the carriage in which Andrew Jackson rode to Washington, D.C., for his inauguration. Young Samuel, then, grew up in a household of reasonable means where the father could provide his sons with a good education.[7]

Samuel H. Stout received his college preparatory training at Moses Stevens's classical and mathematical seminary in Nashville. He entered the University of Nashville at the age of thirteen, graduating with an

letters to Stout from his nephew Thomas Hill, dated October 15, 1863, February 11, 1864, and April 29, 1864, can be found in TSLA, box 1, folder 6.

6. TSLA, box 2, folder 11. Lt. H. D. Wheatly to "Cousin Holl," June 24, 1864, Emory, box 2, folder 2; S. V. D. [Samuel Van Dyke] Hill to "Uncle Holl," January 16, 1864, Emory, box 2, folder 2; S. H. Stout, "David Crockett," chap. 3, UTX, box 2G380. Stout, "Clinical Lectures: Asiatic Cholera," 89.

7. TSLA, box 2, folders 11 and 13. "Katherine T. Stout," entry in Barns, *Texas Writers of Today*, 430–31. S. V. D. Stout apparently did not have much education himself. The letter he wrote to his son Samuel on April 28, 1850 is nearly illegible and the spelling is terrible. TSLA, box 1, folder 10. The 1850 census, taken just a couple weeks after S. V. D. Stout's death on August 8, shows him as the owner of thirteen slaves and his wife, Catherine, as the head of the household with $25,000 worth of real estate. 1850 Census, Population Schedules: Tennessee, Davidson County, roll 875, p. 100; Slave Schedules: roll 902, p. 633; Clipping from unidentified newspaper, August 9, 1850, TSLA, box 1, folder 17.

A.B. degree in 1839 and receiving an A.M. degree in 1842. Philip Lindsley, president of the university from 1824 to 1850, strove to make it an excellent institution, equal to a European university. Actually, however, the institution probably was more equivalent to a modern high school than to a college. Student enrollment peaked at 188 in 1836, declining to 80 in the year of Stout's graduation. During his college career Stout gave several public speeches, preserving the texts in a manuscript book. In April 1839 he spoke on the subject of conflicts of opinion in the past, citing Mohammed and the Muslims, the Crusaders, and Martin Luther as examples. He concluded that the way to preserve the Union was to avoid conflicts of opinion, especially avoiding party spirit, and voting out any office holder who would oppose a good idea simply because it was proposed by someone of the opposite party.[8]

Stout apparently pleased his teachers with his oratorical skills because he delivered a "Speech on the Natural Sciences" at the commencement exercises of the University of Nashville, held in the Presbyterian Church on October 2, 1839. The purpose of studying the natural sciences, Stout claimed, was "the investigation of the rules by which the universe is & has been governed from its creation." In keeping with the oratorical style of the period, Stout paid flowery tribute to Copernicus, Galileo, Newton, and Franklin, and often lapsed into a few lines of poetry. He also lauded Tennessee because it was one of the first states to have a state geologist.[9]

Upon Stout's graduation from the university, Professor Moses Stevens offered Stout a teaching position at the seminary. During the two years he held this post, Stout also began to study medicine with his brother

---

8. Stout's master of arts degree was probably honorary. Typically, an alumnus was eligible for the degree from his college if he had maintained good behavior for three years after graduation and if he paid a small fee. Coulter, *College Life in the Old South*, 143; "Samuel Hollingsworth Stout, A.M., M.D., LL.D.," 210; Davenport, *Cultural Life in Nashville*, 2–5, 10–12; Crew, *History of Nashville*, 392. The speech was delivered April 3, 1839, in the Episcopal Church, Nashville. "Speech," TSLA, box 2, folder 11.

9. "Speech on the Natural Sciences," TSLA, box 2, folder 11. The book also contains "Thoughts on Man," dated December 21, 1839, but there is no indication that he actually delivered it as a speech. Stout's ideas seem to be typical of the Baconian philosophy of the period as discussed in Daniels, *American Science in the Age of Jackson*, chap. 3 especially. Gerard Troost (1776–1850), professor of geology, mineralogy, chemistry, and natural history at the University of Nashville, was Tennessee's first state geologist, serving from 1831 to 1850. Wilson, Jr., *State Geological Surveys and State Geologists of Tennessee*, 2, 4. Stout was one of nineteen graduates. Crew, *History of Nashville*, 392.

Josiah, a graduate of the Medical Department of the University of Pennsylvania in 1840, and Josiah's partner, R. C. K. Martin.[10]

Even the best medical training of the 1840s was inadequate according to late twentieth-century standards. The first medical school in America had opened with two instructors at the University of Pennsylvania in 1765. By the early 1800s several dozen medical schools, some associated with universities and others privately conducted, competed for students and financial remuneration. Students paid fees of fifteen to twenty dollars per course directly to the faculty member involved. A popular medical lecturer could make a good deal of money in this way, but an instructor's popularity did not necessarily mean that his students left the class as qualified medical practitioners. In fact, the competition for students tended to lower standards both for admission and graduation. Before the 1820s the medical school curriculum became more or less standardized at seven courses: theory and practice of physic (medicine), chemistry, surgery, anatomy, materia medica (pharmacy), institutes of medicine (physiology), and obstetrics and diseases of women and children. This standard curriculum did not change much until the 1870s. By the 1840s, the better medical schools, like the University of Pennsylvania, had a professor for each subject, while some of the smaller schools required professors to teach several subjects or omitted some of them.[11]

To enter a medical school in the 1840s, a prospective student needed to be a white male who could read and write. He did not need to know Greek and Latin, nor did he need to have a college degree, although certainly many young men, like Stout, did have a good classical background. One feature of the curriculum at the University of Pennsylvania that made it a better school than most was a longer term of instruction. Beginning in 1836 the term lasted five months—from mid-October to mid-March. From 1847 to 1853 the school experimented with a five-and-a-half-month term but dropped it when competing schools did not lengthen their terms as well. During each term the student studied all seven subjects. To graduate, he had to attend for two terms (the second

---

10. "Samuel Hollingsworth Stout, A.M., M.D., LL.D.," 210; University of Pennsylvania Alumni Catalogue questionnaire, filled out by Katherine Tannehill Stout, July 1918, University of Pennsylvania Archives, Philadelphia, Pennsylvania. Martin, a graduate of the University of Pennsylvania, began to practice medicine in 1833 and continued to do so until his death in 1870. Crew, History of Nashville, 529.

11. Corner, Two Centuries, 58–60, 65, 87–88; Breeden, Joseph Jones, 23.

term was exactly the same as the first), study for three years as an apprentice to a reputable doctor, and write a thesis.[12]

Before the organization of medical schools, doctors had learned medicine through apprenticeships. Even in the mid-nineteenth century many practitioners, especially rural ones, never attended medical schools. A "cursory survey" of 201 physicians conducted in East Tennessee in 1850 revealed that thirty-five had medical degrees, forty-two had attended medical courses to some extent, ninety-five were orthodox or regular physicians who had no academic training, and twenty-nine were Thomsonians or homeopaths (members of the several groups who propounded gentler or more natural remedies in opposition to the "heroic" prescriptions of purging, bloodletting, and massive doses of drugs containing mercury and arsenic often advocated by the orthodox "regular" physicians). A medical degree did not necessarily make one a better doctor as much depended on the quality of the mentor or "preceptor." Stout later waxed philosophical about midcentury medical training when he wrote a brief biography of a nondegreed doctor who had developed a radical, but apparently effective, treatment for smallpox. "A year and a half or two years of study and instruction under such [good] private preceptors . . . ," Stout said, "was worth more to the students than attending a full course of lectures in a crowded medical school."[13] The preceptor provided

---

12. Corner, *Two Centuries*, 95, 98, 100; Duffy, *The Healers*, 171–72, 175; Rothstein, *American Medical Schools*, 48–63; Breeden, *Joseph Jones*, 23. Stout later reminisced that during his second term at the University of Pennsylvania (1847–48) there were about one thousand medical students there and at the Jefferson Medical School, its same-city rival. Nearly half of these students, Stout claimed, came from the South, and most of them had a bachelor's degree or were at least well educated in classics, mathematics, natural philosophy, and chemistry. Stout, "Reminiscences," 232. Corner notes that, despite the lengthened term, 508 students enrolled in the University of Pennsylvania medical department in 1847, the largest student body to that point. Corner, *Two Centuries*, 100.

13. Members of the medical sects were especially prevalent in rural areas. Stout was, however, by training and practice, a "regular" physician and supervised "regular" physicians during the Civil War. Duffy, *The Healers*, 101, 110-19, 181. According to Duffy and John Harley Warner, by the mid-nineteenth century, at least partly due to the influence of the various medical sects, regular physicians were resorting to "heroic" remedies less often, but they nonetheless defended the heroic principle. Warner, "Power, Conflict, and Identity," 936–38. Stout, "Smallpox—The Osborn Treatment," 13. Despite Stout's generous view of nondegreed doctors, during the Civil War the Confederates required a doctor to have a medical degree before he could be commissioned in the medical service. A nondegreed doctor could still hold a position as a contract physician, however. S. P. Moore, "Confidential Instructions to

what the medical schools did not—opportunities for close observation and experience. Even at the University of Pennsylvania students were not required to do any dissection. From a great distance away in the lecture amphitheatre they watched their anatomy professor perform a dissection and give the explanations, but if they wanted any practical experience they had to attend extra courses at the Philadelphia School of Anatomy, or other smaller private schools, during the April–November interim when the medical school was not in session. Opportunities for clinical experience were also extremely limited, making the role of the preceptor crucial.[14]

Stout attended his first term in 1842–43, after several years of at least intermittent practice with his brother and Dr. Martin. He studied "Theory and Practice of Medicine and Clinical Practice" with Dr. Nathaniel Chapman, chemistry with Professor Robert Hare, and anatomy with Dr. William Edmonds Horner. Chapman had been at the University of Pennsylvania for years, initially as professor of materia medica, a subject he treated in a long-enduring book. By the time Stout studied with him, Chapman had been teaching the theory and practice of medicine for more than twenty years. Although he had a rather odd, and sometimes outdated, combination of medical ideas that came from various "systems" of medicine propounded in the past, Chapman was talented in proposing treatments. One former student remembered Chapman as a popular and witty lecturer, once students got used to his speech impediment so that they could understand what he was saying.[15]

Although many medical doctors, including Chapman, did not think it was necessary for doctors to know chemistry, the University of Pennsylvania included the subject in its medical school curriculum. Robert Hare, who held the post, was a noted chemist but had not earned a medical degree, a situation that initially provoked other faculty members to discriminate against him until in 1818 Yale, Harvard, and Columbia each granted him an honorary degree. As with dissection during this period, so with chemistry—the instructor performed the experiments before a large lecture class. Hare, as was typical of chemistry instructors, focused on introductory and inorganic chemistry. He devoted little time

---

the Army Medical Board at Chattanooga, Tenn.," March 21, 1863, UTX, box 2G425; D. W. Yandell to Stout, August 18, 1862, Duke.

14. Corner, *Two Centuries*, 76, 92–93, 95; John Harley Warner, "Physiology," in Numbers, ed., *Education of American Physicians*, 42–43.

15. Corner, *Two Centuries*, 66–67, 92; Gross and Gross, eds., *Autobiography*, 2: 278-81.

to organic or "animal chemistry," the type most useful for a physician. While Hare was apparently a dull lecturer, his experiments never failed. He had one of the best sets of chemical equipment available at the time, purchased with his own funds, which he donated to the Smithsonian when he retired in 1847. He was succeeded by an excellent lecturer, his pupil James Blythe Rogers, whose lectures Stout would have attended during his second term (1847–48).[16]

According to George W. Corner, the University of Pennsylvania Medical School's historian, the anatomy professor, William Edmonds Horner, was the "most distinguished anatomist the country had produced." Like Chapman, Horner had been at the University of Pennsylvania for more than two decades by the time Stout enrolled in 1842. Given the great difficulties of teaching anatomy by lecture and demonstration to a class of four hundred, without modern conveniences, Horner apparently did his best to make sure the students could see and hear as well as possible. He repeated each procedure and explanation four times, once in each direction. Horner was also one of the first American physicians to use the microscope seriously.[17]

George Bacon Wood, the professor of materia medica, was one of the youngest and most popular medical school professors. Wood was extremely knowledgeable about pharmaceutical plants and coauthored a substantial reference book on the subject, which ran through fourteen editions. He had a large garden and conservatory where he grew medicinal plants to illustrate his lectures. In 1850, after Stout had graduated, Wood succeeded Chapman as professor of medicine.[18]

Three other professors taught at the medical school while Stout attended, and he had to take their courses also. Hugh Lenox Hodge taught obstetrics and diseases of women and children since faulty eyesight prevented him from performing surgery.[19] The surgery professor, William Gibson, was known for his bad temper as well as his skill in lecturing and operating. Although he performed a number of operations

16. Corner, *Two Centuries*, 54, 70, 71, and 102; Gross and Gross, *Autobiography*, 2: 297–98; James Whorton, "Chemistry," in Numbers, ed., *Education of American Physicians*, 80–81; *NCAB*, 8: 151–52.

17. Corner, *Two Centuries*, 76; Gross and Gross, *Autobiography*, 2: 275.

18. Emory, box 4, folder 13; Corner, *Two Centuries*, 84, 99, and 103; Gross and Gross, *Autobiography*, 2: 394–96.

19. Hodge devoted himself to his subject and published an influential obstetrics text in 1869. Corner, *Two Centuries*, 87, 122; *NCAB*, 10: 244.

that were unusual at the time, his most unusual feat was performing two Caesarean sections on the same woman and saving the baby both times.[20] Dr. Samuel Jackson, professor of the institutes of medicine, was a popular and interesting lecturer. However, he presented some outdated theories in the developing field of physiology.[21]

It is not known whether Stout studied at any of the private dissecting schools, but there is evidence that he attended an extra preterm course of some sort in 1847. An important part of this course was making rounds with Dr. William Wood Gerhard, one of the two doctors who ran the dispensary associated with the medical school. Gerhard had studied in Paris with Pierre C. A. Louis, a great French pathologist who was in the forefront of the development of new methods in careful observation of symptoms and results of cases. Gerhard himself determined the difference between typhoid fever and typhus, which was a major contribution at the time. Thus, Gerhard introduced Stout to the very latest theories.[22]

As Stout walked the wards with Gerhard, he noted the patient's name, age, date of admission, and symptoms, as well as Gerhard's diagnosis and prescription. While these prescriptions included drugs, they also included "cupping," a method of bloodletting from areas where the patient had pain. Concerning R. Farrel, an "intermittent fever" patient, Stout wrote, "In the hospital they have rather got out of the habit of using cups and leeches in cases like this. But they are very useful." Many of the patients had typhoid fever, typhus, or dysentery. In one case Stout reported, but did not see, a man, delirious from typhoid fever, threw

20. Corner, *Two Centuries*, 69–70; Gross and Gross, *Autobiography*, 2: 326–28. Francois Marie Prevost (1771–1842) performed two successful Caesareans on a Louisiana slave woman between 1820–25, so Gibson was not alone. Nonetheless, the operation was so unusual that only seventy-nine are known to have been performed in the United States from 1822 to 1877. Duffy, *The Healers*, 140–41.

21. Gross and Gross, *Autobiography*, 2: 371–73. While admission tickets exist for Stout's courses with Chapman, Hare, Horner, and Wood, no direct evidence survives of his contact with Hodge, Gibson, and Jackson. Emory, box 4, folder 13.

22. Gerhard is discussed in Corner, *Two Centuries*, 91–92. NCAB, 23: 340; Allen Johnson and Dumas Malone, eds., *Dictionary of American Biography* (New York: Charles Scribner's Sons, 1931, 1969), 7: 218. Stout's notebook from this course is in Emory, box 4, folder 15. It is a 3¾″ x 6¼″ hardbound notepad with no page numbers. The French clinicians stressed the importance of directly observing, rather than making assumptions about, diseases. P. C. A. Louis, who especially influenced Americans, counted the percentage of times a "particular symptom or lesion" appeared in a certain type of disease. Rosenberg, *The Care of Strangers*, 83–84.

himself out of a window twenty-five feet above the ground, with fatal results. A crucial goal in the treatment of all these patients seemed to be to keep the bowels "open." To some extent, the physicians with whom Stout studied still advocated the bleeding and purging treatments espoused by their fellow Philadelphian Benjamin Rush in the 1790s.

Stout also recorded notes on two of Pennsylvania Hospital surgeon Edward Peace's lectures about venereal disease. On September 2, 1847, Peace discussed the history of these diseases, claiming that "the leprosy of the ancients" is "the syphilis of the moderns." Using scriptural passages about Job's and David's afflictions, which he believed were syphilis, as well as quotations from Juvenal and Livy, Peace argued his case, claiming that "from the time syphilis was described leprosy has ceased to be known." Peace also gave prescriptions for "ghonoerhoea." Peace's view was not typical of the era, for most physicians understood that these venereal diseases resulted from sexual contact.[23]

Stout, then, studied, in most cases, with some of the best informed medical men of his day, men who used microscopes, performed unusual surgical operations, and were acquainted with the latest research methods. But he also absorbed some outdated theories from instructors who were unaware of, or opposed to, new knowledge. In many subjects, however, important medical discoveries, like the role of bacteria, simply had not yet been made when Stout was a student.

To graduate from medical school the student had to write a thesis on a medical topic. The subject Stout chose for his thesis is not known,

---

23. Perhaps the fact that Stout learned the importance of bloodletting but did not see it practiced frequently supports Warner's contention that regular physicians defended "heroic" principles but resorted to heroic practice less often. Warner, "Power, Conflict, and Identity," 936–38. These "heroic principles" of massive bloodletting and continual purging with mercury and other cathartics came to prominence when advocated by the influential Philadelphia physician Benjamin Rush during the yellow fever epidemic of 1793. Although often dangerous or fatal to the patient, these remedies remained the staples of medical treatment until well into the nineteenth century. Duffy, *The Healers*, 94–96. Peace does not seem to have been expressing a common opinion. A medical reference book published in Philadelphia in 1848 noted that leprosy and syphilis may exhibit similar skin symptoms, but "the most esteemed authors consider that they should form a separate class," because of the commonly known "venereal origin" of syphilis. *The Cyclopaedia of Practical Medicine*, 3: 127. While there is no consensus among modern physicians on the nature of the highly contagious leprosy of Biblical times, it was not the same as present-day leprosy (Hansen's Disease), nor was it sexually transmitted syphilis. Richard G. Sellers, M.D. to Glenna R. Schroeder, August 8, 1988. Stout's brief biography also mentions that he studied privately with Gerhard and Peace. "Samuel Hollingsworth Stout, A.M., M.D., LL.D.," 210.

but, if he was like most students at the time, he based his paper on information from lectures and textbooks, not on any original research that he performed.[24]

During his final medical term, Stout applied to take the examination for a commission as assistant surgeon in the United States Navy. To receive a commission, the applicant had to be between the ages of 21 and 28, apply to the secretary of the navy with proper testimonials of his character and qualifications, and, upon invitation from the secretary, appear before an examining board which "rigidly scrutinizes the pretensions of each candidate; taking into consideration his physical qualifications and moral habits, as well as his professional requirements." Stout received permission to appear for examination on January 25, 1848, in Philadelphia. Not only did he take this test, but he also apparently took his university examination for the medical degree early, passed it, and went home to Tennessee before the official graduation date of April 8. The exact sequence of events cannot be established, but Edward Peace wrote to Stout on March 2 that Stout had not only passed the naval exam, but had also ranked first among the more than fifty applicants. When Stout received his official commission, he declined to accept it, probably partly because the Mexican War had ended and he would no longer be able to gain much in the way of surgical experience. However, he wrote to John Y. Mason, the secretary of the navy, that he declined because he had "been compelled by domes[tic] and private considerations of [the] most sacred character,—unfo[re]seen at the time of applic[ation] for the office. . . ." Just over a week later, on April 6, 1848, Samuel Hollingsworth Stout married Martha Moore Abernathy of Giles County, Tennessee.[25]

---

24. Corner, *Two Centuries*, 95. On the alumni questionnaire that Katherine Stout filled out about her father for the University of Pennsylvania in 1918 she stated that she did not know the topic. University of Pennsylvania Archives. A copy of Stout's thesis apparently has not survived.

25. "Information for Persons Desirous of Entering the Medical Department of the Navy," printed, undated flier, UTX, box 2G380. Washington Barrow to Stout, December 16, 1847, Emory, box 1, folder 1. Daniell, *Types of Successful Men*, 309, treats Stout's early examination, presumably from information furnished by Stout himself. Stout's early departure from medical school may not have been peculiar because some schools were quite casual about attendance, allowing a student to enter late and leave early— as long as he paid. N. S. Davis, *History of Medical Education and Institutions in the United States* (Chicago: S. C. Griggs, 1851), 181, as noted in Rothstein, *American Medical Schools*, 97. Edward Peace to Stout, March 2, 1848, TSLA, box 1, folder 10;

From 1843 to 1847 Stout was not in medical school, and he engaged in other activities. Sometime between the conclusion of the medical school term in the spring and July of 1843, Stout moved to Eaton, Gibson County, Tennessee, located in the western part of the state. Whether he was teaching school or practicing with another doctor is unknown, but it seems that Stout had some intention of settling in Eaton, for in July 1843, he bought a lot in the town. Apparently, he was not satisfied there, however, and was considering alternatives such as a military medical career. In October 1843 Surgeon General Thomas Lawson wrote to Stout in Eaton, and enclosed a circular describing how to apply for appointment to the army medical staff.[26]

Stout apparently did not pursue the military medical option any further at this time, and, at some point in 1843, he accepted a position as teacher and principal at the Elkton Classical and Mathematical Seminary, a boys' school in Giles County, Tennessee. Moving to Giles County, located on the Alabama border, almost due south of Nashville, meant a return to middle Tennessee. Here Stout's second career, as an educator, once again intersected his medical training. Stout remained in Elkton until about June 1847.[27]

During his tenure at the Elkton Seminary, Stout took the opportunity to share his educational philosophy with the parents of his students. "Education . . .," he said, "in its salutary influence upon mankind is the physical, moral or religious, and intellectual training of the young in such a manner as to secure to them, when at maturity, the full enjoyment of health and vigor both of mind and body and firmly fixed moral or religious principles." To Stout, then, education was not simply developing the memory and stuffing it with facts, but also helping to develop the mind to think and reason. Stout believed that a classical education using languages was the best way to develop the mind, no matter whether the child eventually became a farmer or a professional. In fact, Stout mentioned that he thought girls ought to have the same mental discipline

---

Stout to Hon. Richard Coke, January 26, 189[3], ibid., folder 12; Stout to Hon. John Y. Mason, Secretary of the Navy, March 29, 1848, Emory, box 1, folder 1. The right edge of the page is cut off. "Samuel Hollingsworth Stout, A.M., M.D., LL.D.," 210.

26. Copy of "indenture" for sale of land, Emory, box 4, folder 8. Thomas Lawson to Stout, October 25, 1843, TSLA, box 1, folder 7.

27. "Samuel Hollingsworth Stout, A.M., M.D., LL.D.," 210. B. F. Mitchell to Stout, May 7, 1847, TSLA, box 1, folder 10.

as boys. That they were not taught languages was, Stout felt, "a relict of that ancient one which was always putting woman in station inferior to the sphere which she is justly entitled to occupy."[28]

During this period Stout met his future wife, Martha Abernathy. Martha's father, Thomas E. Abernathy, a wealthy planter near Elkton, may well have been on the school board. Martha's only surviving brother, Burwell, was just Stout's age and probably a friend. In any event, Martha, born January 19, 1830, was eight years younger than Stout and was only eighteen when they were married in April 1848.[29]

After their marriage the young couple moved to Nashville where Stout practiced with his brother Josiah and treated patients during the cholera epidemic of 1848–49. He apparently attempted to begin a periodical, the *Central Medical and Surgical Journal*, of which he proposed to be editor and proprietor. The subscription price was two dollars per year with the first number to be printed when the subscription list was large enough. Apparently Stout was unable to recruit enough subscribers, however, as he never published an issue. Stout had joined the Tennessee Medical Association in 1840 and probably during this time served as its secretary.[30]

While living in Nashville, Stout also expressed an interest in history. He was among those who met in the library rooms of the Merchants Association on May 1, 1849, to form the Tennessee Historical Society for "the collection and preservation of facts relating to the Natural, Aboriginal and Civil History of the State of Tennessee." Stout was one of the active members who did the most to help keep the young society alive. At one of the meetings during the society's first year Stout read

---

28. Stout, "An Address," TSLA, box 2, folder 11. This speech was delivered on December 24, 1845. Stout seems to have sided with the classicists in the debate over whether a classical or a "utilitarian" education was best for a child. Stout apparently had a more positive view of women and their capabilities than the average educator of his time. Even Catherine Beecher, certainly one of the foremost educators of women during the period, taught her students natural science, moral philosophy, history, mathematics, and literature, but not classical languages. Sklar, "Women, Education of: History," 559–60.

29. Obituary from unidentified Giles County paper and other materials in TSLA, box 2, folder 11. Langston, [Obituary] "Mrs. S. H. Stout," 499.

30. Daniell, *Types of Successful Men*, 310; Hamer, *The Centennial History of the Tennessee State Medical Association*, 455–56, 529–34. Josiah is listed as recording secretary 1844–46 and 1846–48. Samuel is not listed as an officer, but the association records are missing for 1847–49. Alumni questionnaire, University of Pennsylvania Archives.

a paper on "The Asiatic Cholera Epidemic in Nashville During the Present Year."[31]

Josiah Stout's departure for the California gold fields may have influenced Samuel's decision to move back to Giles County or his wealthy father-in-law might have offered financial aid.[32] In any case, on February 2, 1850, Samuel H. Stout purchased 155 acres of land, about seven-and-a-half miles south of Pulaski on both sides of the Pulaski to Elkton turnpike, from Pleasant Proffitt for $2,500. The land adjoined that of his brother-in-law Burwell Abernathy, and the Stouts apparently lived with Burwell while their house was under construction.[33]

By the time the Stouts settled on their farm, which they named Midbridge, they had begun their family. Thomas Edward, named for his maternal grandfather, was born in Nashville on January 24, 1849. Four other children, three sons and a daughter, joined the Stout household before the Civil War, although one of them, Wilkins Tannehill, died in early childhood.[34]

Stout began his career as a farmer with ten slaves.[35] During the 1850s he also practiced medicine. Generally only a few physicians, usually

31. Moore, "The Tennessee Historical Society," 197–99, 207.

32. Unsigned to "Dear Parents," April 18, 1850, from "Havannah" [Cuba], TSLA, box 1, folder 12; Josiah Stout to ?, April 19, 1850, indicates that he is on his way to Chagres, Panama, en route to San Francisco, TSLA, box 1, folder 10. Catherine [Stout Hill] to Brother [Stout], November 29, 1850, ibid.

33. Deed, February 2, 1850, registered in Giles County, Register's Office Book U, 189, TSLA, box 1, folder 18; Stout, "Some Facts," pt. 12, 24 (October 1902): 570; 1850 Census, Population Schedules: Tennessee, Giles County, roll 879, dwelling and family 933.

34. [Obituary] "Thomas Edward Stout," *Confederate Veteran* 28 (November 1920): 429. Wilkins Tannehill, the second child, was born October 2, 1851, and died August 15, 1854. *Cemetery Records of Giles County, Tennessee*, 99. Burwell Abernathy Stout is listed in the 1860 census as being six years old, and in the 1870 census as seventeen. Thus he was born about 1853 or 1854. Samuel Van Dyke Stout, named for his paternal grandfather of course, is listed as three years old in 1860, thirteen in 1870, but born in May 1855 and thus forty-five years old in 1900. He and his family were living with Thomas in Atlanta in 1900. 1860 Census, Population Schedules: Tennessee, Giles County, roll 1251, p. 132; 1870 Census, Population Schedules: Georgia, Fulton County, roll 151, p. 20. Margaret Jane, only six months old when the 1860 census was taken, was born in December 1859. 1900 Census, Population Schedules: Texas, Dallas County, Dallas, roll 1625, vol. 27, enumeration district 122, sheet 5, line 14.

35. Five of the slaves were female children ages six months to nine years who would not have provided much help initially. 1850 Census, Slave Schedules: Tennessee, Giles County, roll 903.

those trained in Europe, earned enough money from their medical practice to make a living. Most of them "either eked out a bare living from medicine or else used it as a supplement to farming or business." A surplus of physicians kept fees low, and the rural practitioner frequently had to accept payment in goods and services. When writing in the 1890s, Stout painted a somewhat rosier picture of the antebellum southern rural practitioners who became the mainstay of the Confederate medical corps. In doing so, he was probably describing his own experiences. Stout stated that the rural doctor was generally well educated in the arts and in medicine. "Combining agriculture and the practice of his profession, he was generally prosperous. Practicing for his neighbors of all classes, both rich and poor, he was a friend to all, and in general an adviser, in regard to matters social, educational and political. He had an office to which his patrons often resorted to discuss the topics of the times. He had a library of miscellaneous books, as well as medical. He was a subscriber to newspapers and literary magazines as well as to medical journals, and those, too, that were the very best of their kind." While riding to and from visits to patients the doctor had a chance to observe local medicinal plants. But the distance from his patients strongly influenced the nature of the doctor's practice. He was not able to visit them as often as a town doctor might visit his patients, and thus the rural practitioner "studied pathology with zealous intelligence," trying to make a careful diagnosis. Because he could take only the medications his saddlebags would hold, he simplified his prescriptions to the few remedies that worked best. Since the rural doctor worked in a relatively isolated situation, he had to be prepared to treat any type of ailment, and also to practice surgery. Stout the gentleman farmer was thus rather typical and probably more successful than most rural practitioners.[36]

As a substantial member of his community, Stout was involved in the Masonic order at Elkton, serving as worshipful master of the lodge and also holding the office of secretary of the Giles County Fair Association. In addition, he served on the Board of Directors for the Central Southern Railroad, and perhaps also for the Nashville and Decatur Railroad.[37]

---

36. Duffy, *The Healers*, 177–79. Stout, "Reminiscences," 232–33. "Samuel Hollingsworth Stout, A.M., M.D., LL.D.," 210, said he "made phenomenal pecuniary success."

37. T. L. Williams to Stout, April 9, 1895, TSLA, box 1, folder 10; John Baird to Stout, July 24, 1856, ibid.; Committee of Decatur, Alabama, to Stout, July 24, 1858, UTX, box 2G379; Daniell, *Types of Successful Men*, 313–14.

By 1860 Stout had prospered in his role as a farmer and physician. At that time he owned twenty slaves, real estate worth $21,300, and personal property worth $21,885.[38] The father of a growing family and a pillar in his community, Stout could reasonably look forward to a future of comfort and increasing prosperity. The course of national events, however, brought a sudden and permanent halt to his comfort and eventually thrust him into a position of considerable administrative responsibility.

Because information about Stout's life before the outbreak of the Civil War is so fragmentary, it is difficult to discern just what factors might have prepared him to fulfill his administrative duties with such skill. Young Stout had one of the best medical educations available in the United States at the time and apparently kept abreast of new developments by reading the latest medical journals. While these things may have given him confidence in his medical abilities, they could not make him a successful hospital administrator because such skills were not taught in medical schools, nor even considered necessary, since laymen, not physicians, administered the few hospitals then in existence. Stout might, of course, have been influenced by some well-organized medical school professor. Perhaps his mentor in the private course, William Wood Gerhard, who had a strong reputation as a methodical investigator, encouraged Stout's latent tendencies toward organization. Undoubtedly Stout's years of experience as a school teacher contributed to his effectiveness in personnel management. Probably, also, Stout simply had a natural bent toward, or gift for, administration which enabled him to respond well in a crisis situation. Beyond this, however, there is no evidence suggesting that any of these proffered explanations should be preferred above the others.

---

38. 1860 Census, Population Schedules: Tennessee, Giles County, roll 1251, p. 132; Slave Schedules: Tennessee, Giles County, roll 1282, p. 24. In April 1857 Stout purchased seventy-five acres adjoining his land from C. W. Westmoreland for $1,875. Deed entered in county register book Y, p. 547, May 1, 1857, in Emory, box 4, folder 8. It is not known whether he ever owned more than these 230 acres. According to Stephen V. Ash's study of thirteen counties which comprised Tennessee's "heartland," Giles County's free white inhabitants had an average wealth of $1,000–1,500, a farm of 120–196 improved acres, and an average farm cash value of $5,000–12,220. Giles was one of the wealthiest counties in an area of wealthy counties. Only one in ten slaveholders in the entire thirteen-county region had more than twenty slaves. Stout seems, therefore, to have been very prosperous. *Middle Tennessee Society Transformed*, 5–7, 10.

CHAPTER 2

PREPARING FOR ONE
CHANCE INSPECTION

While Samuel Hollingsworth Stout was a physician and planter in rural Tennessee for more than ten years before the outbreak of the Civil War, he was, nonetheless, aware of events going on in the country at large as national emotions, building for years, crested and broke in the election of 1860. Although the extent of Stout's personal participation in the election is unknown, his interest in it is evident from his collection of a large number of newspaper clippings on the subject which he pasted in a scrapbook. In later years, when applying for an appointive position, Stout claimed to have been a faithful Democrat, though his stand in 1860 is not known. In an account of his Civil War medical service written in 1897, Stout explained that Tennessee had few ardent secessionists or unconditional Unionists. Instead, most of the population were rural and "home loving," "therefore they were loath to take any step likely to lead to bloodshed or to interrupt the calm tranquility of their firesides."[1]

All such "home-loving" reluctance came to an end, according to Stout, because, in attempting to supply Fort Sumter, the Union government committed an "Act of War," leading the Confederates to resist the act

---

1. Stout scrapbook, UTX, box 2G380. It also contains many pages of his own writings tracing political parties in the United States. Whether Stout put this material together in 1860 is not certain, but it seems to be the source for his manuscript "History of Political Parties in the United States to 1860" (UTX, box 2G379), which has much later handwriting. Stout to Richard Coke, January 26, 189[3], TSLA, box 1, folder 12. Stout, "Outline," 56–57. As Stout lived in a rural area, and did not identify himself with the secessionists or the unconditional Unionists, he probably shared the home-loving opinion. Giles County, Tennessee, had displayed a slight Democratic majority in each presidential election since 1840. This tendency held true in 1860 as well when Southern Democrat John C. Breckinridge captured the county with 1,511 votes. Although Constitutional Unionist John Bell won the state's electoral votes, he only won 1,313 popular votes in Giles County. Voters even cast 86 ballots for Stephen A. Douglas. Thus Stout could have voted for any of these three candidates. (Abraham Lincoln was not on the ballot in Tennessee.) Burnham, *Presidential Ballots*, 748.

and capture the fort. When President Abraham Lincoln called for 75,000 troops from the loyal states to put down the so-called insurrection, Isham G. Harris, the governor of Tennessee, refused to supply his state's quota, saying, "Tennessee will furnish not a single man for the purpose of coercion, but fifty thousand if necessary for the defense of our rights and those of our Southern brothers." Most of the conditional Unionists, at least those with whom Stout was acquainted in middle Tennessee, backed their governor and prepared to join the provisional state military forces.[2]

Having twice previously considered a military medical career, Stout at last actually embarked upon one in May 1861. He did not have to seek out a position in the Confederate army, but he decided to enlist when the parents of the boys from Giles and surrounding counties serving in the Third Tennessee Regiment invited him to become the regimental surgeon. Upon the recommendation of the medical board of the Provisional Army of Tennessee, Governor Harris granted Stout a commission as surgeon, with the rank of major of cavalry, on May 17.[3]

Col. John C. Brown,[4] a native of Giles County and a long-time friend of Stout, was the commanding officer of the Third Tennessee Regiment, which, about 1,100 strong, went off to join the First and Eleventh Tennessee Regiments in training at Camp Cheatham in Robertson County. Although Robertson County was north of Giles County, on the Kentucky border, the distance was not great enough to prevent a number of relatives and friends from visiting the recruits. In fact, according to Stout, the first weeks of the war for these men, as for other soldiers North and South, were not a true test of military life but rather a giant picnic. Many of the men in the Third Tennessee came from well-to-do

---

2. Stout, "Outline," 56–57. "Resisted" and "captured" were Stout's words for the Confederate actions at Fort Sumter. Harris's statement is quoted in James M. McPherson's *Ordeal By Fire: The Civil War and Reconstruction*, 150. In another article Stout strains to explain that Tennessee did not secede but voted for "separation" and to ally with the Confederate government. Stout, "Reminiscences," 225–26.

3. Stout, "Outline," 80; Stout, "Some Facts," pt. 3, 23 (February 1901): 101; pt. 10, 24 (March 1902): 160. Stout's commission is in Va. Hist. Soc., Mss1ST465a14.

4. John Calvin Brown (1827–89), a lawyer before the Civil War, was Stout's best man at his wedding. He was commissioned colonel of the Third Tennessee Regiment on May 16, 1861, the day before Stout became the regimental surgeon. Boatner, *The Civil War Dictionary*, 91; Stout, "Days of Long Ago," *Pulaski Citizen*, August 16, 1894, clipping in TSLA, box 2, folder 14.

farming families, and at least seventy-five brought along a slave. Stout also took a slave to camp, an older man named Uncle Isham. According to Stout's daughter, Kate, Uncle Isham volunteered to accompany Stout to care for his two horses, a task Isham performed faithfully throughout the war.[5]

Unfortunately the military "picnic" soon turned into a nightmare as epidemic childhood diseases, especially measles, laid half to three-quarters of the regiment low within their first month or two of service. This situation was not peculiar to the Third Tennessee as all regiments, North and South, composed primarily of rural recruits who had never been exposed to measles, were subject to such epidemics. Some patients had other diseases as well, such as typhoid fever or diarrhea, resulting from poor sanitation or unaccustomed diet, which compounded the problem. This sudden influx of ailing men caught Stout before he had gotten his medical facilities fully set up. His assistant surgeon, W. E. Perry, and Surgeon J. B. Murphree, who was sent by the Army Medical Board, helped Stout, as did some other physicians who had enlisted in the regiment as officers and privates. Despite this aid and his knowledge of military regulations, however, Stout found himself "powerless to keep the sick under adequate discipline, and to prevent a panic among the stricken and their friends who swarmed in the camp, when their absence was more to be desired than their presence." These visitors did more harm than good. They supposed that the patient should be kept warm with hot tea and alcoholic beverages in an unventilated room to make the measles break out. Despite the pleasant weather, they thought that staying in a tent would be fatal to the patient. Stout had no alternative to keeping the patients in tents, but he claimed that the nine who died in camp were ones whose friends had smuggled them whiskey. Once the disease ran its course, Stout was able to send most of the convalescents home on furlough, which allowed him time to organize his regimental hospital.[6]

---

5. Stout, "Some Facts," pt. 3, 23 (February 1901): 101; pt. 7, 23 (December 1901): 585. Katherine Stout Moore, "Some Horses in History," apparently unpublished manuscript, TSLA, box 2, folder 13. Stout trusted Isham with various errands as well. In March 1863, for example, Stout sent him to see about renting a house on Lookout Mountain near Chattanooga. Stout to Mr. Foster, and George D. Foster to Stout, both March 19, 1863, UTX, box 2G427.

6. Stout, "Outline," 58–59; "Some Facts," pt. 3, 23 (February 1901): 101–2; pt. 4, 23 (March 1901): 149–50. Stout's report for the Third Regiment on June 20, 1861, showed 73 cases of measles and 125 cases of other diseases. Emory, box 4, folder 6.

On July 7, Stout and his two assistant surgeons officially requested that the regiment move to a site that no one had previously occupied due to a worsening "typhoid element" among the diseases evident in the camp. "The succession of epidemics with which this regiment has been scourged," Stout explained, "has enfeebled the men, and the men owing to the absence of hospital facilities having been treated when sick in their quarters, the very ground has become in spite of the efforts of the officers to prevent it, odorous with effluvia from the secretions and excretions of sick men." It is possible that this report influenced the decision to move the regiment to Camp Trousdale, located on the Louisville and Nashville Railroad, sometime after July 16, although once it had settled there, similar conditions soon prevailed. An undated "Report of the Sick at Camp Trousdale" stated that in addition to the usual measles many soldiers suffered from typhoid fever, dysentery, and diarrhea. It called for further movement of the camp, combined with strict inspections to keep the site clean. The report also urged the convalescents not to eat unwholesome foods such as unripe fruit, pies, unfermented cider, musk melons, cucumbers, and sweetmeats. At Camp Trousdale Stout progressed in organizing his hospital, which occupied a tent. He reported that he treated a number of patients with a "slow fever" (which was not typhoid) and "sequela of measles." These "sequela" were nearly any disease that attacked the measles-weakened system and, in the army at large, caused numerous fatalities and left many permanent invalids.[7]

Not very many documents survive from Stout's period of regimental service. Among those that do, several indicate the frantic pace at which Stout was working. On June 26, 1861 Stout responded to a complaint that he had not signed a list of patients sent to the general hospital. He explained that it was not an intentional omission, nor was he unaware that a signature was required. The problem resulted from an oversight while he was sending off three carloads of patients in great haste. Several weeks later Stout, at Camp Cheatham, applied for a short leave

---

Discussions of the disease problems rural troops encountered in camp can be found in Cunningham, *Doctors in Gray*, 188–89; Adams, *Doctors in Blue*, 13–17; and Steiner, *Diseases in the Civil War*, 12–13.

7. S. H. Stout, W. T. Perry, and James B. Murfree, Third Tennessee Regiment, Camp Cheatham, no addressee given, June 7, 1861, UTX, box 2G425; Stout, "Some Facts," pt. 6, 23 (June 1901): 294; "Report of Sick at Camp Trousdale," no author given, undated, TSLA, box 2, folder 2. The after-effects of measles are discussed in Cunningham, *Doctors in Gray*, 189–90.

of absence until July 24 because, he said, he was "Feeling an urgent necessity for physical and mental quietude after the severe labors of the last two months."[8]

The Third Tennessee Regiment was among the troops that moved across the state line into Kentucky in September 1861. Stout rode in a baggage car on the first Confederate train that pulled into Bowling Green on September 18. There he was finally able to make his regimental hospital into a model institution, "using Mr. W. B. Patilloe's house as a hospital at the rate of fourteen dollars per month." With winter approaching, the switch of medical facilities from a tent to a house would provide better protection for the patients. Through no fault of Stout, sanitation remained a problem. On October 8 Stout protested, both orally and in writing, to Colonel Brown that "a detail from the 18th Tennessee Regiment (Col. Palmer's) were digging a sink [latrine] in close proximity to the hospital of the 3rd Tennessee regiment." Since Stout had been working hard "to secure to the sick as well as the healthy men of the regiment cleanliness in their quarters and purity of atmosphere," he felt "that the use of a sink" next "to the hospital, as the receptical of the feces of a regiment of men is injurious to the sick and necessarily hazzards their lives and those of their attendants."[9]

Thanks to his application for a naval medical commission in 1848, Stout was already well-acquainted with the United States Army regulations, the basis of both the regulations of the Provisional Army of Tennessee and the Provisional Army of the Confederate States. But, in addition to this background, Stout also had the assistance of some knowledgeable Nashville friends who had served in the Mexican War. Stout and Col. Thomas Claiborne knew each other well as young men and moved to Gibson County together in the early 1840s. Their paths diverged in 1844 when Stout accepted the teaching job in Giles County and Claiborne joined the United States Army. They did not meet again until 1861. At Bowling Green, Claiborne, now a Confederate, was on the staff of Gen. Albert Sidney Johnston, in which capacity he inspected the

8. Emory, box 1, folder 2; also SHC–UNC, Stout microfilm, reel 2. Stout to Lt. Col. T. M. Gordon, July 16, 1861, Emory, box 1, folder 2. It is not known if Stout received his leave, but it is possible since the next extant dated item is a list of sick leaves recommended July 24–25. UTX, ledger 4L219.

9. Stout, "Some Facts," pt. 6, 23 (June 1901): 294–95; Connelly, *Army of the Heartland*, 65; Memorandum, October 1, [1861], UTX, ledger 4L219; Stout to Col. John C. Brown, October 8, 1861, ibid.

hospital of the Third Tennessee Regiment. Claiborne spent a good deal of time showing Stout the problems in his hospital and "giving minute directions" about how to maintain order, on whom to make requisitions, and how and why the hospital fund was so important for the provision of necessities and delicacies. Perhaps it was Claiborne's instructions about the hospital fund that caused Stout to engage in his "first official dispute." The regimental commissary refused to pay the hospital funds until Stout, who had kept all his records, threatened to press charges against the commissary. In any case, Stout considered Claiborne his "teacher" in hospital organization. His other advisor, Dr. F. Josephus Robertson, organized the first military hospital in Nashville, in the old Lunatic Asylum, and remained in charge of it until his death in February 1862, about the time of the fall of Fort Donelson.[10]

Shortly after Gen. Albert Sidney Johnston took charge of the Western Department of the Confederate Army, he selected Dr. David Wendel Yandell of Louisville, Kentucky, as his medical director. Yandell called a meeting of all his subordinate surgeons near Bowling Green and asked for their help as he tried to organize the medical department of the army, a "herculean" task, as Stout put it. The quartermaster and subsistence (or commissary) departments were not yet completely organized or prepared to fulfill their roles in supplying the hospitals, a deficiency that caused many problems for Yandell and the other doctors. At this point Stout "had the only regimental hospital at Bowling Green organized and administered in accordance with army regulations." Apparently Stout offered himself and his hospital as facilities for teaching newly enlisted civilian surgeons about the process of organizing and running a regimental hospital. That Yandell took Stout up on his offer is evidence that Stout was not idly boasting about his abilities, but that he did, in fact, have a hospital that was, at least comparatively, exemplary.[11]

Yandell, however, soon decided to use Stout's organizational abilities in another way. The nonregimental hospitals that Yandell tried to organize around Bowling Green were not especially successful, so he also set up thirteen hospitals in Nashville during the fall of 1861. By impressing

---

10. Stout, "Reminiscences," 227; "Some Facts," pt. 4, 23 (March 1901): 150–52; "Outline," 78. In his "Reminiscences" Stout implied that he knew how to do everything and with whom to deal simply as a result of his study of the regulations. While he no doubt did learn a great deal on his own, it was only in his longer account, "Some Facts," that Stout acknowledged the assistance of Claiborne and Robertson.

11. Stout, "Some Facts," pt. 8, 24 (January 1902): 50–52; "Reminiscences," 227.

homes and businesses whose owners refused to rent them, Yandell had found places for 800 men by November, and ultimately, according to Stout, had beds for about 13,000. In November 1861 Yandell sent Stout to Nashville to take charge of one of these so-called general hospitals.[12]

The Gordon Hospital, Stout's new responsibility, was by no means prepossessing. The building itself was the Gordon warehouse (hence the hospital's name), located on Front Street near Broad Street, and facing a wharf. Since it was designed to be a warehouse, the building lacked many requisites for a proper hospital, including ventilation. Several windows and doors in the front of the building, plus a skylight, provided the only circulation for the 213 patients, ranging from convalescents to very sick, who occupied the building when Stout took his first tour of the premises.[13]

Stout also found a total lack of organization in the Gordon Hospital. No one kept even a basic register of the patients and their complaints, a problem that Stout began to rectify at once. But he also faced more serious problems. The staff consisted of three assistant surgeons, three black cooks, and two civilians who acted as steward and watchman. The hospital had no guard, which allowed a number of patients to wander off the night before Stout made his report. Presumably the hospital had some nurses, although Stout did not mention them. The whole

12. A "general" hospital admitted men from any regiment. Adams, *Doctors in Blue*, 149; Baird, *David Wendel Yandell*, 37–41; Stout, "Some Facts," pt. 8, 24 (January 1902): 52. Stout's figure may be a misprint since other sources estimate the Confederate hospital capacity in Nashville at about 3,500. Durham, *Nashville: The Occupied City*, 15. Stout repeatedly said that he was transferred to the hospital service in October 1861. See for example, Stout, "Reminiscences," 227, and "Some Facts," pt. 6, 23 (June 1901): 294–95. Other documentation places Stout in Nashville about mid-November. A note from L. T. Pim, acting medical director, November 11, 1861 ordered that "Surgeon Stout is required to report to Surgeon Yandell for duty at Nashville tomorrow." Emory, box 1, folder 2; also SHC–UNC, reel 2. Stout inspected his new hospital and wrote a report to Surgeon Yandell on November 13, 1861. TSLA, box 1, folder 11. Finally, a list of "Discharges on Surgeon's Certificate and Deaths" at the Gordon Hospital for November 1861 included a note that said "I took charge of this hospital Nov. 14th 1861." UTX, box 2G417. Stout later said he was willing to transfer to the hospital service because most of the sick and wounded were being sent to Nashville and so there was not much use for his regimental hospital. "Some Facts," pt. 10, 24 (March 1902): 160.

13. Stout, "Some Facts," pt. 10, 24 (March 1902): 160–61; Stout to Yandell, November 13, 1861, TSLA, box 1, folder 11. Stout's report says 213, with some in private houses. In 1902, when he described the scene in the *Southern Practitioner*, he obviously did not consult his papers as he stated that there were 650 patients there.

institution was under the control of a local ladies hospital society.[14] In his report Stout indicated that the ladies were "rendering valuable services," but actually he and they did not see eye-to-eye. The women thought they should continue to manage the hospital, but Stout rejected such an arrangement. He intended to have it under his control and to run it by strict military regulations. On November 15, his second day in charge, Stout issued a "Notice" warning the soldiers that hospital regulations would "be as strictly enforced as circumstances will permit." He decreed that soldiers were not to leave the hospital without permission from the surgeon or assistant surgeons, that visitors would be carefully regulated, that those who damaged public property would be punished, and that hospital officers were to enforce the rules. These rules were a temporary expedient to introduce a much-needed standard of behavior and organization. Later Stout issued a more extensive and detailed set of regulations.[15]

To understand why Stout believed that hospital discipline was so important, it is necessary to know something about hospitals in the nineteenth century. These institutions, located in the large, mainly Northern cities, were essentially refuges for the worthy poor who had no home, or no one to care for them there, and for unfortunate transients who fell ill away from home. The hospital provided the illusion of home—a warm bed, food, and nursing. Anyone with the choice would certainly choose to be cared for in their own home, for medical treatment did not, at that time, involve any specialized procedures which could not be performed at home. Hospitals were primarily charity institutions with carefully regulated discipline of the patients, allegedly for their moral as well as medical benefit.[16]

Thus, at the time of the Civil War, very few soldiers had ever been hospital patients. Hospitals, in this case, were certainly necessary for those soldiers who could not go home—initially, at least, most of them—

14. All hospital and soldier's aid societies in the South were local or, at most, statewide. There was nothing national in the Confederacy like the United States Sanitary Commission. Cunningham, *Doctors in Gray*, 141–43.

15. Stout to Yandell, November 13, 1861, TSLA, box 1, folder 11; Stout, "Notice," November 15, 1861, UTX, box 2G417. Stout details some of his difficulties with the ladies of the Nashville Hospital Association, led by Mrs. Felicia Grundy Porter, in pt. 10 of "Some Facts," 24 (March 1902). Stout's later set of "Rules and Regulations of the Gordon Hospital Front St. Nashville, Tenn." is not dated. Mus. Confed., no number.

16. Rosenberg, *The Care of Strangers*, 4–5, 19, 27–28, 35.

and those who needed specialized surgical care resulting from battle wounds. However, at first virtually all officers and men objected to being treated in a hospital. "The surgeon of a regiment or a hospital was regarded by the populace generally as a sort of inhumane monster. Mothers in parting with their soldier boys would implore their Captains and Colonels to keep their precious children out of those horrid places, the hospitals," and many officers promised to do so.[17] First of all, then, discipline was necessary simply to keep patients in the hospital.

Discipline also seemed the only way to confront large numbers of extremely individualistic Southern soldiers, many of whom had no concept of the rudiments of sanitation or chose to ignore what they did know. In addition, few doctors had any experience with hospitals beyond, perhaps, a visiting acquaintance while in medical school. Consequently, they needed instruction in proper management and discipline so that they could care for the large numbers of sick and wounded and perhaps return them to duty.

Stout had been in charge of the Gordon Hospital for less than a week when he faced two major difficulties: a malodorous sanitation problem and uncooperative supply officials. As Stout described it to L. T. Pim, the surgeon in charge of all of the hospitals at Nashville, "At present the drain of the water closet is stopped up and the second story of the hospital is flooded with filthy water. I have no money with which to have repairs done, or with which to buy provisions. Commissary Schoaf refuses to have any thing to do with the hospitals. Says he has no time to attend to them. You will oblige me if you will give me instructions in writing. If it is not Commissary Schoaf's business to supply the hospital, together with Quartermaster Stevenson and Purveyor Blackie, in their respective departments you will confer a favor by informing me whose business it is." This was by no means the last wartime struggle Stout would have with recalcitrant quartermasters and commissaries. While no evidence explaining the specific resolution of the overall supply problem survives, it can be assumed that Stout was able to get enough supplies eventually since the hospital continued to operate until the fall of Nashville in February 1862.[18]

Obstructed plumbing was another matter, however. This problem arose because many of the soldiers had no idea how to use indoor

---

17. Ibid., 98; Stout, "Some Facts," pt. 15, 25 (January 1903): 29.
18. Stout to Surgeon Pim, November 20, 1861, TSLA, box 1, folder 11.

facilities, and they found the water closet a convenient repository for sticks, cloth, paper, and other items. Stout sent repeated requisitions to the quartermaster for repairs. The quartermaster, however, refused to comply. Finally, the condition of the hospital became so intolerable that on December 9 Stout received permission to move all the patients elsewhere and to close the hospital temporarily for cleaning and disinfecting. Stout took this opportunity to organize and train his workers according to military regulations, and to phase the ladies association out of hospital administration.[19]

It is not surprising that the women resented Stout's authority, for they had been in charge of the hospital since its establishment. The ladies had employed civilian physicians to prescribe for the patients and local druggists to fill the prescriptions. This, in itself, was less of a problem than that no one kept records of these transactions. In addition, the women had hired the cooks and laundresses, who were often lazy and sometimes dishonest, absconding with hospital property rather than responding obediently to Stout's discipline. The women had also allowed numerous visitors to invade the hospital, not only relatives and friends of the patients but also mere curiosity seekers, thus inconveniencing the medical staff and sometimes injuring the patients. These visitors often brought fruits and pies that were not appropriate for the patients' diet. Stout recounted the story of a very handsome and spoiled soldier, whom he suspected of being a "malingerer," who died of apoplexy because he gluttonously ate pies all night which had been surreptitiously slipped to him during the day.[20]

On December 16, just about the time the Gordon Hospital was clean and ready to reopen, Stout was suddenly ordered by General Johnston to return to his regiment and resume his position as its surgeon. The place was not vacant, however. James A. Bowers had taken the position and, assuming it to be a permanent assignment, was unwilling to give it up because he had invested a good deal of money in equipment. Stout obeyed orders and went to Bowling Green, but Colonel Brown, the regimental commander, sent him right back to Nashville, where Yandell

---

19. Stout, "Some Facts," pt. 10, 24 (March 1902): 161–62; L. T. Pim to Stout, December 9, 1861, UTX, box 2G417.

20. Women's hospital visiting committees were common by the time of the Civil War but did not generally have many responsibilities. Rosenberg, *Care of Strangers*, 117. Stout, "Some Facts," pt. 10, 24 (March 1902): 161; pt. 11, 24 (April 1902): 215–16. The term "malingerer" was used for a person feigning sickness.

once again ordered him to take charge of the Gordon Hospital. The problem, as it turned out, was much more involved than conflicting orders or administrative cross purposes; it related to Stout's original commission as a surgeon in the Provisional Army of Tennessee.[21]

When the state of Tennessee turned over the troops of the Provisional Army of Tennessee to the Confederacy, making them national rather than state troops, Gen. A. S. Johnston decided that the automatic transfer included all soldiers, but not surgeons or quartermasters, who had to be dealt with as individuals, perhaps to weed out incompetents. Colonel Brown and the other regimental officers had applied for Stout to be granted a Confederate commission. While waiting for that commission, Stout performed his regimental medical duties, and was paid by the quartermaster for the period from August 7 to October 7 as though he were a Confederate surgeon. Yandell assigned Stout to the Gordon Hospital, but Adjutant and Inspector General Samuel Cooper, in Richmond, decided that regimental surgeons could not be assigned to hospital duty. Cooper's decision led to Johnston's order returning Stout to his former regiment. Yandell sent Stout back to the hospital because Johnston decided that Cooper's order did not apply to Stout's case. Since Stout did not have a Confederate commission, he was only a contract surgeon.[22]

Stout was incensed at the idea of being merely a contract surgeon. Such persons were generally temporary recruits from private practice (possibly disabled for extensive field service), men awaiting an examination for a commission, or those who, through lack of education or experience, were unable to get a commission but were supposed to be adequate medical practitioners. In a letter, written in the third person, to the surgeon general on December 19, Stout protested: "Surgeon Stout does not consider himself employed by contract. He considers himself rightfully Surgeon of the 3rd Tennessee Regiment and will not accept any position that may imply a degradation from that rank. He will serve for the present as surgeon of the Gordon Hospital because he was ordered there not because he is employed by contract." In yet another letter he exclaimed, "If my services are worth any thing to the country, it is

---

21. W. W. McKall, Special Order No. 137, December 16, 1861, TSLA, box 2, folder 4; James A. Bowers to Stout, December 17, 1861, Emory, box 1, folder 3; John C. Brown, no addressee, December 21, 1861, Mus. Confed., no number.

22. D. W. Yandell to Stout, December 16, 1861, Emory, box 1, folder 3; also SHC–UNC reel 2; Stout to Secretary of War, January 4, 1862, Mus. Confed. ST–2–1, also Emory, box 1, folder 4.

welcome to them but if my sphere of usefulness is to be contracted by degrading me from my rank, I prefer the position of private soldier." Stout applied for a Confederate commission and eventually received it in the spring of 1862.[23]

When the Gordon Hospital reopened, the ladies of the hospital association were chagrined to discover that they had very little to do in the reorganized hospital. For example, since Stout used the money in the hospital fund to purchase vegetables, butter, eggs, and other items needed by the sick, donations of delicacies from the ladies were no longer as necessary as they had been previously. Among the vegetables purchased with the hospital fund were quantities of onions. Stout wanted each convalescent to eat an onion every day to prevent scurvy. Needless to say, the reek of onions soon pervaded the hospital, causing several ladies to complain that the strong odor nauseated them. While the women accepted Stout's explanation for the onions, they continued to complain about other matters and threatened to appeal to the surgeon general or to Medical Director Yandell. Stout informed them that it would not do any good unless they could prove that he was "guilty of malfeasance or misfeasance in office." He assured the women that he wanted their help but that he refused to stand for their opposition as he intended to run the hospital according to military regulations. The ladies finally agreed to cooperate.[24]

By early January 1862 the Gordon Hospital had about 240 beds served by one surgeon, three assistant surgeons, one ward master, one steward, nineteen nurses, and two cooks. The hospital did not have a matron, but that was not unusual this early in the war. According to a report he issued at the end of January 1862, Stout received 727 patients in November and December, of whom 58, or around eight percent, died. In January new patients totaled 305 while only 14, or less than five percent, died. Stout explained the reasons for this difference: "Though the proportion of grave cases, (in January,) to the number received in hospital, was greater than

---

23. Stout to Surgeon General, December 19, 1861, Emory, box 1, folder 3; Stout to ?, no date (this is the third page of a letter the rest of which is missing), TSLA, box 1, folder 11. Stout, "Some Facts," pt. 7, 23 (December 1901): 584–85. In pt. 11 Stout mentioned the orders but said it was not necessary for him to explain the reasons. 24 (April 1902): 215. In his later writings Stout was both casual about "such oversights" and a bit defensive about having a Confederate commission dated nearly a year later than the commission which he had received from Tennessee.

24. Stout, "Some Facts," pt. 10, 24 (March 1902): 162–64; pt. 11, 24 (April 1902): 213–14.

that of those received in the months of November and December. Yet there was a diminuation of the percentum of mortality . . . due in my opinion to the following causes, 1st The better organization of every department of the hospital. 2nd, The greater quiet, and better control of the diet of the patient's. 3rd The wards of the hospital are better ventilated. 4th The thorough repairs which the privies have undergone have contributed to render the hospital atmosphere more pleasant and pure." Stout also pointed out that in January he placed no patients in private homes, which reduced mortality because in November and December sixteen of the seventy thus placed had died. Stout reported too that in January, accompanied by an assistant, he had visited each patient twice daily, giving them attention that he had been unable to provide in November and December.[25] By the end of January 1862, then, the Gordon Hospital was organized and running relatively smoothly. Such a stable situation, however, was not characteristic of the wartime Confederacy, and, once again, factors beyond Stout's control intervened to disrupt his establishment.

The security of Nashville depended upon two forts that protected the Confederate "heartland" from invasion by water. Fort Henry, on the Tennessee River, fell to the Federal navy on February 6, 1862. Better-defended Fort Donelson, situated on the Cumberland River, was captured by troops under Gen. Ulysses S. Grant on February 16. Had Stout still been with the Third Tennessee Regiment, he would have gone to help defend the fort, and, along with the regiment, he would have been captured. With the fall of Fort Donelson, Nashville was immediately vulnerable, and A. S. Johnston decided not to defend the city even though it was a major supply depot. Due to flooding, the Cumberland River rose almost as far as the sidewalk in front of the Gordon Hospital. Stout said that the Federal gunboats could have sailed up the river with ease, but they did not arrive until Friday, February 21.[26]

---

25. Stout erroneously reported the deaths for November and December as 7.01 percent. Miscellaneous "Morning Reports," dating from late December 1861 to early January 1862, UTX, box 2G417; "Remarks to accompany 'Report of Sick and Wounded' in Gordon Hospital for the month of January 1862," ibid.

26. According to Thomas L. Connelly, the "heartland" of the Confederacy included Tennessee, northeast Mississippi, north-central Alabama, and north-central Georgia, an area that was valuable for its raw materials such as food products, minerals, and livestock, as well as a variety of manufacturing establishments. *Army of the Heartland*, 3. An account of this campaign is Cooling, *Forts Henry and Donelson*. Stout, "Some Facts," pt. 12, 24 (October 1902): 564–65, 569.

Although the Yankees did not arrive in Nashville on that fateful Sunday when Donelson fell, panic did. Stout reported that he was eating at the City Hotel when "some one pretending to be a courier of Captain Lindsey, commander of the post, rushed down the street on horseback, and stopping before the door of the Gordon Hospital, cried out in a commanding voice, 'The Yankees are coming; are just below the city. Captain Lindsey has sent me to order every sick and wounded man, able to do so, to leave his bunk, and try as best he can to make his way to Murfreesboro.'" By the time Stout got back to the hospital, he found all the weak, panic-stricken patients, many of them barely able to walk, out in the street. He had a hard time trying to persuade them to get back into bed. Infuriated, Stout declared that had he been able to find out who the horseman was, he would gladly have seen the man hanged from the nearest lamp post for needlessly alarming the patients.[27]

Stout, realizing that it was only a matter of time until the Federals really did arrive in Nashville, began trying to get railroad transportation for his patients. His major problem was that the quartermaster, responsible for providing this transportation, was nowhere to be found.[28] Stout did find Medical Director Yandell, however. Yandell had decided to take all the doctors from Missouri and Kentucky with him when he evacuated because, since their states had not seceded, he feared that they would be executed as traitors. As a Tennessean, Stout would be treated as a prisoner of war. Thus, Yandell proposed to leave him behind with the patients who could not travel. Stout was by no means amenable to this idea. Even though he had grown up in Nashville, he had not lived there for at least twelve years. It was no longer "home" to him. He believed that the people had changed and he would not be able to find anyone to help him care for his patients. Local citizens were already moving the sick and wounded Federal prisoners into schools and public buildings which they had not allowed the Confederates to use as hospitals, in the hope that the Yankees would have mercy on them when they saw that the prisoners

---

27. Ibid., 566. The story is also recounted in "Outline," 59. Durham, *Nashville: The Occupied City*, 7ff treats various aspects of the panic which affected citizens and officials as well as the patients.
28. V. K. Stevenson, president of the Nashville and Chattanooga Railroad, loaded his family and belongings on a private train and fled Nashville on February 16. As Durham expressed it, "He was singularly unaffected by the fact that he was a major in the Confederate Army and that his departure from assigned duty as quartermaster at Nashville was unauthorized." Ibid., 15.

were well-treated. Stout, in fact, could not bear the idea of remaining in Nashville under these conditions, especially since he thought that all but a half dozen or so of his patients could be transported elsewhere. Those few who could not move he proposed to leave with a competent contract surgeon.[29]

At the suggestion of a friend, Stout went to see Gen. Johnston, who had previously been impressed by an inspector's report about the Gordon Hospital and was only too glad to order Surgeon Yandell to relieve Stout of duty in Nashville and allow him to evacuate. Several days later a very reluctant Yandell gave Stout his orders, and on February 20, 1862, Stout left Nashville for his home, Midbridge, on a thirty-day leave of absence. At this point Stout was thoroughly disgusted with the hospital service. He was frustrated with people who were offended because he said that the Gordon warehouse was poorly suited for hospital purposes. He was also perturbed by visitors who would only minister to patients from their own states, ignoring all others. No doubt recalcitrant quartermasters, interfering women, and the recent frustrations with his commission also contributed to his discouragement. "I wanted to enter upon field service in any position, it mattered not how humble, so that I could be in the vicinity of the boys of Brown's 3rd Tennessee Regiment when they were released from prison."[30]

Stout's wish was not granted. A few days before Stout's leave ended he went to see General Johnston at Decatur, Alabama, not only to deliver a message from another officer but also to see where he was about to be assigned. The doctor and the general talked for several hours, since heavy rainfall prevented Stout from leaving. Stout never saw Johnston again—the general was on his way to Corinth and, ultimately, his final battle at Shiloh.[31]

---

29. Stout, "Some Facts," pt. 12, 24 (October 1902): 566–68. It is useful to remember that Yandell was from Kentucky, which probably helps to explain his great concern about how the Yankees would treat Kentucky and Missouri physicians. Durham estimates that the Confederates had housed about 3,500 patients in twenty-five to thirty buildings plus private homes. The Union wounded, who arrived on February 16, were placed in Zollicoffer Barracks (an unfinished hotel) and the hospital at the military academy of the University of Nashville. Durham, *Nashville: The Occupied City*, 15–16.

30. Stout, "Some Facts," pt. 12, 24 (October 1902): 568–70; pt. 11, 24 (April 1902): 215–16. Stout's own accounts are the only materials located that describe his experiences during the last few days before Nashville fell. No doubt many potentially useful papers were lost or destroyed with the evacuation of the city.

31. Stout, "Some Facts," pt. 13, 24 (November 1902): 623–24.

Stout's assignment sent him in the opposite direction, to Chattanooga, where he was to take charge of the hospitals. He also received instructions from one of the surgeon general's inspectors to clean up the hospitals and to send all the patients who could travel to the hospitals in Atlanta. Stout did not protest this assignment, but he thought that it was beneath him and that it had been made to get him out of the way. Few persons besides Johnston saw any strategic value in Chattanooga at this point.[32]

When Stout arrived in Chattanooga on March 22, 1862, he found that the town was indeed unimpressive. "Little more than a village," Chattanooga's streets were "unimproved." In fact, "filthy mud holes were reeking with the debris, thrown there by a large army passing hastily through en route to the bloody field of Shiloh." He found a few patients in the filthy Waverly House Hospital, a former hotel. The situation was so bad there that Stout closed the hospital and moved the patients to the Academy Hospital, a former school, which was in somewhat better condition. It is no wonder that Stout had a low opinion of his new position. Except for the patients, Stout could find no soldiers or officers, let alone a post commander, quartermaster, commissary, or provost marshal anywhere in the town. The military seemed to be conspicuous by its absence. The next day Stout met another gentleman in a similar situation—Brig. Gen. Samuel B. Maxey, the new post commander who had, so far, been unable to find anyone to command. Within the next few weeks Maxey was able to organize the post and was very helpful to Stout in making sure that the patients were well cared for.[33]

Chattanooga continued to be an undesirable post for the next several months. The one commissioned surgeon and the hospital steward at the post when Stout arrived were both eager to be transferred elsewhere and soon were. Although he urged several doctors passing through Chattanooga to request assignment to the post, Stout could find no one who was interested. As a result, he had to depend on contract physicians and teach them their duties. Overall, Stout found that they learned well. As not very many patients were kept in Chattanooga at first, and as no military activity was occurring in the vicinity, Stout found that he had a good deal of time to study the army regulations thoroughly and ensure

---

32. Ibid., 624.
33. Despite his serious responsibilities, Stout apparently had some sense of humor, as he described the way he and Maxey joked about their ridiculous position. Maxey did not remain in Chattanooga more than a month or so as he wished to return to field command. Ibid., 624–26.

that his hospitals were organized accordingly. Apparently due to the military situation after Shiloh, Stout was unable to receive orders from Medical Director Yandell. As a result, he contacted Gen. Edmund Kirby Smith, who was then in charge of the Department of East Tennessee. Smith put Stout under the control of his own medical director, S. A. Smith. The cooperation of Medical Director Smith helped Stout in his organizing endeavors.[34]

Eventually the hospital business in Chattanooga picked up. When an artillery battery, plus two newly recruited Georgia regiments, took up their assignment at the post, Stout once again faced a measles epidemic which kept him busy. In addition, Stout's hospital began to receive patients from the trenches at Corinth, Mississippi, most of whom were sick with or convalescing from typhoid fever, dysentery, and diarrhea. Discovering that many of these patients were too ill to travel beyond Chattanooga, Stout found that he needed to increase his facilities. It is probably at this point that he organized the Newsom Hospital to care for the patients that the Academy Hospital could not contain.[35]

Gen. Braxton Bragg became head of the Army of the West, in November to be renamed the Army of Tennessee, on June 20, 1862. After a few weeks of reorganization, discipline, and morale building, Bragg sent most of his army by a circuitous route (the only one available with transportation other than wagons) from Tupelo, Mississippi, via Mobile and Montgomery, Alabama, to Chattanooga. Bragg himself seems to have arrived in Chattanooga on July 29 and, without further delay, he and a group of prominent surgeons proceeded to make an unannounced inspection of Stout's two hospitals. About four o'clock that afternoon, Stout's hospital steward, Dr. J. Eber Fry, appeared at Stout's office to tell him that an inspection had taken place. Stout quoted Fry, "I have seen many inspecting officers, but General Bragg is the most thorough

---

34. Ibid., 625–26; pt. 14, 24 (December 1902): 669–70; pt. 15, 25 (January 1903): 26; "Outline," 63.
35. Stout, "Some Facts," pt. 14, 24 (December 1902): 670; pt. 15, 25 (January 1903): 31; "Outline," 62. The Newsom Hospital was named for Ella Newsom, "a young, handsome, and wealthy widow" from Arkansas, who had already served as a nurse, matron, and financial benefactor in a number of hospitals, particularly at Corinth, Mississippi, after the Battle of Shiloh. The patients and surgeons appreciated her so much that they named the new hospital for her even before she arrived in Chattanooga to serve as chief matron of the Academy Hospital, where she remained until she became ill from overwork. "Some Facts," pt. 22, 25 (September 1903): 522; Cumming, Journal, 29, 31–32, note 10.

inspector I ever met with. He did the inspecting in person—the other officers for the most part looking on. He inspected every bunk, turned down the coverlets and sheets, and even looked under the bunks. He inspected the medicines, the kitchens and outhouses, and looked over the register, the prescription, diet, order and case books. I never saw anything like such an inspection." Stout admitted, "I confess I felt a little resentful, because the General had not been courteous enough to invite me, the chief medical officer at the post, to accompany him on that inspecting tour." Not many minutes passed before Stout received an order to report to Bragg's medical director, A. J. Foard, the next morning at nine o'clock.

Stout appeared at Foard's office as commanded and was surprised when Foard told him that, "General Bragg ordered me to summon you to my quarters, and to say to you that the two hospitals you are in charge of here, are the only ones he has inspected since he left Pensacola that are such as they ought to be for the care and treatment of sick and wounded Confederate soldiers. Where and how," Foard questioned, "did you learn to organize and manage military hospitals?"[36]

It was one chance inspection. Stout in no way anticipated it. Bragg had no idea what he would find when he performed it. But the results of that inspection were crucial to Stout's Civil War career. His months of studying the regulations, consulting inspectors, and applying what he learned to hospital organization were about to net him a larger field of responsibility.

When the war began Southern doctors were not prepared to do battle with the afflictions of the soldiers. Although many physicians volunteered to aid the Confederate cause, they found themselves at a loss when faced with half a regiment of men suffering from the measles or an improvised hospital crammed with filthy, bleeding wounded. Few doctors had experience caring for the ailing en masse, since few civilian hospitals existed and these few could be found only in the larger cities. Confronted

---

36. Lash, *Destroyer of the Iron Horse*, 61; McWhiney, *Braxton Bragg vol. 1*, 264–65, 268–71. Bragg was accompanied by, among others, A. J. Foard, his medical director, Stanford E. Chaille, his medical inspector, and Dr. Josiah Nott, a famous Mobile physician who was sometimes also a hospital inspector for Bragg. Stout, "Outline," 62. A biography of Nott is Horsman, *Josiah Nott of Mobile*. Nott's relationship to Bragg's staff is discussed on pp. 277–79. Stout, "Some Facts," pt. 16, 25 (February 1903): 95–96. The Pensacola hospitals Bragg so much admired had been administered by Foard.

with such unanticipated conditions some doctors faltered and failed. But most medical officers muddled along as well as they could, neglecting some areas of hospital discipline to achieve success in others. It was a rare doctor who had the administrative skills, perhaps even genius, to put all aspects of a hospital together: to learn how to adapt to military regulations, how to use the hospital fund to the best advantage, how to keep a hospital clean, and how to discipline and supervise subordinates and patients without causing a mutiny. Bragg had performed many hospital inspections and he knew what he could expect to find. When, surprisingly, instead of a half-prepared affair, he found two well-managed institutions at Chattanooga, Bragg determined to increase the responsibility of their obviously competent organizer—Stout.[37]

---

37. Lack of preparedness also characterized the Northern medical corps, of course.

CHAPTER 3

"THAT ATTENTION AND CARE, TO WHICH THEY ARE ENTITLED"

As Samuel Hollingsworth Stout sat in Medical Director Foard's office and listened to him deliver General Bragg's commendation of the hospitals which Bragg had inspected, Stout had every reason to be pleased. Bragg's approval was a sure sign that Stout's hospitals were indeed well organized, since the general was a notorious stickler for administrative detail. Stout was probably aware that Bragg was difficult to please, but he may not have heard the story, possibly apocryphal, of Bragg's ultimate perfectionism. During Bragg's career in the United States Army, he had been assigned to duty in Florida, at one point serving both as company commander and company quartermaster. According to the story, as quartermaster he refused to fill a requisition which he had made as company commander. After a good deal of correspondence with himself, he finally referred the issue to a most exasperated post commander. By 1844, seven years after his graduation from West Point, Bragg had the unenviable reputation of being "the most cantankerous man in the army." His reputation did not change much while he was in Confederate service.[1]

While Stout appreciated Bragg's compliments, he did not at first attach to them any great significance. As far as he knew, he still reported to Medical Director S. A. Smith and expected to join Gen. Edmund Kirby Smith's forces at Knoxville. On August 3, 1862, S. A. Smith ordered Stout to report to him to organize hospitals as soon as Foard could get some other man to take his place in Chattanooga.[2] Thus began a tug of war over Stout which lasted for several months. Both Smiths knew what a good administrator they had, and proposed to keep him on their

---

1. Stout, "Some Facts," pt. 16, 25 (February 1903): 96. McWhiney, *Braxton Bragg vol. 1*, 33, 51.
2. Stout later recalled that the order to report to Smith arrived in the afternoon of the day he spoke with Foard. Stout, "Some Facts," pt. 16, 25 (February 1903): 94–97; S. A. Smith to Stout, August 3, 1862, Emory, box 1, folder 5.

staff, while Foard and Bragg realized what a good administrator they had found and were not about to let him go.

Both sides seemed to have a legitimate prior claim on Stout's services. Smith had been supervising and encouraging Stout ever since he arrived in Chattanooga in late March 1862. In fact, Smith was trying to secure a superintendency for Stout. Bragg, on the other hand, claimed that Stout was still a part of the Army of Tennessee, because he was assigned to his post by the late A. S. Johnston. Stout was still on the Army of Tennessee roster and reported to Smith merely because it was more convenient while the Army of Tennessee was campaigning in Mississippi. Upon receiving a second order from Smith, Stout informed Foard that he would have to obey orders even if Foard had not found a replacement for him. Foard disagreed, however, and commanded Stout to remain in Chattanooga or Bragg would have him arrested.[3]

Stout was now in an awkward position, and he remained in the predicament for several months. Part of the difficulty related to planning for the upcoming invasion of Kentucky, which involved the troops of both Bragg and Kirby Smith. Many problems occurred because neither commander was actually in charge of the campaign. Because both Medical Directors Foard and Smith would accompany their respective armies to the field, they both found it particularly urgent to leave a responsible administrator in the rear to supervise their hospitals—hence the demand for Stout.[4]

Foard and Bragg took action to keep Stout and also to expand his responsibilities beyond Chattanooga. Bragg's Special Orders No. 160 of August 22, 1862 announced that "In addition to his present duties as Post Surgeon at Chattanooga, *Surgeon S. H. Stout* will have control of the Hospitals at Tunnell [sic] Hill, Ringgold, Dalton, and, also, those hereafter established between Chattanooga Tenn. and Atlanta Georgia, subject to the orders of the *Medical Director* of the Department, to whom he will make consolidated reports weekly." Smith did not know

---

3. While the army of which Bragg took command in June 1862 was not actually known as the Army of Tennessee until November, the later name is used here for simplicity. Stout, "Some Facts," pt. 13, 24 (November 1902): 625–26; pt. 16, 25 (February 1903): 97–98. S. A. Smith to Stout, July 1[?], 1862, Emory, box 1, folder 5.

4. In his later accounts Stout generally tended to minimize conflicts, and in this instance he wrote as though the problem only persisted for several days. Stout, "Some Facts," pt. 16, 25 (February 1903): 97–98; "Outline," 64; S. A. Smith to Stout, August 23, 1862, Emory, Stout microfilm. Information about the unsuccessful Kentucky campaign and the Battle of Perryville can be found in McWhiney, *Braxton Bragg vol. 1*, chaps. 13 and 14, and Connelly, *Army of the Heartland*, chaps. 11–14.

about this order when he wrote to Stout on August 23 urging him and his subordinate medical officers to report to Smith's headquarters as soon as possible. "I have written to surgeon Ford [sic] to send you and hope there will be no difficulty on the matter. You do not know how much I want *you* for to superintend the hospitals in the rear of this column." As Smith soon found out, Foard was willing to send anyone but Stout. Foard assured Stout on September 1 that General Smith had no authority over him as he was still under other orders.[5]

Shocked by his new assignment, Stout did not see it as a promotion and said that he would rather have remained in a position where he could care for the sick and wounded directly. But, he claimed that he had too strong a sense of honor and duty to shirk his new responsibilities, and he soon decided that "as the position of superintendent of hospitals afforded many opportunities of comforting the sick and wounded and weary soldiers, I determined to avail myself of the powers entrusted to me to that end, believing the finger of the Divinity had pointed me out for that work to General Bragg and his Medical Director."[6]

The controversy over Stout's position, only partly resolved because Stout remained in Chattanooga, continued until late December. Special Orders No. 32 from the headquarters of Maj. Gen. Samuel Jones in Knoxville, issued on October 25, essentially put Stout in the same position to which Bragg had already assigned him, supervising the hospitals from Cleveland, Tennessee, on the east to Chattanooga on the west to Dalton, Georgia, on the south. Hospitals below that point were under the command of Surgeon J. P. Logan, in Atlanta.[7]

S. A. Smith probably felt that a portion of General Orders No. 50 from the Adjutant and Inspector General's Office, Richmond, which said the Department of East Tennessee included all of Georgia north of the railroad from Augusta to Atlanta to West Point, provided conclusive evidence that Stout came under Smith's control, for this area contained the hospitals of which Stout was in charge. Smith triumphantly informed

5. Extract from Special Orders No. 160, August 22, 1862, Mus. Confed., ST–2–12; S. A. Smith to Stout, August 23, 1862, Emory, Stout microfilm; Foard to Stout, August 21, and September 1, 1862, both Emory, box 1, folders 5 and 6 respectively. In the letter of August 21 Foard told Stout about his new responsibilities before the official order was promulgated.
6. Stout, "Some Facts," pt. 16, 25 (February 1903): 98.
7. Special Orders No. 32, Department of East Tennessee, October 25, 1862, Mus. Confed., ST–3–7.

Stout of this fact in a letter of November 20. But Smith's jubilation was premature, for, in a letter of November 30, Foard urged Stout to hasten hospital construction in Chattanooga and informed him that new hospitals being opened in Rome would be part of his domain. Foard also reminded Stout that he was to make his reports to Foard only and to take orders from Bragg's department only.[8]

The controversy continued with problems over who supervised the post surgeon at Cleveland, since Stout and Smith each sent a post surgeon. Supervision of hospitals in Atlanta also became an issue because many of Bragg's sick and wounded troops, who could travel some distance from the front without further injury, went to those hospitals. Stout recommended, when asked, that Atlanta remain under Logan, but he suggested that Logan send daily and weekly reports to him. At the end of December Kirby Smith issued an order placing the Atlanta hospitals under Bragg's control and, ultimately, under Stout's command. "Is the question now settled?" Logan asked on December 26. But he doubted it: "I would hope so but for previous experience." In fact, however, the question was settled. From that point on, both Stout and Logan reported to Bragg and Foard.[9]

While Stout's uncertain position was awkward, it was not the focus of his activities during the late summer and fall of 1862. Stout was much too busy creating a hospital department. When Foard departed for Kentucky, he left Stout a small staff—a surgeon, an assistant surgeon, and a clerk—to assist with the organization.[10] In addition, the hospitals in Chattanooga played a major role in caring for the large number of sick soldiers of Bragg's army when it retreated from Kentucky. On November 3, 1862, Stout instructed his surgeons in charge of hospitals to prepare for the arrival of two hundred sick that evening. He distributed the responsibilities among the various hospitals, and reminded his subordinates, "I hope that the medical officers appointed for these duties will be prompt, and kind, and see that the sick soldiers have that attention

8. S. A. Smith to Stout, November 20, 1862, and Foard to Stout, November 30, 1862, both in Emory, box 1, folder 7. A part of the departmental boundary confusion is mentioned in Connelly, *Army of the Heartland*, 188.

9. The problems at Cleveland are discussed in David E. Ewart to Stout, December 3, 1862, Emory, box 1, folder 8, and also SHC–UNC, Stout microfilm, reel 2; Foard to Stout, December 19, 1862, Emory, Stout microfilm; and Charles E. Michel to Stout, December 27, 1862, SHC–UNC, reel 2; Stout to Foard, December 18, 1862, Emory, box 1, folder 9; J. P. Logan to Stout, December 26, 1862, SHC–UNC, reel 2.

10. Stout, "Outline," 63.

and care, to which they are entitled and that none are neglected or overlooked. Wardmasters and Stewards should all be taught to promptly extend aid to the sick at all hours. In no instance in future will I over look, negligence, or even indifference on the part of the officers of the hospitals under my charge."[11]

By the end of 1862 Stout was able to make several reports on the status of his hospitals. He was in charge of all the hospitals at Tunnel Hill, Catoosa Springs, Ringgold, and Dalton, Georgia, as well as Chattanooga and Cleveland, Tennessee. In this capacity he assigned medical officers as needed, and, because he maintained accurate daily reports, he knew where among the 4,300 beds in the district he could find vacancies to accommodate new patients. From July through November the hospitals in the district treated 14,087 cases, sending 466 to hospitals outside the district (probably in Atlanta), returning 8,113 to duty, discharging 304, and furloughing 1,115. Eighty-four patients chose to desert and 869 died, leaving 3,136 in the hospitals on November 30.[12]

Stout's system of hospitals experienced a major test when the casualties from the Battle of Murfreesboro or Stone's River, fought December 31, 1862, to January 2, 1863, began to arrive.[13] The wounded, including Federals as well as Confederates, inundated Chattanooga. Surgeons and nurses worked for several days and nights without respite, caring for those in the hospitals who could travel no further, as well as for those at the depot who awaited transportation. Every corner of every hospital was filled, and as soon as patients were able to travel, they were shipped out of Chattanooga to make room for the more severely wounded. Some surgeons working at the depot stood so long that their boots had to be cut from their swollen feet. Trying to feed this crowd taxed the hospitals' culinary resources. Hospital Matron Kate Cumming reported that the cooks also had to go with little or no sleep for several nights

---

11. Cumming, *Journal*, October 27, 1862, p. 63. Cumming was serving at the Newsom Hospital. Stout [to Surgeons of Hospitals at Chattanooga], November 3, 1862, Emory, Stout microfilm.

12. Stout to Sir, November 17, 1862, Emory, box 1, folder 7. Preparations were not yet complete at Rome. Thirteen hundred and fifty of the beds were located in the three hospitals in Chattanooga. Information on hospital capacity is found in Stout to Sir, December 15, 1862, TSLA, box 1, folder 11. The patient statistics are found in Stout to Foard, December 16, 1862, UTX, ledger 4L230.

13. For studies of the battle see McDonough, *Stones River*; Peter Cozzens, *No Better Place to Die: The Battle of Stones River* (Urbana: University of Illinois Press, 1990); Connelly, *Autumn of Glory*, chap. 3; and McWhiney, *Braxton Bragg vol. 1*, chap. 15.

preparing the beef, bread, and coffee which was all the food available for the patients.[14]

The strain of continuous work and lack of sleep soon began to tell on the medical attendants. On January 5, 1863, Frank Hawthorn, surgeon in charge of the Foard Hospital, wrote to Stout, "I have the honor to report the distressed condition of this Hospital. The nurses are sick or broken down. There were not at first not [sic] more than enough nurses to take care of the sick in the house & they have all been used at the trains until they are exhausted. The Surgeons of whom there are only two are both tired & sick. I am myself worn out & have not only the work of the house to do but double duty as an Asst Surgn besides. I deem it my duty to make these facts known to you that you may take whatever step you may think necessary." Stout circulated Hawthorn's letter to the surgeons at the other hospitals asking each to send one or two assistant surgeons and "a corps of nurses" to aid their beleaguered brethren. Unfortunately, the other surgeons could spare no staff for the situation in their own hospitals was similar. With 750 patients at the Newsom Hospital, for example, Surgeon in Charge Francis Thornton found it "impossible" to send any nurses, although he sent an assistant surgeon. Dr. Hamilton at the Academy Hospital also could do no better than to send one assistant surgeon.[15] In the wake of Murfreesboro, Stout and his subordinates had a chance to see how well their hospital structure worked. Stout felt that the hospital discipline previously adopted was invaluable in helping the medical corps to survive the postbattle chaos.[16]

Several months after Murfreesboro, Stout received his final promotion. As with his previous changes of position, this one also generated controversy, but not because Stout was in any way unqualified for the job. The problem began with an order from the Adjutant and Inspector General's Office in Richmond, dated March 12, 1863, which removed the so-called general hospitals, those behind the lines to which the sick and wounded were sent from the field, from the responsibility of the army medical directors. Army medical directors remained in charge of field medical arrangements while medical directors of hospitals, a new

14. Stout to A. A. Gen. G. W. McCawley, January 4, 186[3], Mus. Confed. ST–2–2; Cumming, *Journal*, entries for January 2, 3, and 11, 1863, pp. 74–76; Stout, "Some Facts," pt. 23, 25 (October 1903): 569.
15. Hawthorn to Stout, and notations on the back, January 5, 1863, Emory, box 1, folder 10, also SHC–UNC, reel 2.
16. Stout, "Some Facts," pt. 23, 25 (October 1903): 569.

position, took charge of hospital arrangements and reported directly to the surgeon general, rather than to the army medical director. Splitting the responsibilities of field and general hospitals was a logical idea that offered the potential for better administration in both areas. Stout gave the credit for the idea to Bragg, who had already created such a general hospital position for Stout, rather than to the surgeon general, who, Stout believed, simply applied Bragg's scheme throughout the army.[17] The controversy developed because Bragg already had Stout in charge of general hospitals for the Army of Tennessee, and the surgeon general, not understanding Stout's responsibilities, tried to assign someone else to his position.

The first indication that something was awry came to Stout in a general order, which he forwarded to Bragg's new medical director, Edward A. Flewellen, who had replaced Foard in early 1863.[18] Flewellen replied that Bragg was "determined to resist the control of the hospitals established for his army in any such way as that indicated in the G.O. enclosed by you." In any case, Flewellen did not think the order applied to the Army of Tennessee. Presumably the order was the previously mentioned one of March 12, and Bragg was afraid that the war department or surgeon general would assign someone to his hospitals without consulting him.[19]

Bragg attempted to make Stout's position clear in Special Orders No. 81 on March 28. "S. H. Stout, Senior Surgeon of the Post at Chattanooga, will, subject to the orders of the Medical Director, have the general superintendance of all hospitals which have been, or may hereafter be established in the District of the Tennessee, which includes those at Chattanooga, Rome, Atlanta, and all intermediate points. Medical officers on duty in the Hospitals in said District, will forward through Surgeon Stout all Reports, Returns, and official Communications, and will make to him such reports, and exhibits as he may from time to

---

17. In his later account, Stout claimed the assignments that precipitated the difficulty with his position were made in February 1863, but no papers pertaining to the issue have been located which are dated earlier than March. Ibid., pt. 19, 25 (May 1903): 277; "Outline," 68; Cunningham, Doctors in Gray, 71, 106. General Orders No. 28, S. Cooper, A & IGO, Richmond, March 12, 1863, OR, ser. 4, vol. 2, p. 425. Although Stout attributed the new position to the surgeon general, that officer told Flewellen that it was a creation of the war department about which he knew nothing until the order was published. S. P. Moore to Flewellen, May 13, 1863, N A, chap. 6, vol. 748.

18. E. A. Flewellen to Stout, March 24, 1863, Emory, box 3, folder 9.

19. Flewellen to Stout, ibid., and April 16, 1863, TSLA, box 1, folder 4.

time call for."[20] While Bragg's statement was official, it was certainly not conclusive for the surgeon general. On April 16, Flewellen reported to Stout that he believed the surgeon general would appoint a medical director anyway, without consulting Bragg. In a letter of April 19, Flewellen urged Stout to write to the surgeon general himself, applying for the job and asking if the new officer would report to the commanding general, as Bragg did not want any outside influence in his hospitals. In the draft of a letter, probably to Surgeon General Samuel Preston Moore, Stout wrote, "In the uncertainty which hangs over my official status I feel much embarassment. Having labored long and earnestly to build up and discipline the hospitals in this district, I can but feel an interest in the question as to whether I am to be permitted to continue in charge of them, or be superceded by another. I cannot ask that my superiors [sic] officers shall continue me in a position in which I have reasons to believe I have secured their approbation by earnestly & laboriously endeavoring to discharge my duty, yet an early solution of the question will much relieve my mind, though the decision may be adverse to my own claims to be entitled a med. director while performing the duties, & incurring the responsibilities of an officer of that grade."[21]

Stout and his claims were not without friends in various places. Thomas J. Foster, an Alabama congressman, personally presented Stout's case to the surgeon general, probably at the behest of Stout's coworker Dudley D. Saunders. While Foster informed Stout that he could not promise positive results from his actions, he conveyed his hope that they had been helpful. He also suggested that a petition signed by a number of surgeons and endorsed by Bragg would probably gain Stout the nomination.[22]

On May 4 Stout wrote to Flewellen once again, explaining that while he had no official information, he had heard that the new director would be Surgeon Lewis T. Pim, who was the head of the Army Medical Board which was examining surgeons in that area. Stout asked Flewellen to give this information to Bragg so that he could issue orders that would make

---

20. Special Orders No. 81, Bragg, March 28, 1863, Emory, box 1, folder 14, also Mus. Confed. ST–4–14.

21. Flewellen to Stout, April 16 and April 19, 1863, both in TSLA, box 1, folder 4; Stout to Sir, April 21, 1863, TSLA, box 1, folder 11.

22. Thos [?] J. Foster to Dudley, April 21, 1863, TSLA, box 1, folder 15. There is no evidence that the recommended petition was drawn up. Warner and Yearns, *Biographical Register of the Confederate Congress*, 89–90.

the transition to a new director easier. Clearly Stout was discouraged as he lamented, "my labors have been either so unsuccessful or unappreciated as to call for a change in the management of the hospitals, which it has been the single object of my life, for many months, to perfect, and render satisfactory to the Army, and the General Commanding."[23]

Various persons attempted to assure Stout that Bragg and others valued his work, but this was no great comfort to Stout when he found out that he had been appointed medical inspector, and not director, for the hospitals. Stout fumed to Foard that he had not and would not accept a post which had so far been a "*contemptible* sinecure." If "inspector" were merely a new title for his present job, Stout had no objection, but he flatly refused to take a subordinate position while another man occupied his place. Unknown to Stout, on May 29, the same day as he vented his disgruntlement, John Withers, assistant adjutant general, by command of the secretary of war, issued Special Orders No. 128, which made Pim the inspector and Stout the director. Not until June 3, however, did news of the appointment make its way to a delighted Stout.[24] The issue

23. Stout to Flewellen, May 4, 1863, Emory, box 1, folder 6.
24. C. B. Gamble to Stout, May 6, 1863, Emory, box 1, folder 16; George S. Blackie to Stout, May 29, 1863, Atlanta Hist. Soc., also, Emory, box 3, folder 10. Blackie commented, "If you are displaced, believe me you and I will not be, by many hundreds, the only Tennesseans who will regret it." Special Orders No. 115, A & IGO, Richmond, May 14, 1863, Emory, ibid., also TSLA, box 2, folder 4. Stout to Foard (copy to Flewellen), May 29, 1863, Emory, box 1, folder 16; Special Orders No. 128, John Withers, A. A. G., May 29, 1863, N A, chap. 6, vol. 748; Stout to Stanford Chaille, June 3, 1863, TSLA, box 1, folder 4. It is interesting to look at Stout's later treatment of the difficulties surrounding his appointment as medical director. His "Outline," written in 1897, and three biographical sketches, published during Stout's lifetime, for which he probably contributed the information, noted no controversy. The only article that even mentioned that Stout had any competition for his position was pt. 19 of his series "Some Facts." He treated the problem so briefly that he implied the whole situation was solved in February 1863. Stout, "Outline," 68; Evans, ed., *Confederate Military History* 11: 639; Daniell, *Types of Successful Men*, 310; "Samuel Hollingsworth Stout, A.M., M.D., LL.D.," 212; Stout, "Some Facts," pt. 19, 25 (May 1903): 276–77. Why did Stout gloss over a period of such traumatic uncertainty which seemed at the time to threaten his reputation and capacity as a hospital administrator? Probably the passage of time helped to moderate Stout's recollections. His accounts were written thirty-five to forty years after the fact, and the trauma of uncertainty had been dulled. Furthermore, Stout was not using his own source materials, so his dates were not accurate, and he may well have forgotten just how long it took to resolve the problem. It is possible, too, that Stout decided this story was not very important since he was ultimately vindicated and retained his

had never been a question of whether Pim would be good or bad in the position but a question of why Stout should be removed for no reason when he had done such a good job of organizing the hospitals.

Once his position was confirmed, and once it became clear that he was to carry on his previous duties, Stout reiterated a request that he had made in April. He believed that it was not "for the good of the service" for one man to hold both the position of post surgeon at Chattanooga and the position of superintendent of hospitals for the wider district. Because Chattanooga was an important post, Stout needed to remain there to carry out his responsibilities. Yet, superintending all the hospitals prevented him from performing his post duties thoroughly. He requested that his assistant, Dudley D. Saunders, be appointed to the post surgeon position, a request that was granted on June 12.[25]

Crucial to an understanding of Stout's responsibilities as medical director, is some knowledge of the way in which the Confederate medical department as a whole was supposed to be organized. In many respects the Confederate army and government structure were closely modeled on that of the United States, and the medical department was no exception to this practice. An "Act for the Establishment and Organization of a General Staff for the Army of the Confederate States of America," passed by its congress on February 26, 1861, created, among other offices, that of surgeon general. This officer was to hold the rank of colonel and be paid three thousand dollars per year to oversee the administration of the medical establishment, both in the field and the hospital. The Confederates briefly had two acting or temporary surgeon generals, David C. DeLeon and Charles H. Smith, before Samuel Preston Moore took office on July 30, 1861, a position which he held for the rest of the war.[26]

---

job. Whatever else this incident demonstrates, it shows that Stout's later recollections must be used with caution and compared with his papers where possible. Stout said "that whatever statements of facts have been or will be made in the course of this 'narrative' ["Some Facts"], the future historian proposing to utilize them may regard them as official." The problem, however, is that because Stout did not take advantage of his own resources, his recollections in some places are not as accurate as he supposed. Stout, "Some Facts," pt. 14, 24 (December 1902): 667.

25. H. W. Walter, A. A. G., Army of Tennessee to Stout, June 10, 1863, Emory, box 1, folder 17, also Mus. Confed. ST–4–27, and Duke. Stout to Flewellen, April 14, 1863, TSLA, box 1, folder 11; Stout to T. G. Richardson, June 3, 1863, Emory, box 1, folder 17, also TSLA, box 1, folder 11; Special Orders No. 157, Army of Tennessee, June 12, 1863, Emory, box 1, folder 17, also UTX, box 2G424.

26. Cunningham, Doctors in Gray, 21–22, 27. The Confederates were fortunate, at least from the standpoint of consistency, in having only one surgeon general. The Union

Moore received his medical degree in 1834 and his commission as assistant surgeon in the United States Army in 1835. Promoted to surgeon in 1849, Moore served American troops in Missouri, Kansas, Florida, Texas, Wyoming Territory, New York, and Mexico, and, finally, became medical purveyor (a supply agent) in New Orleans. Moore was not politically inclined, but he resigned when Louisiana seceded and moved to Little Rock, Arkansas, to establish a private practice, agreeing only with great reluctance to become Confederate surgeon general. Moore was generally an able administrator, but his insistence on the formalities of military discipline and his brusqueness with his subordinates combined to make him a less than popular figure.[27]

The small medical force established in the act of February 26, 1861, was augmented by various other laws until by August 1861 President Davis had authority to appoint as many surgeons and assistant surgeons as necessary. Medical officers were divided into two groups—those who cared for the soldiers in the field and those who attended them in the hospitals. Some doctors, like Stout, served in both capacities at one time or another. Often an officer transferred from field to hospital service when his health deteriorated to the point at which he could no longer perform duties in the field. He might then be assigned to hospital duty while a healthier hospital physician replaced him in the field. In more than one case surgeons in charge of hospitals sent Stout lists of doctors able for field service, but marked some of the men as absolutely indispensable to the hospital service.[28] Some aspects of the medical system, such as rank, for example, applied to both the field and the hospital services. But since this study deals only with the general

---

medical department, thanks to various political or sanitary commission-inspired upheavals, went through four surgeon generals. See Adams, *Doctors in Blue*, and Frank R. Freemon, "Lincoln Finds a Surgeon General: William A. Hammond and the Transformation of the Union Army Medical Bureau," *Civil War History* 33 (March 1987): 5–21.

27. Lewis, "Samuel Preston Moore, M.D.," 380–86. See also Cunningham, *Doctors in Gray*, 30–31, 271. One medical officer who reported his personal unpleasant experiences with Moore was S. C. Gholson in "Recollections of My First Six Months in the Confederate Army," 35–47.

28. Cunningham, *Doctors in Gray*, 21–22. Moore to Flewellen, November 28, 1863, NA, chap. 6, vol. 748, gives Flewellen authorization to transfer medical officers from field to hospital and vice versa. One list of doctors is found in D. D. Saunders to Stout, October 28, 1863, UTX, box 2G413. "Medical officers," rather than doctors or physicians, is the term generally used in Civil War correspondence.

hospitals behind the lines, the specific organization and functioning of the field service will not be treated.[29]

Medical officers in the hospitals were divided into three ranks: surgeons, assistant surgeons, and acting assistant surgeons. Surgeons had the best qualifications in experience and education. Some had been medical school professors. Generally they had five or more years of practice to their credit, although some outstanding recent graduates, such as Ferdinand Daniel (see Appendix B), became surgeons directly. Surgeons were likely to have major administrative responsibilities. Assistant surgeons were generally younger and less experienced than surgeons. They usually had direct charge of one or two wards of patients (about seventy men under optimum conditions), for whose care they were responsible. The results of an examination by a three-man board of qualified surgeons determined appointments as surgeon or assistant surgeon, or pronounced an unfortunate candidate unqualified for a commission. These examinations were both oral and written. A typical written exam for promotion to surgeon was four pages long and contained forty-eight questions which asked the meaning of various terms, the proper dosages of various medications, the antidotes to certain poisons, the route of blood circulating from particular organs to the heart, the circumstances rendering amputation necessary, procedures for the treatment of gunshot wounds, and the nature, diagnosis, and treatment of particular diseases. Acting assistant surgeons were not commissioned officers, but physicians hired by contract to assist temporarily. While some of these doctors were well-qualified men awaiting an opportunity to appear before the examining board, others had failed the examinations or were physically unqualified for long-term service.[30]

---

29. For information about the field medical service see *Doctors in Gray*, chap. 7, and *Regulations for the Medical Department of the Confederate States Army.*

30. *Regulations for the Medical Department* (in 1861 and 1863 editions) details the rules and roles to be filled by various officers and the examining board. S. P. Moore, "Confidential Instructions to the Army Medical Board at Chattanooga, Tenn.," March 21, 1863, UTX, box 2G425. A sample of the numerous examination papers at UTX is Thomas Hart Benton Williams's examination for promotion to surgeon. From Homewood, Mississippi, the twenty-eight-year-old Williams was assistant surgeon of the Ninth Mississippi Regiment. He passed the exam. Box 2G423. Stout served as recorder on an examining board in Knoxville during the fall of 1862. Stout to S. A. Smith, December 3, 1862, Emory, box 1, folder 8. Two of Stout's best medical officers, S. M. Bemiss and Robert C. Foster, began their Civil War careers as contract physicians. Stout to Sir, January 30, 1863, Emory, box 1, folder 11.

Among the administrative responsibilities assigned to a few of the very best surgeons was the position of post surgeon, a title later changed to surgeon in charge of hospitals. This position existed in towns where there were two or more hospitals. The surgeon who held it supervised all the hospitals and medical officers there, received and transmitted orders for the post, relayed hospital reports and other messages to his medical director, negotiated with local citizens for the use of buildings by the hospitals, and tried, to the extent possible within his authority, to solve whatever local problems arose. Among Stout's most trusted post surgeons were Joseph P. Logan in Atlanta, and Dudley D. Saunders in Chattanooga and, later, Marietta. Generally the post surgeon was not in charge of any hospital himself.[31]

Each hospital at the post had its own surgeon in charge who assigned the patients to their wards and visited and prescribed for them when possible. He selected the cooks, nurses, and laundresses, supervising them as well as the assistant surgeons and other workers, and seeing that regulations were properly followed. In a hospital of any size the surgeon in charge had so many administrative responsibilities that he had little time for patients. Paperwork of all sorts flourished in the Confederate hospitals. Every day the surgeon in charge had to make a "Morning Report," indicating any change in the number of persons in the hospital and the names of those affected. These daily reports had to be consolidated into weekly and monthly reports. Each month the surgeon in charge of the hospital also had to make a personnel report, not to mention daily keeping a hospital register, case book, prescription book, diet book, copies of all his correspondence, and making miscellaneous other reports. It was absolutely essential for a surgeon in charge to have a clerk. In addition, the surgeon in charge requisitioned medical supplies from the medical purveyor, food from the commissary, and wood, bunks, facilities, and transportation from the quartermaster. Instances in which requested supplies were not forthcoming are legion.[32]

---

31. A. J. Foard commanded the use of the proper title in a Circular of February 13, 1863, Emory, box 1, folder 12. The title post surgeon will continue to be used to avoid confusion when discussing the differences between the surgeon in charge of hospitals and the surgeon in charge of a particular hospital. Tebault, "Hospitals of the Confederacy," 501. In general Tebault's recollections of the Confederacy are effusively, verbosely rosy. Some of these generalizations about the responsibilities of various types of medical officers come from wide reading in the Stout papers. Many specific incidents will be cited at a later time.

32. Regulations for the Medical Department, 8, 10; Tebault, "Hospitals of the Confeder-

Medical purveyors were doctors in charge of supplying medicines (including their indigenous substitutes), alcoholic stimulants, and other hospital supplies. Standard supply tables regulated the quantity of drugs that could be dispensed to a hospital at a particular time. Commissaries provided staple foods such as flour, beef, and pork. Other items necessary to the sick, such as vegetables, were grown on the hospital grounds or purchased with the hospital fund, which the commissaries also dispensed. Quartermasters had large responsibilities for requisitioning or constructing hospital buildings, and providing tools, tents, straw, fuel, clothing, and transportation. Unfortunately, many quartermasters, at least in the West, seemed to regard hospitals as nuisances and were slow to meet hospital needs. In many instances quartermasters insisted that bulky hospital property, especially bunks, be abandoned when the hospitals moved, yet when the hospitals arrived at their new location, the quartermasters were unable or unwilling to supply them with replacements for the missing items. The sins of quartermasters were a source of frequent complaint among Army of Tennessee medical officers.[33]

One other avenue for procuring supplies was also open to the surgeon. This was the hospital fund, which was supposed to be used for luxuries needed by the sick but not procurable through the commissary. The source of these funds baffled many recently civilian surgeons. Each soldier was supposed to receive a daily ration, which by law had a particular monetary value. The sick and wounded were usually unable to eat much, if any, of the standard army ration. At the end of the month the monetary value of all the uneaten rations became the hospital fund.

acy," 501; Cunningham, *Doctors in Gray*, 74. In late 1864 a reminder to surgeons in charge of hospitals listed twenty-one reports sent through seven routes. Stout Circular No. 43, December 14, 1864, UTX, box 2G425. A list of "Records to be inspected" included twenty types of registers. Loose sheet in Flewellen Hospital Order Book, Emory, Stout microfilm.

33. George S. Blackie to My dear Doctor [Stout], November 6, 1862, UTX, box 2G387. Blackie, headquartered in Atlanta, was the purveyor with whom Stout dealt most frequently. Stout, "Some Facts," pt. 19, 25 (May 1903): 282; pt. 5, 23 (April 1901): 195. Problems in Columbus, Georgia, are described in George B. Douglas to Stout, July 12, 1864, UTX, box 2G395. Stout recounted specific difficulties in Stout to Brig. Gen. M. J. Wright, July 8, 1864, Mus. Confed. ST–8–16; Stout to Moore, October 10, 1863, Emory, box 1, folder 20. Stout said "It is my conviction, founded upon experience and observation, that quartermasters and commissaries recently appointed from civil life, are more given to the evasion of their duties than officers of any other staff departments." He blamed them for causing the soldiers much needless suffering. Pt. 15, 25 (January 1903): 27.

This money could be spent in nearly any way that would increase the comfort of the patients. Chickens, eggs, and butter, as well as milk cows, vegetable seeds, and horses and wagons for transporting provisions came from this fund. Even chamber pots could be a hospital fund purchase, but the doctors were not supposed to buy medicine with it. Stout spent a good deal of time instructing new military doctors how to figure and use the fund. He speculated that as much as one million dollars was lost and much needless suffering resulted during the early part of the war because of lack of knowledge about this money.[34]

Surgeons who were not in charge of hospitals, as well as assistant surgeons, did not have responsibilities for dealing with other departments. Instead they had direct responsibility for the care of the patients on their ward, prescribing medicines, dressing wounds, and determining diets, under the general supervision of the surgeon in charge. Each of these men also had to take their turn as "officer of the day." This person was on duty for twenty-four hours beginning at 7:00 A.M. He was to be formally attired in sash and sword, to be available for any emergency during the night, and to inspect the entire hospital, making a report the next morning about what he found. Most of these reports were quite prosaic, but on occasion some bored officer wrote a creative piece for his own amusement. Ferdinand Daniel, for example, was stationed at a hospital in Covington, Georgia, during the summer of 1864. For several weeks the hospitals in that town were nearly empty since most of the patients had been sent further away to make room for the wounded from an anticipated battle. The battle was delayed and the seventeen medical officers at the post spent their time fishing, picnicking, and going riding with the local girls. This situation made the position of officer of the day all the more tedious. On one occasion Daniel whiled away the time writing pages and pages of endless verbosity, merely to state that the bread was burnt. Another morning the officer going off duty jokingly told Daniel that there was a pig in the "sink" behind ward three, when there actually was not. Daniel reported the following to his superiors, "Surgeon Warmuth in reporting mentioned that a pig in sporting on the brink of the sink, attracted by the od'rous vapors began to cut up divers capers, and essayed at last to take a peep into the depths of the nasty deep; but

---

34. Stout, "Outline," 78–79; "Some Facts," pt. 5, 23 (April 1901): 194–98; pt. 19, 25 (May 1903): 280–82. Stout, "Circular," September 21, 1863, Flewellen Hospital Order Book, Emory, Stout microfilm. Cumming describes problems with the hospital fund in *Journal*, September 28, 1862, and May 9, 1863, pp. 58 and 91.

owing to a little dizziness he got his pig-ship into business. I heard a squealing, which, appealing to every feeling of my nature, I quickly ran to get a man to lend a hand to help the porcine creature. The pig, in the meantime, became apprehensive that the stink of the sink (which was very offensive), would produce a fit of indigestion, revolved in his mind the knotty question, 'To be, or not to be.' He soon decided that if taken by our hands we'd save his bacon (not the Friar, but the fried), then another effort tried. Striving then with might and main, he landed on the land again, and scampered off with caper fine, a happier and wiser swine." Stout returned the report with the notation "not approved" and added, "this dignified officer is expected to make a more dignified report."[35]

A hospital could not function without many other assistants. Of particular importance were stewards. Hospital stewards were usually enlisted men, sometimes civilians, "sufficiently intelligent, and skilled in pharmacy" to serve as the hospital druggist. The steward was to keep track of all the hospital supplies and rations, oversee their issue, and supervise the cooks and nurses. That the steward held an important position is evidenced by the fact that stewards were the only able-bodied white men between the ages of seventeen and forty-five employed in hospitals who were exempted from field duty in a circular from the surgeon general's office, issued on July 8, 1864.[36]

Each ward had a wardmaster who was responsible for its cleanliness and who supervised the nurses on his ward. He assigned new patients to their beds, collected and carefully listed, labeled, and stored their effects, and issued hospital clothing. In addition, the wardmaster received all the bedding, furniture, utensils, and other materials issued to his ward by the steward, and was responsible for a weekly account detailing any loss or damage to hospital property.[37]

On November 25, 1862, Confederate authorities initiated a system of female matrons for each hospital. The system provided for two chief matrons "to exercise a superintendence over the entire domestic economy

35. Tebault, "Hospitals of the Confederacy," 501; Daniel, *Recollections of a Rebel Surgeon*, 119–20. A typical report, from the Hardee Hospital in Forsyth, Georgia, is J. H. Brack to William Webb, May 4, 1864, Emory, box 2, folder 18.
36. *Regulations for the Medical Department*, 8–9, 14. S. P. Moore, Circular No. 11, July 8, 1864, Flewellen Hospital Order Book, Emory, Stout microfilm.
37. *Regulations for the Medical Department*, 8; S. E. Chaille, Fairgrounds Hospital #2, Atlanta, No. 25, August 15, 1863, UTX, ledger 4L218; Smith, *The Soldier's Friend*, 182.

of the hospital," two assistant matrons to superintend the laundry and patients' clothing, and two ward matrons for each ward of one hundred patients to see that they received proper bedding, food, and medicine. No doubt these numbers could be adjusted, depending upon the size of the hospital. Several matrons kept diaries or wrote accounts of their service in which they detailed their activities: fixing special delicacies, such as toddies and eggnog, for small appetites; washing hands, faces, and wounds; feeding the weak; dispensing liquor as prescribed; padding crutches; encouraging the patients spiritually and praying with them; writing letters to the patients' families with news of their whereabouts or accounts of their demise; and comforting the dying. Kate Cumming, working at the Newsom Hospital in Chattanooga, described the schedule which she and her assistant matron kept. They arose at 4:00 A.M. and often kept busy until midnight. It is little wonder that many matrons got sick after a few weeks or months and had to go elsewhere to recuperate. Initially many doctors and civilians opposed having women in the hospitals in any capacity, but Stout and Cumming believed that the soldiers appreciated their presence and that most women did good work.[38]

The medical *Regulations* required one nurse for every ten patients, but getting and keeping enough nurses, whether white or black, male or female, was one of the major problems confronted by the medical department. The only women with any training as nurses when the war began were the members of various Roman Catholic sisterhoods, most notably the Sisters of Charity, who maintained their hospitals in perfect

38. General Orders No. 95, A & IGO, Richmond, November 25, 1862, in *Regulations for the Medical Department*, 55. A pamphlet labeled "General Orders No. 93," dated November 22, 1862, contains this same act. UTX, box 2G425. Among the matrons who served in the Army of Tennessee hospitals were Kate Cumming, Mrs. Susan E.D. Smith, and Mrs. Fannie Beers. Their works have been cited already. An account by a matron at the Chimborazo Hospital in Richmond is Phoebe Yates Pember, *A Southern Woman's Story*. S. P. Moore, Circular No. 6, March 17, 1864, Flewellen Hospital Order Book, Emory, Stout microfilm; Smith, *The Soldier's Friend*, 183–84; Cumming, *Journal*, entries for May 8, 1862, March 10, 1863, and May 24, 1864, pp. 23, 83, 186–87. Sick matrons are mentioned in ibid., October 8, 24 and 27, and December 30, 1862, pp. 61, 63, 69; Beers, *Memories*, 51. Cumming reports restrictive doctors and reluctant friends on April 9 and September 8, 1862 (among other places), pp. 3, 55, but says that "I think as soon as surgeons discover that ladies are really of service, that prejudice will cease to exist. The patients are delighted to have us, and say that we can cause them to think of the dearest of all places to them now— home." May 23, 1862, p. 28. She reports Stout's commendation of helpful women, August 10, 1863, pp. 113–14. Stout, "Some Facts," pt. 22, 25 (September 1903): 523.

order. The Sisters of Charity were much in demand, but there were less than two hundred of them.[39] Some nurses were men detailed from the ranks, most of whom had had no nursing experience. While some of these soldiers were found to be unqualified and soon relieved from nursing, others became quite skilled. The problem with training able-bodied men, however, was that they were subject to recall for field service at a moment's notice. Many convalescents who were unable for field duty also attempted to serve as nurses, a carryover from antebellum hospital practices. They too usually were untrained and had to return to the field as soon as they were physically fit. But an additional problem with convalescents was that they were often too disabled themselves to serve as nurses. B. W. Avent, surgeon in charge of hospitals at Kingston, complained to Stout in December 1863, "a number of men have been sent to this Post recently for duty in hospital, a large majority of whom, are entirely unfit for such duties. Some are sick, some with one arm, some with one leg others stiff with Rheumatism &c &c, Cases permanently disabled, most of them have been placed under treatment, and are not now on duty in hospital, and will, in my judgment, never be able to do effective service." Louisa May Alcott, whose month as a nurse in a Washington, D.C. hospital terminated in typhoid fever, complained about similar conditions in Northern hospitals. "I should like to enter my protest," she said, "against employing convalescents as attendants, instead of strong, properly trained, and cheerful men. . . . Here it was a source of constant trouble and confusion, these feeble ignorant men trying to sweep, scrub, lift, and wait upon their sicker comrades. One, with a diseased heart, was expected to run up and down stairs, carry heavy trays, and move helpless men; he tried it, and grew rapidly worse than when he first came: and, when he was ordered out to march away to the convalescent hospital, fell, in a sort of fit, before he turned the corner, and was brought back to die."[40]

---

39. *Regulations for the Medical Department*, 10. Simkins and Patton, "The Work of Southern Women," 490–91; Cumming, *Journal*, April 18, 1862, p. 12; Flewellen to Stout, February 12, 1863, TSLA, box 1, folder 4; W. M. Gentry to Stout, March 1, 1864, ibid., folder 6. A study of the various Catholic sisterhoods and their contributions to nursing care both North and South is Maher, *To Bind Up the Wounds*. Frank Hawthorn was unusual since he did not want any Sisters of Charity. He did not want to replace the women already doing good work at the Academy Hospital, many of whom really needed the job. Hawthorn to Stout, February 17, 1863, UTX, box 2G392.

40. Rosenberg, *The Care of Strangers*, 35–36. Stout to A. Adj. Gen. H. L. Clay, July 6, 1862, TSLA, box 1, folder 11; George M. Shattuck to Dr. Pim, June 5, 1862, N A,

Conditions were hardly better in relation to securing cooks and even laundresses. Soldiers sometimes served in both categories. Commanding officers encouraged doctors to employ civilians and blacks (slave or free) as much as possible to relieve soldiers for field duty. In his study of masters and slaves in Civil War Georgia, Clarence L. Mohr has analyzed data from nineteen of the twenty-nine hospitals under Stout's control in 1863 before the Battle of Chickamauga. Of their 834 employees (excluding doctors), 355 were soldiers, 95 were white civilians, and 384 were slaves, leading him to speculate that from 450 to 500 slaves were working in Georgia hospitals at this time. Although he has no detailed later statistics, Mohr believes that black hospital employment could have doubled that figure by the end of the war, especially in areas with little competition from industry.[41]

While most of the generalities of hospital administration have been illustrated by citing examples from the Army of Tennessee, the same regulations and personnel requirements held true for hospitals in Virginia as well.[42] A great variety of capable and cooperative personnel, from doctors and matrons to cooks and laundresses, were absolutely crucial to the successful functioning of hospitals, as Stout was well aware. The problem was, of course, that finding these workers and keeping them capable, cooperative, and disciplined was much easier theorized and ordered than done, especially given conditions in the Confederacy as the war progressed.

Foard file; Stout, Circular No. 3, August 15, 1863, UTX, ledger 4L218. B. W. Avent to Stout, September 11, 1863, Emory, box 1, folder 18; Avent to Stout, December 13, 1863, UTX, box 2G405. Alcott, *Hospital Sketches*, 68, 78.

41. Cumming, *Journal*, October 12, 1862, February 21, 1863, pp. 61, 81; Flewellen, "Circular," no date (but probably early 1863), N A, chap. 6, vol. 749. One civilian volunteered his services with the following note, "i am a man not beaing able for duty in the field i thought that i would do verry well for a nurse in the horse pittal[.]" Robert B. Carson to ?, May 25, 1863, UTX, box 2G379. Mohr, *On the Threshold of Freedom*, 128–35. In mid-June 1864 S. P. Moore authorized Stanford E. Chaille in Macon to pay four hundred dollars per year to hire slaves. Moore to Chaille, June 27, 1864, N A, chap. 6, vol. 741, pt. 2.

42. This can be seen in numerous examples from the eastern theatre of the war in Cunningham, *Doctors in Gray*. The situation was, in many respects, similar in Union hospitals as well. Adams, *Doctors in Blue*, passim.

CHAPTER 4

"STEADILY IMPROVING IN EFFICIENCY AND FAITHFUL ATTENTION TO DUTY"

"When Genl. Bragg placed me in charge of all the hospitals of his department," Stout later wrote, "I well remember the chagrin manifested by many medical men and professors of colleges from the cities, who unmistakably manifested their disappointment. Some I heard of as saying 'Who in the hell is that fellow *Stout?*' Several personally asked me where I hailed from. I told them good humoredly and with a gentle tone of sarcasm, 'I had been living for more than a dozen years in a hollow beech tree in the back woods of Giles County Tenn.'"[1] When Stout became superintendent of hospitals for Bragg's army, at which time he took on the duties and responsibilities which he continued as medical director, he was relatively unknown. He had held no prewar teaching position that would have given him a widespread reputation and consequent respect. People who were acquainted with Stout's hospitals in the field, in Nashville, and in Chattanooga realized that he was a very good administrator; but these people were few in number,

This situation could easily have led to disaster. Rank was a matter of concern to the medical corps, just as it was to the rest of the military. Stout was responsible for the assignment of doctors (as well as matrons and stewards), and he was supervising men who had established reputations, such as B. W. Avent, previously the surgeon general of the Provisional Army of Tennessee. It would not have been surprising if Stout had found his path blocked by quarrels and disrespect. But this did not happen. Instead, Stout managed as many as several hundred doctors at one time, who usually cooperated with him, if not with each other.[2]

---

1. S. H. Stout to Ferdinand E. Daniel, September 21, 1898, TSLA, box 1, folder 12.
2. An undated "List of Medical Officers on duty in the Hospitals of the Army of Tennessee," probably written in early 1864 (since there were still hospitals in Dalton and Kingston, but there were already hospitals in Alabama), contains 225 names. Mus. Confed., ST–11–7.

To understand Stout's successful supervision of his subordinates, it is important to examine his philosophy of personnel management. While this could be deduced solely from the ways in which he handled various cases, Stout also described his philosophy in a letter to Tobias G. Richardson in March 1864,[3] as well as in parts of his *Southern Practitioner* series written in 1903.

First of all, Stout believed that surgeons should be told their duty and then expected to do it. He gave the men general principles to follow, leaving "the details of their mode of application . . . to the judgment the honor and the conscience of the officer." Inundating the doctors with a mass of details for every possible case tended, Stout believed, to promote the evasion of duties rather than their fulfillment. Under Stout's system most doctors functioned at least adequately when encouraged to do their duty and instructed in areas where they were deficient. "[I]n special cases, where there is neglect of duty, intoxication, incompetency— either physical or mental or both, by a wise exercise of their authority, medical directors and the Surgeon General can secure the punishment of delinquents and offenders and retire, those not qualified." Stout saw his men "steadily improving in efficiency and faithful attention to duty under the policy." In fact, Stout felt strongly that "No severe orders, which indicate a desire on the part of those in authority to convert the members of our profession into mere machines . . . can ever secure their hearty obedience, and they are damaging to the esprit du corps [sic] of the profession."[4] While Stout was a student of the military regulations and while he advocated military discipline, he said forty years later that one could make "no greater mistake" than to try to carry out regulations intended for peacetime while in the middle of maneuvers and battles that made them impracticable.[5]

---

3. Richardson, former assistant (field) medical director of the Army of Tennessee, had gone to Richmond as a hospital inspector. There he found a good many aspects of the hospitals that did not pass his inspection, particularly in personnel matters. As Stout was more experienced at hospital administration, Richardson sent him a letter listing numerous orders that he proposed to issue to rectify the situation, and asking Stout's opinion of them. Richardson's letter has not been found, but from Stout's reply it is evident that Richardson was proposing blanket orders for the whole Confederate hospital system to solve problems that only existed in Richmond. Stout to Richardson, March 28, 1864, Emory, box 2, folder 6.

4. Ibid.

5. Stout, "Some Facts," pt. 19, 25 (May 1903): 279–80.

Stout also inspired cooperation from his subordinates by his own actions and attitudes. He set an example of obedience and subordination to his own superiors. He also set an example by his seemingly tireless endeavors for "professional self-improvement," and his zeal for duty. Stout personally visited all his hospitals at least once each month, and more often when possible, focusing on the places where the worst cases were located. Usually he worked successfully with only four or five hours of sleep each night.[6]

Stout made it known that he was willing to listen to complaints and criticisms from any of his subordinates as long as they came to him through proper channels. When complainers reported poor conditions or infractions of regulations, Stout investigated. In cases where he heard a doctor complain about his own situation, Stout sometimes had to explain kindly and patiently that "the good of the service" required the doctor's cooperation, for the goal of the medical establishment was the best possible care for the sick and wounded soldiers, not the convenience of each individual officer. Stout, however, was sensitive to the needs of his subordinates, and he often rearranged assignments when officers requested it. Stout did not demand that the medical officers give up all comforts either. When T. G. Richardson proposed that doctors live in tents on the hospital grounds to make sure that physicians were always available, Stout strongly resisted the idea. It would be unjust to the medical officers to put them in living conditions which other government functionaries were not required to endure. Doctors would also be less likely to do good work if they were uncomfortable. Stout expressed his operating principle, "I care not how comfortable a medical officer makes himself, how cleanly or finely dressed he goes, so that he does not neglect his duties, or steal the public money and waste the public property." If a doctor could afford the comforts of home, he was welcome to them as far as Stout was concerned.[7]

Of course, Stout realized that inspections and supervision inevitably resulted in criticism and correction, but he believed that some inspectors were entirely too "bossy" and offensive in their comments. Stout said that doctors were often "supersensitive" to professional criticism. They knew more about the details of one of their own cases, for example, than any other person would know. Thus, they often resented criticism of their

6. Ibid., pt. 15, 25 (January 1903): 29–30; pt. 23, 25 (October 1903): 573.
7. Ibid., pt. 15, 25 (January 1903): 29–30; Stout to Richardson, March 28, 1864, Emory, box 2, folder 6; Stout to Daniel, September 21, 1898, TSLA, box 1, folder 12.

diagnosis by a person who had no previous knowledge of the case. Stout claimed that he always tried to treat his subordinates with courtesy and respect, making his critiques positive, patient, charitable, and helpful. This concern for his subordinates, expressed in various ways, apparently helped to build a team spirit among the hospital staff members.[8]

Because Stout believed in leaving the details of hospital administration to his subordinates, he delegated authority and responsibility. He was able to do this because he was very careful about choosing the persons to whom he gave authority. Stout examined not only the medical and surgical qualifications of his post surgeons, who were, of course, the persons to whom he delegated the most authority, but he was also concerned about their attitude toward himself. He wished to ensure against personality conflicts or resentments that would lead to rebellion rather than cooperation. Another factor that Stout had to ascertain was the reliability of reports sent to him by these potential post surgeons.[9] Stout had to depend on post surgeons for accurate reports in several areas. As the hospital system expanded, and then as the hospitals were forced to relocate because of military movements, Stout sent a variety of surgeons, armed with a list of desirable conditions and facilities, to inspect potential sites to determine whether they were suitable for hospital purposes. Toward the end of the war, as communications deteriorated, Stout gave some of his post surgeons considerable discretion to move their hospitals out of the enemy's way without Stout's specific orders, should the need arise.[10] Stout relied

---

8. Stout, "Some Facts," pt. 23, 25 (October 1903): 571–72; pt. 15, 25 (January 1903): 30.

9. Stout, "Outline," 65.

10. Numerous inspection reports survive, often made not just by post surgeons, but also by other reliable medical officers at posts somewhat near the prospective site(s). Criteria desired at the hospital site can be found in S. M. Bemiss to D. C. O'Keefe, December 2, 1863, UTX, box 2G384. Examples of these reports are: L. T. Pim to Stout, March 3, 1863, Emory, box 1, folder 13, and also SHC–UNC, Stout microfilm, reel 2, reporting on Rome and Kingston, Georgia; C. B. Gamble to Stout, March 17, 1863, Mus. Confed. ST–4–11, reporting on Graysville, Ringgold, Catoosa Station, Taylor's, Tunnel Hill, McCamy's Farm, and the Shanties; Richard O. Curry to Stout, September 5, 1863, ibid., ST–5–8, reporting on Cartersville; Albert H. Snead to Bemiss, December 14, 1863, Emory, box 1, folder 25, also SHC–UNC, reel 2, reporting on Jonesboro, Calhoun, Rough and Ready, and East Point; and Charles E. Michel to Stout, September [ca. 19], 1864, UTX, box 2G379, reporting on Fort Valley, and several sites around Eufaula, Alabama. Stout issued such an order from Macon on July 26, 1864, ibid., box 2G428.

on his post surgeons for assistance in personnel management as well. Widespread responsibilities kept Stout from spending extended amounts of time at any but the post where his headquarters were located. Thus he was unable to have personal knowledge of the character and abilities of most of the men he supervised. Stout relied on his post surgeons to provide accurate, confidential information that would allow him to increase the responsibilities of the capable, to diminish the responsibilities of the less able, and to relieve incompetents from duty.[11] Perhaps the best example of Stout's willingness to delegate, however, was his choice, in November 1863, of Samuel Merrifield Bemiss to serve as his assistant medical director. Bemiss, who left Kentucky and joined the Confederacy, was a skilled surgeon, and Stout trusted him to manage the affairs of hospital headquarters as acting medical director when Stout was traveling to visit outlying hospitals.[12] While Stout was able thus to delegate at least some personnel functions to his most trusted subordinates, he was still the court of last resort and chief troubleshooter in personnel matters.

One of Stout's major responsibilities was to assign doctors, matrons, and stewards to the various hospitals. In this activity he cooperated with field Medical Directors A. J. Foard and E. A. Flewellen, as well as Surgeon General Samuel P. Moore. Much mundane correspondence survives that orders a medical officer to a particular hospital and that reports his arrival at his new post.[13] But assigning medical officers could be a difficult, and at times a tricky, proposition. Some doctors asked to be assigned to a particular hospital to work with a certain superior, perhaps

11. Reports of this sort are: F. H. Evans to Stout, December 7, 1863, SHC–UNC, reel 2, and especially J. P. Logan, "Confidential Report in Regard to Merits of Medical Officers, Atlanta April 1864," Mus. Confed., no number.

12. Cumming, *Journal*, November 13, 1863, p. 153.

13. Flewellen told Stout that he could place medical officers ordered to report to him, anywhere "which the interests of the Service requires." January 23, 1863, NA, chap. 6, vol. 749. At one point Stout, on the recommendation of several of his reliable post surgeons, asked Flewellen to "relieve the hospital service" of several "incubi," which Flewellen promised to do promptly. Stout to Flewellen, April 13, 1863, and Flewellen to Stout, no date [but response to April 13 letter], both TSLA, box 1, folder 4. Examples of the reporting letters are W. M. Wright to Stout, August 15, 1864, UTX, box 2G379; George S. King to Stout, December 17, 1863, A. A. Horner to Stout, April 30, 1864, William L. McAllister to Stout, October 23, 1864, and others, all in Duke. Numerous other examples of this sort can be found in all the larger Stout collections.

a prewar friend. Doctors in charge of hospitals often asked for a specific subordinate whose services had been especially satisfactory on some prior occasion. In a few instances, a doctor refused to have a particular medical officer assigned to him because of some past experience.[14]

Doctors were more likely to ask for assignment to a particular post rather than a specific hospital. In many cases the officers requested a change for reasons of health. Those suffering from chronic bronchitis and chronic rheumatism asked to move south to a warmer climate, while diarrhea sufferers desired a change of water. Ironically, some of the doctors with diarrhea believed "limestone water" was the cause of their problem, while others expected it to be the cure.[15]

The medical officers were often frail. Field surgeons, debilitated by chronic diarrhea and other difficulties, applied for hospital positions in the hope that a change of diet and protection from the elements would restore their usefulness. Stout and his superiors attempted to accommodate as many requests as possible, since it was certainly in

---

14. For example, Assistant Surgeon W. G. Lomax wanted to be assigned to the Third Georgia Hospital in Augusta to work with his old college friend Surgeon Baxley. L. T. Pim to Stout, August 24, 1864, and J. P. Logan to Stout, August 25, 1864, both UTX, box 2G379. William L. McAllister had heard that Assistant Surgeon L. W. Yates and his superior at one of the Fair Ground Hospitals in Atlanta did not get along. McAllister, who had worked with Yates for two years and considered him a "faithful conscientious man," asked to have Yates transferred to his hospital, the Buckner, in Newnan, Georgia. McAllister to Stout, June 30, 1864, UTX, box 2G418. B. M. Wible to Stout, May 22, 1863, TSLA, box 1, folder 9, requested that Dr. Bemiss be assigned to Tunnel Hill where he was needed more than at Ringgold. W. M. Gentry wrote to Stout from Montgomery, "Excuse my importuning disposition on the subject of Medical Officers. I like a nice Med. Officer so well, that I want every one I see & having lately seen my friend, DeYampert I must importune for him." Gentry wanted DeYampert to replace an ailing surgeon at a rather unruly hospital. Gentry to Stout, August 26, 1864, Emory, box 2, folder 16. James Mercer Green, post surgeon at Macon, from previous experience in Richmond, did not want Assistant Surgeon G. G. Griffin in his hospitals because "his principles are unsound & I cannot rely on him." As Green had "frequent cause to reprove him . . . for neglect of duty," he became "implacably inimical." Green to Sir [probably Stout], November 6, 1863, TSLA, box 1, folder 11.

15. E. M. Vasser to Flewellen, January 29, 1863, TSLA, box 1, folder 15; Joel H. Williams to Stout, October 12, 1863, Emory, box 1, folder 20; J. M. Green to Sir [Stout?], November 6, 1863, TSLA, box 1, folder 11; F. A. Anderson to Stout, November 11, 1863, UTX, box 2G379. John M. Adams to Stout, January 23, 1865, ibid., box 2G411, wanted an assignment to Shelby Springs, Alabama, which water he had found to be the most helpful for his chronic kidney complaint.

the interests of the medical service that ailing physicians be restored to health. Flewellen lamented, however, "It is impossible to find suitable places for all of the invalid Med. Officers in the service."[16]

Officers transferred from the field had to be replaced by physicians from the hospitals. But surgeons in charge of hospitals or posts were reluctant to send away any officers who were doing good hospital work. And once hospital surgeons arrived in the field, Foard complained, "I find most of the Med. Off. who have been for sometime in hospitals so exceedingly delicate and nice that they cant [sic] Stand camp life and at once get sick when they see that they are to live on corn bread & bacon and sleep in the open air—in other words they have become demoralized from ease & luxury."[17]

While chronic diarrhea, pulmonary and rheumatic complaints, and various typhoid and malarial fevers were the most common ailments, a variety of other conditions appeared among the medical officers. Frank Hawthorn and J. D. Smith suffered eye problems. Surgeon Taliaferro contracted gangrene in one of his hands. W. H. Cunningham had to have all of his lower teeth pulled because of an illness. He asked for assignment to Montgomery where he could have a set of false teeth made and be near his family who would feed him food that he was able to eat. Mental illness was rare among the medical men, but the single known instance of its occurrence created a difficult situation for Assistant Surgeon M. W. King, whose hospital was then in transit to Meridian, Mississippi, in support of Hood's Tennessee campaign. King wrote to Stout that Assistant Surgeon Fleming J. Matthews "is suffering with a decided condition of mental aberation, amounting to confirmed

16. Charles E. Michel to Flewellen, August 12, 1863, TSLA, box 1, folder 15, regarding Paul H. Otey, Second Arkansas Regiment, Liddell's Brigade; W. M. Gentry to Stout, October 13, 1863, UTX, box 2G424; C. C. Abernathy to Stout, March 13, 1864, TSLA, box 1, folder 3. Both Gentry and Abernathy, while suffering from chronic digestive and bowel complaints, also feared longer field experience because they claimed a tendency toward tuberculosis ran in their families. Flewellen's comment, dated February 1, 1863, is noted on E. M. Vasser to Flewellen, January 29, 1863, ibid., folder 15.

17. D. D. Saunders to Stout, October 28, 1863, UTX, box 2G413; J. P. Logan to Stout, November 4, 1863, SHC–UNC, reel 4; Foard to Stout, June 6, 1864, Duke, also Emory, Stout microfilm. In one case a surgeon in Covington wrote Stout in behalf of a colleague whom Stout had ordered to the field. He believed that Stout could not know what terrible asthma Surgeon S. W. Caldwell suffered from or Stout would not send Caldwell out of the hospital. G. S. West to Stout, March 20, 1864, Emory, box 2, folder 5.

Lunacy. He is utterly incapacitated for any duty whatever. It keeps myself & whole Hospital corps in a continued state of painful anxiety."[18]

Another major reason some doctors asked for assignment to a particular post was that they encountered a family problem. Dr. Robert Battey, for example, did not expect his wife to survive the birth of a child, and so he sought, and received, a transfer to his home in Rome, Georgia. Carlisle Terry applied for transfer from the field to his home in Columbus, Georgia, because he had several sick children. Stout had to deal not only with requests from surgeons but also from their wives. In response to one woman's plea that Stout allow her husband to come home to care for the family's needs, Stout noted that he found it "embarassing" to correspond with women "as I can never hope to be able to satisfy them." While medical problems were the most common reason for requesting a transfer, Lucian L. Saunders expressed an explicit economic motive when he asked for a change from Newnan to Griffin. In Griffin he could board with his brother for half the price and better support his wife and three children.[19]

While family problems led to requests for particular assignments, they also occasioned pleas for furloughs and excuses for not reporting as ordered. In December 1864, Robert Battey, whose wife survived her 1863 confinement, and who had since been transferred to Meridian, Mississippi, asked for a thirty-day leave of absence to return to Rome to remove his wife and seven children to a safer place where they would not be harassed by the Confederate cavalry deserters who were

18. D. D. Saunders to S. M. Bemiss (concerning Hawthorn), December 8, 1864, UTX, box 2G404; J. D. Smith to H. V. Miller, July 26, 1864, ibid., box 2G402; W. M. Gentry to Stout (about Taliaferro), August 26, 1864, Emory, box 2, folder 16; W. H. Cunningham to Stout, August 28, 1864, ibid.; M. W. King to Stout, November 19, 1864, TSLA, box 1, folder 7. King reported one surgeon's suggestion, that he leave Matthews in the first hospital they reached.

19. J. P. Logan to Stout, July 16, 1863, UTX, box 2G387. Carlisle Terry, "one of the best Division Surgeons in the Army of Tenn.," had been in the field since the beginning of the war. T. G. Richardson to Doctor, March 29, 1864, Emory, box 3, folder 11. Also J. H. Bryson(?) to My dear Doctor [probably Stout], March 10, 1864, and Carlisle Terry to Stout, March 16, 1864, both in Emory, box 2, folder 5. Mrs. C. J. Cooper to Stout, September 1864 and Stout's notation to Cooper on the back, September 15, 1864, UTX, box 2G381. While W. G. Lomax (footnote 14) wished to work with his friend Surgeon Baxley, he also wanted to be in Augusta so that he could be with his wife while she underwent some medical treatment that could not be provided by an ordinary rural practitioner. Lomax to Stout, September 24, 1864, ibid., box 2G389. Lucian L. Saunders to Stout, January 12, 1864, Emory, Stout microfilm.

then raiding the Rome area. D. D. Saunders, Stout's good friend, asked either to be sent to Alabama on hospital business or to be given a leave of absence. His wife had died and Saunders wanted to take his two small daughters to stay with a relative. G. S. West, then in Augusta, expected to report to Covington, but his wife, who had come to visit, went into labor prematurely, and so West could not leave Augusta. He wrote, "it is very disagreeable thus to be obliged to bring to your notice my Private family affairs, but there is no alternative."[20] Throughout his tenure as medical director of hospitals, Stout found that he had to confront many "private family affairs," and try to allow his surgeons to meet their family responsibilities, while still doing what was best for the medical service.

What about Stout's attention to his own family responsibilities during the Civil War? There is a dearth of manuscript material in this area, probably the result of the activities of his daughters, Maggie and Katie, who weeded many of Stout's personal papers out of the collection in the twentieth century. Information about a few aspects of Stout's relationship with his family survives. Stout's family did not "refugee" out of Giles County, Tennessee. Early in the war no one supposed that the conflict would last long or that the Federals would overrun middle Tennessee. By the time this happened, Stout had considerable hospital responsibilities which did not leave him much time to devote to his family, even if they had been nearby. Probably Stout felt that his duty to his country took precedence over the pleasures and distractions of family life. But Stout did not leave his family defenseless, since his wife's brother lived on the next farm; her father resided nearby; and other relatives and friends lived in the same general area. In all probability, Stout believed that it would be more beneficial for his immediate family to remain among their kin, than to be relocated from one hospital post to another.

---

20. Battey to Bemiss, December 3, 1864, UTX, box 2G413; D. D. Saunders to Stout, February 10, 1864, Emory, box 2, folder 4. B. F. Fields resigned in September 1862, before he actually received his commission, to attend his wife in a difficult childbirth. Even the aid of five other doctors could not save his wife, although the baby lived. After placing his four small children, Fields asked to return to the medical service because he wished to keep busy. Fields to Stout, September 22, 1862 and February 22, 1863, UTX, boxes 2G398 and 2G396 respectively. G. S. West to Stout, December 26, 1863, ibid., box 2G379. A number of other examples can be found, but in one particularly pathetic example A. P. Hall could not report as ordered because he was sick with "bilous fever" and his only child had just died. A. P. Hall to Stout, September 12, 1864, ibid.

Stout was unable to visit his family often. Apparently he came home only three times during the war, and he was gone for one period of thirty-two months.[21] Part of the reason for Stout's lengthy absence was the Federal occupation of Giles County. Obviously an important Confederate hospital administrator like Stout could not venture into enemy-occupied territory. Some military activities and, as Stout put it, "outrages," took place on his property. He later said that the battle of Pulaski began in front of his house. Stout's brother-in-law and neighbor, Burwell Abernathy, suffered a great deal during the conflict. The Federals burned the cotton crops he had harvested in 1860–63 (about one hundred bales) and his cotton gin, took all his livestock and his food crops, and left him in great distress and postwar debt. Stout's immediate family probably experienced similar depredations.[22]

While absent from his family, Stout apparently took whatever means were available to communicate with them, most often sending letters by persons going into the area. This was the case with Stout's single surviving letter, a note written on July 3, 1864, to his four-and-a-half-year-old daughter Maggie, in which he sent her some scraps of material for her dolls. At the end of his note Stout told Maggie to "Kiss Ma and little sister and all the boys for me." Tragically, the "little sister," Mary (or Mollie) Rivers, had died on June 22, and Stout had not yet

---

21. The Stouts' home and Martha Abernathy Stout's relatives in Giles County, are discussed in chapter 1. "Samuel Hollingsworth Stout, A.M., M.D., LL.D.," 212. On the basis of other sources it is probable that the three times Stout visited home were: in July 1861 to rest from his work during the measles epidemic (he requested a leave of absence on July 16), in February-March 1862 after the fall of Nashville and before he went to Chattanooga, and about December 1864 or January 1865 during Hood's invasion of Tennessee. The period from 1862 to about December 1864 would be around thirty-two months. The article also notes that each visit was only for a day or two, but that would not be accurate in every case as his 1862 furlough was about thirty days. Stout to Lt. Col. T. M. Gordon, July 16, 1861, Emory, box 1, folder 2; Stout, "Some Facts," pt. 12, 24 (October 1902): 570; D. D. Saunders to Stout, February 2, 1865, Emory, box 3, folder 12.

22. Lt. W. M. Beckham to Stout, May 14, 1864, Ga. Hist. Soc., collection 764, item 4. Beckham would have visited Stout's family but the Federals were there and Beckham was afraid they would take his horse. Stout, "Some Facts," pt. 13, 24 (November 1902): 623; Burwell Abernathy to Thomas James Paine, August 27, 1866, TSLA, box 1, folder 16. Stephen V. Ash detailed the difficulties experienced by the residents of middle Tennessee, including Giles County. "Few regions even approached the degree and duration of physical devastation, institutional disruption, and human suffering which the heartland endured," he writes. *Middle Tennessee Society Transformed*, 131.

received his father-in-law's letter, sent by flag of truce, informing him of the melancholy event.[23] No doubt Stout grieved over the death of the daughter he had not seen.

In January 1865, Tom, Stout's oldest son, turned sixteen, and by February he had joined the Confederate navy. His military career was short. Tom may never even have served on a ship, but he apparently did get to Richmond, where he held baby Winnie Davis, daughter of Jefferson Davis, and comprised part of the guard for her and Mrs. Davis as they fled the city.[24]

Responsibility for the supervision of the medical officers serving in the hospitals of the Army of Tennessee compelled Stout to try to solve some complex and, on occasion, extremely difficult problems. Among these problems were major personality conflicts which Stout had to resolve to keep the hospitals functioning smoothly. Matron Kate Cumming reported her difficulties with Benjamin W. Avent, the post surgeon at Kingston, Georgia. When she and her assistant matron, Mrs. Williamson, arrived, he greeted them with the information that he did not approve of ladies in hospitals. This was only the beginning of their troubles. When two of the black cooks became ill, Avent refused to allow any of the convalescent soldiers to assist in the kitchen because "such work was degrading to them." Avent refused to erect a shed or any sort of protective covering for the laundresses. Because his mother and grandmother did

---

23. Stout, "Some Facts," pt. 16, 25 (February 1903): 91–92. Stout to Maggie J. Stout, July 3, 1864, Atlanta Hist. Soc. Thomas E. Abernathy to Stout, June 22, 1864, Emory, box 2, folder 12. Mollie died about 7:00 P.M. on Wednesday, June 22. She had gotten sick the previous Friday (her grandfather's shaky handwriting renders the disease illegible), and her illness was complicated by teething. The family planned to bury her by her brother, Wilkins Tannehill, but no tombstone for her survives in that cemetery. Perhaps a wooden marker, long since decayed, was all that the family could arrange, given wartime difficulties. It is probable that Stout never saw this child. If Stout was last home in March 1862, and his wife did not come to visit him (which is possible, even though there is no evidence to suggest that she did), Mollie was probably born around December 1862. She was born at least a few months before November 1863, as she is mentioned in a letter of that date. Pauline Postell to Stout, November 16, 1863, TSLA, box 1, folder 10. Abernathy told Stout that the rest of the family was doing well, but that all of the slaves, except two, had left.

24. F. G. Roche to Stout, February 7, 1865, TSLA, box 1, folder 8; C. A. Rice to Stout, April 27, 1865, Emory, Stout microfilm. Rice reported that Tom had been well when seen a few days previously in Washington, Georgia, en route to Augusta. Katherine Stout Moore wrote a note about Winnie Davis on the back of Tom's picture. TSLA, box 2, folder 5. [Obituary] "Thomas Edward Stout," *Confederate Veteran* 28 (November 1920): 429.

their wash under "the canopy of heaven," no one else needed anything more, he maintained. Cumming found Avent to be quite unreasonable, however, and called him "a real *Pharoah*—expecting bricks without straw." Able to stand the situation no longer, Cumming complained to Stout, who found another place for her and Mrs. Williamson.[25]

One major conflict involved Stout himself in a disagreement with Frank Hawthorn. It began on February 5, 1863, when Stout wrote a note to Hawthorn about his five slaves, who were hired to the Academy Hospital in Chattanooga where Hawthorn was surgeon in charge. Stout hired them out on the condition that they sleep at home. However, the previous night one of the slaves, named Isaac, had been compelled to sleep at the hospital. Stout complained about this to Hawthorn, stating that the "negroes" were so dissatisfied with their position at the Academy Hospital that he planned to send them "further into the interior" as soon as he could find a place for them. Hawthorn, instead of discussing the matter with Stout, went over Stout's head, and asked General William B. Bate, post commander, and Captain J. B. Cummings for an order to force Stout to leave his slaves at the hospital, even though he had said nothing about removing them immediately. It was only after he had gotten the orders that Hawthorn contacted Stout with a rather defensive note about the "urgent necessity" for Isaac to spend the night. Hawthorn excused his conduct: "in a consciencious discharge of my duty I cannot allow immunities & privileges to one person, which are not allowable to all."

Stout was very much offended. He believed that Hawthorn's action "was wholly unnecessary" and probably made a bad impression on the commanding general. Hawthorn implied "an intent on my part to cripple an institution, for the success of which I am responsible." Furthermore, by sending the communications over Stout's head, Hawthorn made it appear that Stout would not forward the message. From this point on, relations between Stout and Hawthorn steadily worsened. Dealings between the two were marked by icy formality, suspicion, and hostility, with each succeeding offense blown out of proportion, until on March 16 Stout relieved Hawthorn from duty and replaced him with D. D. Saunders. The problem was not solved until April, when Surgeons Alexander

---

25. Cumming, *Journal*, July 23, August 1, 3, 7, 8, 10, and 12, 1863, pp. 109, 111–14. In another instance Acting Assistant Surgeon Samuel A. Raborg closed his contract because he had a bitter personal conflict with his superior at the Prison Hospital in Atlanta, Dr. G. G. Roy. Raborg to Stout, August 3, 1864, Emory, box 3, folder 11, also Duke; Foard to Stout, August 16, 1864, Emory, box 2, folder 16.

Hunter and Charles E. Michel were appointed unofficial "mediators." They determined that the "misconception of each others motives" was without "any just cause," although they did think Hawthorn's actions of February 5 were "uncalled for," and that he had made several "error[s] of judgment" in the course of doing what he thought was his duty. "Considering the want of harmony that existed between the aforesaid parties," the mediators agreed, "Dr. Stout was influenced in his action [of relieving Hawthorn] with a view to the future good of the service," but, they recommended that, since Hawthorn was so well qualified, "he be reinstated in his former position; provided an amicable and harmonious official intercourse can be reestablished." Hawthorn was reinstated and did provide valuable service until felled by illness near the end of the war. While Stout strove to be above personal quarrels, in this case he was unable to ignore what he felt was an affront to his official dignity.[26]

Affronts to official dignity, particularly when associated with the question of rank, produced many squabbles, and some insubordination, among Stout's medical officers. In Greensboro, Georgia, Dr. Friend, the senior surgeon at the post, refused to take orders from a junior officer. A. H. Snead in Atlanta similarly would not take orders from an officer he outranked. Other surgeons obeyed orders while protesting to Stout or Bemiss. Alexander Hunter, then at Newsom Hospital in Columbus, Mississippi, objected to being superceded by Dr. Lipscomb merely because of rank. Hunter had previously reported to various junior officers in the department which had, heretofore, not paid much attention to rank. He saw it, most painfully, as "a reflection on my official conduct." Surgeon Hulse, in Union Springs, Alabama, did not complain because he, the ranking surgeon at the post, was only in charge of a ward while an assistant surgeon was in charge of the hospital; he simply requested a transfer to another post. William L. McAllister asked Stout whether it would be possible to get his commission redated to reflect the point when he began serving as an acting assistant surgeon rather than when he passed the board. Foard had once offered to do this, but McAllister

---

26. Stout to Hawthorn, Brig. Gen. William G. Bate to Hawthorn, Hawthorn to Capt. J. B. Cummings, and Hawthorn to Stout, all February 5, 1863, Emory, box 1, folder 12, the last item is also in Mus. Confed., ST–4–4; Stout to Capt. J. B. Cummings, February 6, 1863, TSLA, box 1, folder 11; Stout to Hawthorn, March 16, 1863, UTX, ledger 4L230; Stout to Foard, April 3, 1863, TSLA, box 1, folder 11; A. Hunter and Charles E. Michel, April 6, 1863, Emory, box 1, folder 15. Hunter and Michel were the surgeons in charge of the other two hospitals in Chattanooga. D. D. Saunders to Bemiss, December 8, 1864, UTX, box 2G404.

had never seen any real reason to change the date until recently, when he saw so many maneuverings about rank that he was afraid he might be placed in an awkward position in the future.[27]

Simply because a surgeon had seniority of rank by date of commission did not necessarily mean that he was a better doctor or administrator. In fact, over the course of time, many junior officers gave evidence of unexpected skill. Surgeon Hulse's friends had suggested that he not be placed in charge of a hospital, while Assistant Surgeon Vasser's superior officer felt that Vasser should have been commissioned a surgeon at the very beginning.[28]

One particularly sticky issue of rank and reputation surfaced in the case of Dr. Paul Fitzsimmons Eve. Eve, from Nashville, was considered by at least one later historian to be the most distinguished Tennessee surgeon of his generation. A prolific writer and medical journal editor, he often published accounts of various operations he had performed. Two of his sons also became physicians. Eve's faults included tone-deafness, color-blindness, near-sightedness, and, as Stout discovered to his sorrow, lack of administrative ability. In July 1863, Stout wrote to Surgeon General S. P. Moore that he did not want to embarrass Eve, because he was so popular professionally, but he wanted to see Eve transferred to some more innocuous position, like an examining board. Eve's Gate City Hospital in Atlanta, a former hotel, was so poorly administered that it was an embarrassment to Stout and Post Surgeon Logan. Apparently Eve finally resigned during the summer of 1864 after having served for a short time in a smaller officer's hospital. In an appendix to his "Outline" written for Tennessee Governor James D. Porter in 1897, Stout elaborated in great detail on Eve's incompetence. Eve had petty quarrels with Dr. Logan and other medical officers, and kept a filthy hospital. Although Eve thought his Gate City Hospital was "neat and clean,"

27. J. D. Smith to N. Friend, and Friend to Smith, October 10, 1864, Smith to Sir, October 11, with note from Stout on back, October 15, all in Emory, box 2, folder 18; Smith to Friend, October 10, Friend to Smith, October 11, and Friend to Stout, October 11, with Stout's note on back dated October 15, all in UTX, box 2G402. This difficulty arose because a telegram arrived before an explanatory letter. Bemiss to Stout, July 13, 1864, SHC–UNC, reel 2; Bemiss to Stout, July 14, 1864, Emory, box 2, folder 14, both discussing the Snead case. A. Hunter to Bemiss, December 14, 1864. F. H. Evans to Bemiss, September 1, 1864, UTX, box 2G421, about Hulse. William T. McAllister to Stout, January 8, 1864, Duke(?).

28. F. H. Evans to Bemiss, September 1, 1864, UTX, box 2G421, evaluates both Hulse and Vasser.

every medical inspector pronounced it otherwise. Stout said that when he visited, he "had often to tiptoe, to keep from stepping in filth, sputa, excrement, & urine." Since it was the hospital nearest to the railroad station, anxious relatives of patients often stopped there first in their quest for their kin, which produced a poor reputation for the hospitals in general. The Gate City was finally closed, cleaned, and reopened as a receiving and distributing hospital. In the process of cleaning what Stout described as a "veritable Augean stable," workers found "fecal matter" even in the cellar and on the roof.

Stout's appendix, written for Tennessee Governor Porter's information only, explained why "[t]he name of Dr. Paul F. Eve is purposely omitted from" a list of Tennessee physicians who served the Army of Tennessee "with credit." Even in the 1950s, Sam L. Clark and H. D. Riley, Jr., who edited the "Outline" for publication, apparently felt that this information was much too sensitive to be published in Nashville. They omitted the appendix, except for the list of doctors. Then, in a footnote, they negated everything Stout said: "Dr. Stout lists Dr. Eve among the surgeons who 'performed with efficiency and skill,'" citing a *Southern Practitioner* article by Stout.[29]

Stout also had to face situations that required serious disciplinary action. While intemperance was not a major problem, when a case appeared, Stout dealt with it firmly. "Whenever I hear of a med. officer getting drunk, I notify him, that he must take his choice between a court-martial and resignation." Stout had thus removed one surgeon, and the resignations of two assistant surgeons were on their way to Richmond as Stout wrote this comment to T. G. Richardson.[30] One

---

29. Hamer, *Centennial History of Tennessee State Medical Association*, 158–60, 457; Stout to S. P. Moore, July 11, 1863, UTX, ledger 4L230; Logan to Stout, August 17, 1864, Emory, box 2, folder 16. The original of Stout's "Outline" is in TSLA, and a photostat is in Emory, box 4, folder 26. In the published "Outline" the appendix and footnote are on p. 82. The footnote cites "*So. Pract.* 24 (1902), p. 440," part of Stout's "Address," delivered at the 1902 meeting of the Association of Medical Officers of the Army and Navy of the Confederacy in Dallas. It is printed in the August 1902 issue, pp. 434–54. In justice to Clark and Riley, they did mention in their introduction that they omitted "a small portion of the appendix" (p. 55). While omission of sensitive information can be historically legitimate, this seems to be a case of actual falsification since the footnote says exactly the opposite of what Stout spent several pages detailing.

30. Stout to T. G. Richardson, March 28, 1864, Emory, box 2, folder 6. One of the assistant surgeons was Robert E. Campbell of the Stonewall Hospital in Montgomery, Alabama. On March 15, 1864 he wrote to Stout, admitting that he had "acted indiscreetly," and claiming "I have taken a solemn mental vow, come what may, that I

Simeon S. Osling (or Oslin) not only had "[h]is intellect . . . almost all the time befogged with liquor" but also appeared to be a phony as well. Stout found him "professionally incompetent, and morally unreliable," or, more bluntly, "a liar." Osling claimed that he had passed a board exam but lost his commission; however, a check with the surgeon general's office produced no record of the man.[31] Thefts of hospital property also created periodic problems. At St. Mary's Hospital in LaGrange, the matron, Mrs. Jones, who was also the wife of one of the surgeons, had apparently been stealing milk, eggs, custard, butter, biscuits, chicken, and other food supplies for her own use and that of her friends, thus depriving the sick for whom this food was intended. Surgeon Samuel Annan, who was in charge of the hospital, defended Mrs. Jones, who, in turn, accused Mr. Skillon, the steward, of the thefts. F. H. Evans, post surgeon at LaGrange, removed Mrs. Jones from her position, but the case had not yet been solved when Evans described it to Stout.[32]

Dealing with his own subordinates took most of his time and energies, but Stout also had to cope with problems related to the local citizens. Citizens at times vigorously opposed the establishment of hospitals in their towns, or at least the impressment of buildings for that purpose. Francis Thornton, in Ringgold, for instance, came into conflict with Mrs. Mitchell, head of the local Ladies Aid Society, and her husband, the

---

will never indulge in intoxicating liquors in any shape or form." While his immediate superior, Dr. Cole, was willing to drop the charges, Dr. Gentry, the post surgeon, insisted that Campbell resign or be court-martialed. Campbell felt that he could not resign because his medical books and other property had probably been destroyed in a recent raid in Mississippi, and he had a wife, child, and paralyzed father-in-law to support. Apparently Campbell's pathetic appeal had no effect. TSLA, folder 1, box 4. Other complaints about intemperance can be found in Green to Sir [Stout?], November 6, 1863, TSLA, box 1, folder 11; Flewellen to F. F.(?) Lee, May 1, 1863, N A, chap. 6, vol. 749; J. P. Logan to Stout, August 5, 1864, UTX, box 2G389.

31. Stout to Sir, January 31, 1863, Emory, box 1, folder 11; Stout to Flewellen, February 11, 1863, UTX, ledger 4L230; Stout to A. J. Foard, Stout to S. P. Moore, both February 11, 1863, both ibid.; Moore to Stout, February 18, 1863, ibid.

32. Copies of testimony from James S. Bryant and Nelson Chandler, April 6, 8, and 14, 1864, UTX, box 2G433; F. H. Evans to Stout, May 3, 1864, ibid., box 2G431. Evans described Annan in a letter to Stout, December 7, 1863, SHC–UNC, reel 2. At the Blind School Hospital in Macon, the acting ward master apparently stole a number of items. Although the steward realized that some things were missing, he was so busy preparing to take the assistant surgeon's exam that he did not report the fact or take an accurate inventory for several weeks. James Mercer Green, endorsement on George F. Cooper to Green, May 11, 1864, Emory, box 2, folder 9.

assistant quartermaster. Mitchell complained that Thornton had been unjust to the citizens of Ringgold and created unrest. In a later instance, Mrs. Nancy Denham published unknown charges against William M. Cole of the Stonewall Hospital in Montgomery, Alabama, in the local newspaper, creating such excitement that Cole was relieved from duty, even though he said the charges were false. Yet not all contact between local citizens and hospital physicians was hostile. In several cases citizens petitioned Stout that popular medical officers not be transferred to other posts.[33]

Personnel matters clearly were an important part of Stout's responsibilities as medical director of hospitals. His careful adherence to a few key management principles generally enabled him to administer these personnel matters successfully. Unlike Confederate President Jefferson Davis, who was notoriously unable to delegate the "minutiae" of war to his cabinet members or generals and insisted on meddling with the smallest facets of their responsibilities, Stout was able to select competent subordinates and allow them to administer their designated areas while expending his own energies on overall supervision and troubleshooting. Stout shared this ability to delegate with another of the few outstanding Confederate administrators, Josiah Gorgas, head of the ordnance department.[34]

Yet another important skill Stout possessed was the ability to promote cooperation and teamwork by his own example. He tried to attend to legitimate complaints while encouraging his medical officers to focus on the common goal of healing the patients. He endeavored to correct shortcomings in a kindly way, seeking to avoid embarassing his less capable subordinates, such as the problematic Dr. Eve, rather than allowing the development of the permanent quarrels so characteristic of Confederate leadership.[35] But Stout did not hesitate to insist on proper discipline in his hospitals, and speedily removed inebriates and other transgressors

---

33. William L. McAllister to Foard, December 30, 1862, TSLA, box 1, folder 14, concerns Thornton; William M. Cole to Stout, July 2, 1864, UTX, box 2G414. Petition of Ladies of Augusta to Stout, October 1, 1864, ibid., box 2G389 (to retain H. H. Clayton); Petition of Citizens of Forsyth to Stout, January 9, 1864, ibid., box 2G400 (to retain J. B. Barnette). Citizen opposition to the establishment of hospitals will be discussed in chap. 5.

34. Wiley, *Road to Appomattox*, 14, 15, 17; Vandiver, *Rebel Brass*, 25; Vandiver, *Ploughshares Into Swords*, 64.

35. Davis's quarrels with Gen. Joseph E. Johnston, North Carolina Governor Zebulon Vance, and Confederate Vice-President Alexander Stephens, to name just a few, were

when their sins were confirmed. Stout set an example by obedience to his own superiors, but not blind obedience without discussion if he believed a situation had been misunderstood. Importantly, he refused to indulge in what South Carolina politician James Henry Hammond called "Big-man-me-ism," the idea that "every one thinks every other a jealous fool or an aspiring knave." Such individualism sadly impeded cooperation among Confederates at all levels.[36]

Even admirable principles and skills do not make perfection here on earth. Thus Stout certainly did have personnel problems among his subordinates. Nonetheless, he managed to keep his hospital personnel functioning to an admirable degree considering the rest of the circumstances which prevailed in the Confederacy. For Stout was not merely a personnel manager. His work took place within a broader context—the context of the hospital sites themselves.

---

public knowledge at the time and hardly contributed to cooperation at lower echelons. Wiley, *Road to Appomattox*, 20; Thomas, *The Confederate Nation*, 138–41.
36. Wiley, *Road to Appomattox*, 100–01.

CHAPTER 5

"TO BE BETTER SUPPLIED
THAN ANY HOTEL IN
THE CONFEDERACY"

Of crucial importance to the hospital department of the Army of Tennessee were the hospitals themselves, the battlegrounds for the warfare waged behind the lines. Both the sites selected and the conditions that prevailed once the hospitals were established were major concerns. Normally, doctors sent to inspect potential sites had specific criteria for which they looked. Circumstances beyond the control of these inspectors, however, eventually caused many makeshift locations to become hospital sites.

The most important qualification for a potential hospital site was its proximity to railroad transportation. Inspectors travelled down the railroads specifically to examine the towns along the roads to determine the suitability of their facilities. Wagon or ambulance transportation was so uncomfortable for the sick and wounded that distance from the railroad rendered some potentially suitable sites, such as Gainesville, Georgia, unusable. Railroad officials also had some say about the location of hospitals along their routes. Maj. I. S. Rowland, superintendent of the Western and Atlantic Railroad, opposed the establishment of hospitals on the east side of Tunnel Hill, arguing not only that the grade was too steep but also that trains could stop only at regular stations without ruining the schedule or missing connections with other railroad lines.[1]

---

1. A version of this chapter appeared as an article. Glenna R. Schroeder-Lein, "'To Be Better Supplied Than Any Hotel in the Confederacy': The Establishment and Maintenance of the Army of Tennessee Hospitals in Georgia, 1863–1865," *Georgia Historical Quarterly* 76 (Winter 1992): 809–36. E. A. Flewellen to Dr. [Stout], March 12, 1863, Mus. Confed., ST–4–10; C. H. Lee, Special Orders No. 259, paragraph 7, by command of Secretary of War, October 29, 1863, N A, chap. 6, vol. 748; Flewellen to Stout, December 6, 1863, ibid., vol. 749; E. T. McSwain reported to Stout about Gainesville, July 31, 1863, UTX, box 2G379; M. J. Camden reported Rowland's opinion to Stout, April 9, 1863, ibid. There are numerous other examples of site and inspection reports

A site on the railroad was unsuitable for hospitals if it did not possess the second most important qualification—an adequate and convenient supply of pure water. Hospitals needed water for drinking, cooking, bathing, laundry, and general cleaning. While this water might exist in wells, springs, cisterns, or creeks, sites with a fairly swift stream had an added advantage since then the "sinks" could be built over the stream and waste products would be carried away. This was one feature that led C. B. Gamble to recommend McCamy's farm near Tunnel Hill as a good hospital site. Nearly dry wells, which would mean transporting water from a creek several miles away, were a major objection to locating a hospital at Cartersville, Georgia, in the eyes of Richard O. Curry and other inspectors. Sufficient water was clearly an important consideration for a hospital post. A town with enough water for several hundred inhabitants might not be able to supply several hundred more patients, even though hospitals did not then use water at a rate comparable to late twentieth-century standards.[2]

Closely related to the issue of water supply were factors such as elevation, drainage, and "general salubrity of country around." Malaria was a major scourge in the Confederate army, as it was among Southern civilians. While no one had yet discovered the role of mosquitos in the spread of this disease, people did see a relationship between the disease and the presence of swamps or standing water, which supposedly gave off harmful "miasms." Consequently, contemporary physicians maintained that a hospital site ought to be somewhat elevated and drain quickly after a rainstorm. It was such a view that led James L. Thompson, in a letter to Stout on September 30, 1864, to recommend Opelika, Alabama, as a hospital site. That site, said Thompson, was the highest point on the railroad line, it had dry land and no malaria, and it also had running

---

in all the major Stout collections. It is probably not an exaggeration to say that for most instances cited, there are a dozen other examples that could have been given. Several doctors suggested having the hospitals outside of towns where possible, to avoid their "demoralizing influence." D. D. Saunders to Stout, September 5, 1863, TSLA, box 1, folder 9; E. A. Flewellen to Stout, December 6, 1863, N A, chap. 6, vol. 749.

2. S. M. Bemiss to D. C. O'Keefe, December 2, 1863, UTX, box 2G384; E. A. Flewellen to Dr. [Stout], March 12, 1863, Mus. Confed., ST–4–10; C. B. Gamble to Stout, March 17, 1863, ibid., ST–4–11; Richard O. Curry to Stout, September 5, 1863, ibid., ST–5–8. Albert H. Snead objected to Lovejoy Station as a hospital site because the spring, while convenient, was insufficient for hospital needs and wells would have to be forty to fifty feet deep, as well as bricked to prevent cave-ins. Snead to S. M. Bemiss, December 14, 1863, Emory, box 1, folder 25; also SHC–UNC, Stout microfilm, reel 2.

MAP 1—STOUT'S HOSPITALS

At some point Stout had Army of Tennessee hospitals in each of these towns as well as in Cherokee Springs, Georgia, a former resort near Catoosa Springs, and Vineville, near Macon, neither of which could be precisely located. For sample lists showing the locations of Stout's hospitals at specific times, see Appendix C.

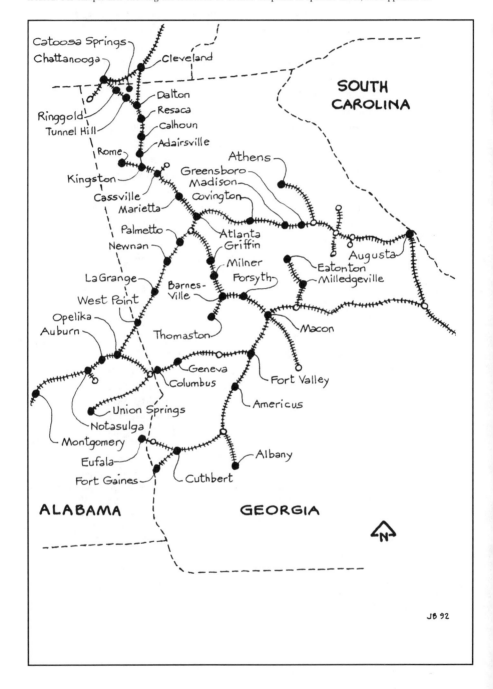

springs and good water in wells dug twenty to thirty feet deep. Beyond Cheraw Station, 400 feet lower than Opelika, he observed, the area was low, flat, and marshy all the rest of the way to Montgomery, and thus was unsuitable for hospitals.[3]

While a good deal of hospital construction did occur for Army of Tennessee patients, in most cases hospitals occupied preexisting build- ings, at least as a nucleus from which to expand. Inspection reports, therefore, generally listed the warehouses, stores, courthouses, hotels, meeting halls, schools, churches, and unoccupied homes in a town that could be converted for hospital use, describing their condition and ca- pacity, as well as any difficulties the government might encounter when attempting to rent or impress the site. Albert H. Snead reported that Jonesboro, Georgia, had a three-story, well-ventilated brick warehouse and a two-story courthouse containing two large rooms upstairs and four downstairs. These buildings, concluded Snead, were vacant and could house about 350 patients while other facilities were constructed. Kate Cumming, who served as a hospital matron at several locations, described the Newsom Hospital in Chattanooga as "the upper part of a long row of warehouses, with windows east and west. The partitions between were taken away, making large wards, where a current of air could blow right through. There were some four or five of these rooms opening into each other." When she moved to Newnan, Georgia, a few miles south of Atlanta, she helped to manage a hospital that occu- pied a square of "dilapidated," but well-whitewashed, stores, and the courthouse. Considerable difficulty arose over the use of a hotel, the Crutchfield House, in Chattanooga, as a hospital. Brig. Gen. William B. Bate, post commander, acknowledged that it was inconvenient for the "traveling public" not to be able to stay at the hotel, but he noted that the size of the building and its location near the railroad depot made its use as a receiving and distributing hospital imperative. Richard O. Curry saw a potential hospital in a forty-by-sixty-foot tobacco warehouse in Cartersville, Georgia. He observed that the building had two stories and an attic, as well as a ten-acre lot that could be used for tents, although he was aware that some large tobacco presses would have to be removed. Also of interest to inspectors were preexisting outbuildings such as the kitchen and dining room which increased the appeal of

---

3. S. M. Bemiss to D. C. O'Keefe, December 2, 1863, UTX, box 2G384; Cunningham, *Doctors in Gray*, 190–91. James L. Thompson to Stout, September 30, 1864, UTX, box 2G390.

the male college at Tuskegee, Alabama, as a hospital for permanently disabled soldiers.[4]

Yet another requisite for hospital sites was the availability of wood. Quantities of firewood were essential for cooking, heating, and laundry purposes. Insufficient wood supplies could lead to poorly prepared meals, lack of sanitation, and, in winter, extreme discomfort and even physical harm for the patients. To haul wood from a great distance was costly and often prohibited by lack of transportation. Wood, in the form of lumber, was also necessary for any new hospital construction, as well as for bunks for the patients. James M. Holloway was excited about Covington, Georgia, east of Atlanta, as a potential hospital location at least partly because seven sawmills existed within ten miles of the town. James L. Thompson also noted sawmills near Salem and Youngsboro, Alabama, as he reported on localities along the West Point and Montgomery Railroad.[5]

Should new construction be necessary or desirable, as it often was, a site required some empty land. Frequently a hospital established in preexisting buildings had to be expanded to accommodate crowds of battle casualties. The simplest and quickest way to expand, especially during the spring and summer, was to pitch a number of tents in a shady grove. Tent camps were so common in 1864 that Stout issued a circular describing the proper way to set up a tent ward: the tents should

---

4. Albert H. Snead to S. M. Bemiss, December 14, 1863, Emory, box 1, folder 25, also SHC–UNC, reel 2. Cumming, *Journal*, September 4, 1862 and December 8, 1863, pp. 53 and 162. William B. Bate to James A. Seddon [Secretary of War], February 17, 1863, UTX, box 2G423; Richard O. Curry to Stout, September 5, 1863, Mus. Confed., ST–5–8; [probably U. R. Jones] to Stout, May 12, 1864, ibid., ST–7–20. Charles E. Michel thought that a female academy in Eufaula, Alabama, could be procured for hospital use by means of persuasion coupled with threats of impressment. Michel to Stout, September [no date], 1864, UTX, box 2G379. Among the schools used for medical purposes was the University of Georgia, where several buildings functioned temporarily as an opthalmic hospital. By September 6, 1864 the eye ward had moved to Forsyth, Georgia. Bolling A. Pope to Stout, June 12, 1864, UTX, box 2G383, and August 4, 1864, box 2G382; Stout, Circular No. 38, September 6, 1864, box 2G429.

5. E. A. Flewellen to Dr. [Stout], March 12, 1863, Mus. Confed., ST–4–10; S. M. Bemiss to D. C. O'Keefe, December 2, 1863, UTX, box 2G384; Frank Hawthorn to Stout, February 7, 1863, Emory, box 1, folder 12; also March 16, 1863, UTX, box 2G427; Stout to Captain Gribble, May 12, 1863, UTX, box 2G423; Francis Thornton to Stout, March 14, 1863, TSLA, box 1, folder 9; James M. Holloway to Stout, December 25, 1863, Mus. Confed., ST–6–6; James L. Thompson to Stout, September 30, 1864, UTX, box 2G390.

be pitched ten feet apart in two rows, leaving twenty feet between rows, and fifty feet between wards. Unfortunately for the patients, many of them were compelled to remain in tents during the winter when there were no other facilities available. By December 1864, movement from one point to another had left most of the hospitals in Lauderdale Springs, Mississippi, in tents, "some of them better suited for a paper mill than a shelter," complained Surgeon Ira Williams. At age fifty-nine, Williams believed that he was too old for such rough working conditions and asked that Acting Medical Director Bemiss either transfer him elsewhere or prepare to bury him.[6]

Kate Cumming thought that patients recovered more quickly in tents, but said that the surgeons seemed to prefer sheds. In fact, D. D. Saunders told Stout that he thought patients were more comfortable in sheds, rather than tents or houses, during the summer. Some of the temporary sheds, such as those built in Newnan, Georgia, were one hundred feet long and twelve feet wide, containing a row of bunks on each side and an aisle in the middle. Because they had board roofs but only canvas sides, which could be raised and lowered as the weather demanded, these sheds could be erected quickly.[7]

More complex and less transient than tents or sheds were the pavilion wards, based on a concept that was not new during the Civil War. The famous British nurse Florence Nightingale had only recently strongly advocated these structures, which were designed to admit sunshine and allow fresh air to circulate in the wards. "Ventilation" was a slogan or, as one historian described it, an "obsession," of hospital site selectors and constructors, North and South, during the Civil War. The pavilion hospitals built in the North and at Chimborazo, the large Confederate hospital in Richmond, contained four or more rows of bunks and were ventilated through windows, where the air entered, and openings under

---

6. B. M. Wible to Stout, April 23, 1863, Duke; Stout, Circular No. 22, July 15, 1864, Tulane; Frank Hawthorn to Stout, February 2, 1863, UTX, box 2G427, also Emory, Stout microfilm; Ira Williams to S. M. Bemiss, December 5, 1864, UTX, box 2G405. A regulation hospital tent was supposed to be fourteen by fifteen feet, by eleven feet high in the center. *Regulations for the Medical Department*, 58.

7. Cumming, *Journal*, March 9, 1865 and June 24, 1864, pp. 246–47 and 190 respectively. D. D. Saunders constructed sheds eighteen feet wide and boarded the sides, leaving eighteen inches open at the top and bottom, and placing windows every twenty feet to promote ventilation. Saunders to Stout, July 31, 1864, Emory, box 2, folder 15. Tents could be used advantageously in isolating contagious cases rather than exposing a whole ward to some additional malady.

a ridge in the center of the roof, where the air escaped. Stout felt that this design had significant flaws, for by the time the fresh air reached the patients on the inner rows it had become impure from "the expired and other gaseous emanations from the bodies of the patients on the outer rows." Stout claimed that he never saw one of these wide wards until he visited Chimborazo in 1864. He had previously developed a slightly different design, which he did not claim was original, "For," he said, "it was dictated by common sense and well-known pneumatic laws. I could not avoid, however, secretly congratulating myself and the sick and wounded of the Department of Tennessee, that in none of the hospital wards constructed under my direction, were the suffering soldiers amid unsanitary environments as I found those occupying bunks in the interior rows of Chimborazo Hospital."

Stout's design differed from other pavilion wards in two respects. First, the wards were narrow, no more than twenty-two to twenty-four feet wide. This dimension permitted only two rows of bunks, with the heads about one foot from the wall and the feet separated by a five-foot aisle. While Stout also used windows and flues in the ridge of the roof, his other major change was to add openings one foot high and two feet wide just above the floor and just below the ceiling at every bed. These gaps could be opened and closed with sliding shutters. When the shutters were opened, the air circulated in under the bunks to the center aisle and then upward and out at the ceiling, allowing the ward to be aired out in a few minutes, even on a cold day, without exposing the patients to drafts. Just how many wards were built to Stout's specifications is not known, but Stout said that during the last two years of the war he "had ample opportunities of testing it by observation and the comparison of results of treatment in hospital wards of a great variety of plan and construction." He claimed that the design was "acknowledged by all medical officers who had opportunities of comparative observation, to have completely solved the problem of securing almost absolute purity of air in hospital wards occupied to their full capacity by badly wounded men."[8]

---

8. The origins of pavilion wards are discussed in Thompson and Goldin, *The Hospital: A Social and Architectural History*, 159ff. While Thompson and Goldin briefly discuss Northern hospitals and Chimborazo (p. 170), they do not mention Stout's adaptation. Some hospitals were designed to promote maximum ventilation even before the Crimean War, when Florence Nightingale promoted the concept. Rosenberg, *The Care of Strangers*, 127–28. Adams, *Doctors in Blue*, 151, 214. Stout discusses his design in three places: "On the Best Models and Most Easily Constructed Military Hospital Wards for Temporary Use in the War," 88–91; "Some Facts," pt. 22, 25 (September

Two other factors were of great concern to those who selected hospital sites, especially in the later stages of the war. The first of these was the availability of foodstuffs, beyond the basics of the army ration, which would tempt the delicate palates of the patients. Chickens, eggs, vegetables, and milk were of great importance in the hospital kitchen. Often, however, troops previously stationed in or raiding an area had stripped it clean of delicacies. These items were difficult to import if they could not be procured in the countryside near the hospital. Stout strongly urged hospitals to plant their own vegetable gardens and keep their own cows. Thus, garden and pasture land in the vicinity of the hospital were added criteria. Once a hospital was established the doctors often contracted with nearby farmers when the hospital gardens could not fully meet the need for vegetables. A successful garden, however, was not only a source of supply but a source of pride. Surgeon Pearson at Forsyth, Georgia, waxed rhapsodic about the "vegatibles" growing in their approximately four-acre garden: "smaller sallads," onions, "eschallotts," English peas, beets, squash, field peas, Irish potatoes, okra, tomatoes, cabbage, turnips, and sweet potatoes. The garden also had eight acres of corn and peas. Pearson hoped to grow enough to keep the hospital supplied during the winter as well.[9]

One final factor that had to be considered in the selection of hospital sites was the relationship of the place to potential battles or raids. While some hospitals had to be fairly close to the battlefield to care for the most severely wounded, they could not be close enough to risk capture in a sudden thrust by the enemy. As Sherman moved his troops further and further into Georgia, he forced the Confederate hospitals north of Atlanta to evacuate to points south of the city. But even there they

---

1903): 517–19; and "Outline" manuscript, 41–44, original at TSLA, photostat in Emory, box 4, folder 24. The discussion of hospital construction is one of the two sections omitted by editors Sam L. Clark and H. D. Riley, Jr., in the version published in the *Tennessee Historical Quarterly*.

9. E. A. Flewellen to Stout, March 12, 1863, Mus. Confed., ST–4–10; J. P. Logan to Stout, September 13, 1863, UTX, box 2G387; Albert H. Snead to Stout, December 14, 1863, Emory, box 1, folder 25, also SHC–UNC, reel 2; James L. Thompson to Stout, September 30, 1864, UTX, box 2G390; J. B. Barnette to Stout, April 11, 1864, Emory, box 2, folder 7; Stout Circular, March 25, 1863, TSLA, box 1, folder 11. C. B. Gamble took particular care to report the pasture and garden qualifications of the sites he inspected. Gamble to Stout, March 17, 1863, Mus. Confed., ST–4–11. S. P. Moore Circular No. 15, August 10, 1864, Emory, Stout microfilm; Robert Battey to Flewellen, April 11, 1863, Duke. J.(?) C.(?) Pearson to John Patterson, May 6, 1864, TSLA, box 1, folder 15.

were not safe. A number of towns experienced raids, especially beginning in the summer of 1864, that compelled the medical staff to evacuate hospitals located there. It became increasingly difficult to meet the other qualifications and also protect the hospitals as the Confederacy edged toward defeat.[10]

Simply locating and choosing a suitable site did not make it easy to set up hospitals there. In Eufaula, Alabama, Surgeon Paul DeLacy Baker thought that he had made arrangements to use a hotel for a hospital. But when he sent his steward to clean the building and prepare it for its new use, he discovered that the proprietress, a Mrs. O'Harra, had changed her mind. Apparently a man had offered to buy the establishment. Baker then asked his superiors for permission to impress the hotel if necessary. Elsewhere other citizens opposed the use of their public buildings by the hospitals. For example, the people of Madison, Georgia, like the inhabitants of some other towns, strongly objected to having their churches used as hospitals. Surgeon James R. Bratton finally convinced the Madison citizens to give him enough material to build six large sheds so that their churches could be spared. In some towns opposition was much stronger than recalcitrant individuals or objections to the use of specific buildings. The mayor and city council of Columbus, Georgia, passed a unanimous resolution asking that the hospitals already established in their town be removed several miles out into the country in "some healthy location." They were afraid that the presence of the hospitals would spread disease among the citizens. George B. Douglas, the surgeon in charge, explained that the mayor's plan would be fine, if it could be carried out, but the need for hospitals was immediate. The buildings being used for the hospitals were not near private residences nor was there any other reason for citizens and soldiers to come into contact and thus spread disease. In fact, Douglas said, the city's health should improve because the hospital workers had cleaned up piles of accumulated garbage. The real cause of the mayor and council's complaint, Douglas maintained, was their objection to the use of the courthouse as a hospital. Despite protests from the town leadership, the hospitals remained and even increased in Columbus. During the last days of the Confederacy, Columbus was a major hospital post and Stout had his office there for a while. In another case, Captain Gormly

---

10. A. J. Foard to Stout, July 6, 1864, UTX, box 2G379; B. M. Wible to Stout, May 26, 1864, UTX, box 2G418; G. S. West, to S. M. Bemiss, September 13, 1864, UTX, box 2G419. Problems related to hospital movements will be addressed in chap. 6.

reported on July 27, 1864, that Cuthbert, Georgia would be a good place for a hospital, as it had college buildings and "hundreds" of ladies and "patriotic gentlemen" who wanted to help the sick and wounded. Perhaps the townspeople did not really understand what having hospitals entailed, or perhaps the quartermaster misinterpreted their sentiments. In any case, when W. L. Nichol moved there a month later, when evacuated from Covington after a raid, he said that he was "surrounded with difficulties. The people are totally insensible to the wants of the army. They are more essentially selfish than any set with whom I have been thrown." The people did not want the hospitals and refused to cooperate at all. Although there were vacant buildings, Nichol had not even been able to get one for an office. "I am entirely out of the world down here," he moaned. "If I swore at all I would say Damn this place."[11] When citizens were not forthcoming with buildings, as well as slaves, food, and other necessary items, Stout did have the power to impress them. Impressment could and, at Chattanooga for example, did, cause serious problems. Stout, therefore, tried to exercise his power with moderation.[12]

The construction of new hospital buildings created problems of another sort, usually related to quartermasters and their inability or unwillingness to provide necessary materials. Several surgeons in Covington, Georgia, complained because the quartermaster had not provided transportation to haul some needed bricks four or five miles to the hospital site. Quartermaster Thomsen defended himself, however, arguing that he only had two four-horse and two two-horse wagons which were kept busy hauling wood for the hospitals and meeting other local needs. Although he had submitted requisitions twice, Thomsen had been unable to get more wagons or livestock. In another instance that occurred in November 1863, S. M. Bemiss noted that the new Erwin Hospital at

---

11. Paul DeLacy Baker to Bemiss, March 27, 1864, UTX, box 2G399; S. Meredith to Stout, December 12, 1863, and J. R. Bratton to Stout, July 10, 1864, both in UTX, box 2G411. In Dalton, Georgia, the pastors of the Baptist, Methodist, and Presbyterian churches agreed that they "must respectfully decline the tender of our houses of worship" for hospitals. G. W. Solvidge(?), J. F. Ellison, and James A. Wallace to [F. H.] Evans, August 25, 1863, UTX, box 2G398. George B. Douglas to Stout, April 13, 1864, Mus. Confed., ST–7–17; F. G. Wilkins, Mayor, to Surgeon General, April 12, 1864, with note on back from Douglas, May 2, 1864, UTX, box 2G421; Stout Circular No. 47, January 25, 1865, Emory, Stout microfilm. M. Gormly to James Mercer Green, July 27, 1864, Duke; W. L. Nichol to Stout, August 29 and 30, 1864, both in UTX, box 2G397.

12. Stout, "Outline," 76–77; Cumming, *Journal*, August 14, 1864, p. 205; William B. Bate to James A. Seddon, February 17, 1863, UTX, box 2G423.

Kingston, Georgia, was nearly complete but would not be ready for patients until cooking utensils arrived. "These buildings would have been ready for occupation some weeks earlier but for the fact, that Maj. McMicken [the quartermaster], ordered the workmen away to build Commissary houses at Chickamauga, and not only removed the workmen, but likewise a large lot of lumber which had been sawed to order and was of such description as to be adapted to the plan of the hospital building."[13] Clearly, then, many quartermasters placed a low priority on hospital construction.

Kate Cumming described the hospital at Cherokee Springs in northern Georgia when she went there to work in August 1863. Under the control of Surgeon S. M. Bemiss (later Stout's assistant medical director), this model hospital for chronic cases was located in a shady valley with numerous mineral springs. Equipped for 500 patients, it was set up in neatly arranged tents, with the sickest patients confined to small wooden buildings left over from the days when the site had been a resort. The hospital included a bath house and a linen and ironing room in other wooden houses on the site. Using stream water, a soldier and his wife did the washing in the open air, protected by shade trees and tents. The hospital had two kitchens, one for the very sick and the other for the convalescents, as well as a good bakery. The convalescent dining room was a newly constructed building with a wooden roof and open sides. The soldiers even had a reading room with papers and books, some of which had just come through the blockade from England. In addition, the hospital chaplain was preparing to erect a chapel. Unfortunately, as so often happened when a hospital was finally functioning smoothly, Cherokee Springs had to be evacuated as a result of military movements around Chattanooga preceding the Battle of Chickamauga.[14]

Aside from the ever-increasing threats of enemy raids and destruction, Stout encountered a number of problems with the hospitals. In some cases, sites did not measure up to their early promise. As a result of his inspections at LaGrange, Georgia, for example, S. M. Bemiss recommended that the Cannon Hospital ward, located in the Methodist church basement, be closed, even though it would mean the loss of space for

---

13. Maj. J. M. Thomsen to Capt. E. M. Foster, March 26, 1864, UTX, box 2G396; S. M. Bemiss to Stout, November 28, 1863, Emory, box 1, folder 24. George B. Douglas at Columbus said that the department quartermaster took no interest in the hospitals at all. Douglas to Stout, July 12, 1864, UTX, box 2G395.
14. Cumming, *Journal*, August 13 and 28, 1863, pp. 115–17, 119.

fifty beds. Because it was built directly on the ground, it could not be kept clean.[15]

Stout also had to cope with the effects of natural disasters. In March 1863, Kate Cumming, then at the Newsom Hospital in Chattanooga, wrote in her diary, "Doctors Foard and Stout paid a visit to the hospital this afternoon, and highly commended all the arrangements, and the order and cleanliness of everything." Only hours after these inspectors left, she reported, "we had a very severe storm, which carried away a part of our roof, and otherwise did a great deal of damage." Another catastrophe occurred on December 27, 1864, when a tornado destroyed a church occupied by part of the Gilmer Hospital in Auburn, Alabama, reducing its capacity by fifty beds. Fortunately, few people were in the building at the time, and only seven were slightly injured, but tents and other hospital materials were also damaged. Surgeon Michel promised to build some other structure out of the debris.[16]

Misfortune also struck some of Stout's hospitals in the form of not-so-natural disasters—fires. For example, in November 1863, F. H. Evans reported the destruction of the buildings, bunks, and medicines of the Cannon Hospital in LaGrange, Georgia, by a fire, which began in the steeple of the chapel being used for a hospital, when a faulty stovepipe caught fire about three o'clock in the morning. When the fire was discovered, it was too late to save the structure. The staff evacuated the patients and as many supplies as possible. Despite valiant efforts, they were unable to keep the flames from spreading to the kitchen and other wooden outbuildings. The patients temporarily occupied some vacant private houses, until the Methodist, Baptist, and Presbyterian churches could be made ready for hospital use. Evans reported that he had inspected all the stovepipes put up by the hospitals, but not the one that caused the fire. Evans assumed it was safe since the owner of the building had put up that pipe. Two days later S. M. Bemiss reported from Marietta that more than one surgeon was not very careful about potential fire hazards. He noted that in several cases he had been compelled to point out stovepipes that were too close to woodwork.[17]

---

15. S. M. Bemiss to Stout, January 10, 1864, Emory, box 2, folder 1, also SHC–UNC, reel 2.

16. Cumming, *Journal*, March 24, 1863, p. 86; Charles E. Michel to S. M. Bemiss, December 30, 1864, UTX, box 2G388.

17. F. H. Evans to Stout, November 26, 1863, Mus. Confed., ST–6–2; S. M. Bemiss to Stout, November 28, 1863, Emory, box 1, folder 24. A stovepipe also caused the

No amount of regular stovepipe inspections could prevent disasters caused by disobedience and negligence, however. Such instances occurred all too frequently, as in the case of two white cooks at the Buckner Hospital in Newnan, Georgia, who built a fire in their fireplace "contrary to orders." During the night a brand rolled out of the fireplace and through a crack in the floorboards, causing a fire that burned down the officer's ward of the hospital. Fortunately, the major property loss was two cook stoves. J. W. Oslin at West Point, Georgia, learned that hospital property was not safe in transit either. Responding to orders issued because of rumors of a Yankee raid, Oslin packed his carefully accumulated supplies for the Reid Hospital into a box car. While the car was sitting on the siding, it caught fire, apparently from sparks spewed out by the locomotive, destroying everything but a stove and a few plates, cups, and provisions, which had been removed from the train previously. One of the most destructive hospital fires, however, was one that broke out in a nearby cotton warehouse in Americus, Georgia, in August 1864. The blaze consumed not only hospital property but also half the business district of the town.[18]

Clearly it was difficult to select appropriate hospital sites, and unforeseen problems often arose that hindered construction or occupation. Nevertheless, Stout had high standards for the management of his hospitals. He wanted them "to be better supplied than any hotel in the Confederacy," spending all the money given them by the government, so "that delicacies and everything else needed for the patients should be provided instead of hoarding it to indicate economy of management at the expense of the soldier's comforts and necessities."[19] To measure up to this standard was a difficult task, given the serious problems of supply. It was a task that only became harder as the war progressed. Many doctors certainly tried to comply with these high standards, but

fire that destroyed most of the S. P. Moore Hospital in Griffin, Georgia, in February 1864. Randal M. Lytle to Stout, February 21, 1864, UTX, box 2G403.

18. William T. McAllister to C. B. Gamble, January 3, 1864, Emory, box 2, folder 1; C. B. Gamble to Sir, January [no date] 1864, SHC–UNC, reel 2; S. M. Bemiss to Stout, January 7, 1864, Emory, box 2, folder 1. Bemiss went to Newnan to inspect the fire damage. J. W. Oslin to Stout, February 19, 1864, UTX, box 2G423. B. M. Wible to Stout, August 31, 1864, UTX, box 2G381; Cumming, *Journal*, September 1, 1864, pp. 214–15.

19. Cumming, *Journal*, July 3, 1863, p. 100; Stout, "Outline," 79. Cumming thought that Dr. Bemiss almost managed to get the Cherokee Springs hospital up to Stout's standard. The only thing lacking was milk. August 13, 1863, pp. 116–17.

they had varied success, as they struggled to make the reality meet the ideal of three facets of hospital management: cleanliness, proper patient care, and diet.

It is hardly necessary to state that Civil War standards of cleanliness were appallingly low according to twentieth-century ideals. Germ theory was unknown and, consequently, sterilization was not practiced. Within the hospitals, doctors and attendants differed among themselves as to what even constituted "clean." For example, Assistant Surgeons Frank M. Dennis and J. E. Nagle, who served on the ambulance trains, complained that the bedding at the Receiving and Distributing Hospital in Atlanta was so filthy that the patients refused to lie on it, as it obviously had not been changed for two or three months. Upon Stout's order, Post Surgeon J. P. Logan assigned a committee of three surgeons to inspect and report on the situation. In their initial report, the three doctors found "the bedding and accomodations [sic] in as good condition and order as the nature of the building and the surrounding circumstances will admit." Stout was not pleased with this report. He wanted the facts, not the doctors' opinion. How clean *was* the bedding? Even though the hospital was only an open shed, Stout suggested that it could be kept cleaner.

In their second report, the three inspecting doctors said that to call the bedding "filthy" was a "gross exaggeration," although they admitted "it was somewhat soiled and dusty," and "not as neat and clean" as "in regular hospitals." In their opinion, "sick soldiers arriving from Camp in all their unavoidable uncleanliness could not reasonably object to the condition of the bedding for a stay of only a few hours." G. L. Jones, acting surgeon in charge of the hospital, defended the state of the facility in a letter of August 28, 1863, which revealed his actions and motivations. "The Sheets and pillow Slips," said Jones, "are washed once every month, being enough for two changes, which I deemed Sufficient, for the temporary use of the sick only occupying them for an hour or two, and not work enough, in my judgement, to justify the regular employment of a Laundress." Apparently the shed hospital remained in use at least until November, when J. E. Nagle complained that the open structure offered no protection from the cold and wind for patients who arrived in the middle of the night.[20]

---

20. F. M. Dennis and J. E. Nagle to Stout, August 24, 1863, and Stout to J. P. Logan, August 25, 1863, both in TSLA, box 1, folder 8; Logan, Special Orders No. 91, August 28, 1863, TSLA, box 2, folder 4; James C. Mullins, D. C. O'Keefe, and William P.

In two different hospitals in Chattanooga, surgeons in charge also demonstrated differing standards of cleanliness in the attitudes they expressed toward the patients' clothing. Kate Cumming complained that at the Newsom Hospital, "When the men come in, their clothes are taken off and clean ones put on; their dirty ones are put in their haversacks, just as they are when taken off. When the men leave to go to another hospital, their soiled ones are put on again. I told Dr. Hunter I did not think it was right; he replied, it could not be avoided, as hundreds are coming and going daily. The fact is, it is almost impossible to get people to do washing." Two months later, Cumming visited the Academy Hospital, in the same town, and discovered that the men's clothes were all washed on arrival as a matter of course.[21]

Frank Hawthorn, one of the sternest disciplinarians among Stout's medical officers, had a specific time set aside for cleaning the wards in the Academy Hospital. From 5:30–6:30 each morning, both shifts of nurses were to work together to clean everything. Ventilation, too, was an important part of keeping a hospital clean. Although some disinfectants, such as lime, were used in the hospitals, even the appearance of cleanliness might be only superficial. For example, Sam R. Watkins, who was slightly wounded in the ankle and heel during the fighting around Atlanta, and sent to a hospital in Montgomery, Alabama, recounted that "Everything seemed clean and nice enough, but the smell! Ye gods!" In some cases the source of a malodorous situation was more easily discerned. At the Clayton Hospital in Forsyth, Georgia, pigs broke out of a sty and rooted around under the hospital, bothering the patients with an "unpleasant and unhealthy odor" until someone rounded up the animals and repaired the fence.[22]

One hospital where standards of cleanliness reached an abysmal low point was located on Lookout Mountain near Chattanooga. The surgeon

---

Harden to Logan, August 28, 1863, TSLA, box 1, folder 15; Stout to Mullins, O'Keefe, and Harden, August 31, 1863, TSLA, box 2, folder 4; Mullins, Harden and O'Keefe to Stout, September 3, 1863, and G. L. Jones to no addressee, August 28, 1863, both in Emory, box 1, folder 18; J. E. Nagle to Stout, November 10, 1863, TSLA, box 1, folder 8.

21. Cumming, *Journal*, March 10 and May 20, 1863, pp. 84–85, 93–94.
22. Frank Hawthorn, "Rules of the Academy Hospital," no date, UTX, copies in boxes 2G379, 380, and 392. Cumming "thought the smell of the lime was better as a disinfectant than all the camphor or cologne in the world." *Journal*, September 4, 1863, p. 53. Watkins, "*Co. Aytch*," 186–87. Davis, "A Confederate Hospital," 18. Davis quotes the Clayton Hospital letter book, in private hands.

Samuel H. Stout about the time of the Civil War. Samuel H. Stout Papers, Special Collections, Robert W. Woodruff Library, Emory University.

Andrew Jackson Foard about the time of the Civil War. *Southern Practitioner* 24 (March 1902).

Samuel P. Moore before 1889. *Southern Practitioner* 23 (August 1901).

Dudley D. Saunders about 1901. *Southern Practitioner* 23 (July 1901).

. The Crutchfield House hotel in Chattanooga served as an Army of Tennessee hospital. This photograph was taken after the Union occupation of the town. National Archives (111-B-607).

The Academy Hospital in Chattanooga. At the far right is the original building of the Masonic academy. The other buildings were constructed by the Confederates for the hospital. This photograph, taken after the Union occupation, also shows two ambulances. National Archives (111-B-587).

Edward A. Flewellen about 1902. *Southern Practitioner* 24 (April 1902).

Samuel M. Bemiss about 1878. Atkinson, ed., *Physicians and Surgeons* (1878).

Kate Cumming after the Civil War. Cumming, *Gleanings from Southland* (1895).

Ferdinand E. Daniel and his grandchild no later than 1903. Samuel H. Stout Papers, Special Collections, Robert W. Woodruff Library, Emory University.

THIS
SOUVENIR

of The

Re-Union of
Confederates

Dallas, Texas.

April 22, 23, 24 and 25, 1902,

IS PRESENTED TO HIS COMRADES
BY

ÆT. 80,

WHO WAS SURGEON OF
COL. JNO. C. BROWN'S
(AFTERWARDS MAJ. GEN. AND GOVENOR)
THIRD TENN. REG.,
AND

MEDICAL DIRECTOR OF HOSPITALS
OF THE
ARMY AND DEPARTMENT OF TENN.

HIS RESIDENCE IS
177 WASHINGTON AVE.,
DALLAS, TEXAS.

TELEPHONE NO. 495.　COME AND SHAKE HANDS.

Souvenir card distributed by Stout to veterans who attended the Confederate reunion at Dallas in 1902. Samuel H. Stout Papers, Special Collections, Robert W. Woodruff Library, Emory University.

in charge, Randal M. Lytle, asked for a guard of at least thirty-five men as he was unable to keep either the nurses or the convalescents under control. Lytle was fighting nurses who continually disobeyed orders about "the deposit of excrement from the sick ward," and convalescents "caught *evacuating the contents of their bowels*" near, but not in, the "sinks."[23] In another case, at the St. Mary's Hospital in Dalton, Georgia, there apparently was not enough tableware for all of the patients to eat at one time. As a result, the patients ate in two groups. The problem, according to W. H. Means, post adjutant, was that the dishes were not washed between servings, leaving the second group to eat from dirty dishes. In February 1863, H. Hinkley, a surgeon for Preston's Brigade in Breckinridge's Division, wrote to E. A. Flewellen to convey complaints brought by his men returning from a hospital, also in Dalton. The men said that "the wounds are all (in the same ward) washed with same sponge and basin," a situation which Hinkley recognized as spreading the highly contagious wound infection erysipelas.[24] While standards of cleanliness varied from doctor to doctor and hospital to hospital, it is clear that some people had a better than rudimentary knowledge of sanitation and attempted to combat sanitary abuses.[25]

Certain standards did exist for the care of the sick and wounded. The ideal was a ratio of seventy patients for each medical officer and ten patients for each nurse. Every patient should have his own bed in a space of 800 cubic feet with clean bedding sufficient for the season, and ample food of the type appropriate to his assigned diet. But a battle, either an actual conflict or the threat of one, or some other emergency, could send a hospital into near chaos. Paul DeLacy Baker graphically described such a problem at Eufaula, Alabama, in July 1864: "Late last night, I had emptied upon me, without any sort of notice, between 200 and 300 wounded men. I am compelled to lay these men, filthy and lousy, upon the floor of the houses I have prepared for bunks, without any kind

---

23. R. M. Lytle to Stout, August 3, 1862, Emory, box 1, folder 5, also SHC–UNC, reel 2.
24. W. H. Means to F. H. Evans, June 15, 1863, Emory, box 1, folder 17; H. Hinkley to E. A. Flewellen, February 21, 1863, UTX, box 2G379. The second hospital may have been the St. Mary's as well, since in both cases the staff seemed to exhibit an aversion to the use of more than the minimum amount of water.
25. It was important that Stout, with his leadership role, was an advocate of hospital cleanliness. But Stout was certainly not alone in this regard. Other informed doctors, such as the researcher Joseph Jones, observed better patient results in cleaner facilities. Breeden, *Joseph Jones*, 204–12. Standards of cleanliness were also a problem in Northern hospitals. Adams, *Doctors in Blue*, 168–69.

of appliance or convenience necessary to the required cleanliness. I have, for these men sent on in advance of all necessary materials, no pans, no tubs, no spittoons, no medicines, no nurses, no ward masters, no adequate medical assistance, no Hospital clothing, and, consequently, cannot have the clothing of these men washed without turning them naked in the Houses or in the streets." Baker had no food for the new patients either, and some of them had not eaten for two days. As the war neared its close, scenes like Baker related, which fell far short of desired standards, became more and more common.[26]

Food was of great interest to all but the very sickest of the patients. The medical department realized that all patients could not eat the same food and devised a variety of diets, depending upon a patient's health. The most elaborate listing of such diets is found in a circular from the surgeon general's office of July 6, 1863. It listed the proper items, down to their exact weight in ounces, that were to comprise the daily serving for ten different diets: Tea Diet, Spoon Diet, Beef Tea Diet, Milk Diet, Light Meat Diet, Chicken Diet, Half Diet, Fish Diet, Roast Half Diet, and Full Diet. The ability to follow this elaborate scheme fully would certainly have made hospital meals the equivalent of the best a hotel could offer. But most hospitals, of necessity, simplified the specifications to Full Diet, Half Diet, and Low Diet, or perhaps only two diets—one for the sick and the other for convalescents. Even under good conditions during the early part of the war, Cumming complained of the "sameness" of the hospital diet. While the diet contained some variety even in March (for example, dried fruit, potatoes, rice, mush, beef and chicken soups, and bread), what the patients had to eat they had every day.[27]

Sometimes the quality of the hospital diet depended upon the ability of the hospital cooks. To help those who had little experience in preparing meals, the medical *Regulations* of 1863 included "Soyer's Directions for Cooking in Hospital." Fifteen recipes in the back of the volume gave instructions for preparing stewed mutton with soup for one hundred men, Beef Soup, Beef Tea, Thick Beef Tea, Essence of Beef, Chicken Broth,

---

26. B. M. Wible to Stout, December 7, 1863, UTX, box 2G390, and S. P. Moore Circular, July 6, 1863, box 2G425 and ledger 4L215. Paul DeLacy Baker to Stout, July 24, 1864, Emory, box 2, folder 14. Staffing ideals are discussed in chap. 3. The collapse of the hospitals will be treated in chap. 6.

27. Surgeon General's Office, Circular, July 6, 1863, UTX, ledger 4L215; Jno. R. Jones to R. M. Lytle, April 8, 1864, Emory, box 2, folder 7; Cumming, *Journal*, March 10, 1863, p. 84; Daniel, *Recollections of a Rebel Surgeon*, 150–51.

Plain Boiled Rice, Sago Jelly, Arrow-Root Milk, Arrow-Root Water, Rice Water, Barley Water, Crimean Lemonade (made with lime juice), Citric Acid Lemonade, and a miserable concoction called Toast and Water. The book directed, "Cut a piece of crusty bread about 1/4 lb.; toast gently and uniformly to a light yellow color; then place near the fire, and when of a good brown chocolate, put in a pitcher; pour on it 3 pints boiling water; cover the pitcher, and when cold, strain—it is then ready for use. Never leave the toast in, as it causes fermentation in a short time. A piece of apple, slowly toasted till it gets quite black, and added to the above, makes a very refreshing drink." No doubt the patients found the drink more "refreshing" if they did not know what was in it. Cumming related that she prepared a drink of arrowroot and eggs, flavored with preserves and wine, for her patients, who drank it because she would not tell the ingredients.[28]

Several patients expressed their displeasure with hospital food. Sam Watkins remained in a hospital in Montgomery only one night. Supper, he reported, "was a thin slice of light bread and a plate of soup . . . I ate it, but it only made me hungry." Watkins, however, found that "the bill of fare was much better for breakfast," although he did not say what it was. Ferdinand Daniel reported another instance of a patient's dislike for hospital meals. This patient, who was recovering from typhoid fever, had been assigned a diet of rice and milk. Eventually he revolted: " 'Take it away,' he said; 'I had just as soon lie down and let the moon shine in my mouth as to eat rice.' "[29] Such dissatisfaction was common, but it often received no sympathy. Thus, when a "Tennessee patient" wrote to Stout complaining about the food at the Madison Hospital in Montgomery, Surgeon in Charge C. J. Clark said the complaints had no foundation. Clark explained that they had four trained cooks, and two matrons who prepared special diets. He further defended the hospital menu by listing the quantities of food that had been purchased during the preceding month: 27 bushels apples, 46 bushels Irish potatoes, 500 bunches onions, 333 dozen eggs, 282 gallons milk, 74 bushels sweet potatoes, 167 pounds butter, 7 bushels tomatoes, 2 bushels butter beans, 402 chickens, 147 pumpkins, 31 gallons molasses, 6 1/2 barrels flour, 55 bushels turnip sallad, 216 dozen ears green corn, 2 bunches red pepper, 6 1/4 bushels okra, 7 1/2 dozen squashes, and 15 bushels peas.

28. *Regulations for the Medical Department*, 73–76. The recipe is on p. 76. Cumming, *Journal*, April 30, 1862, p. 18.
29. Watkins, "Co. Aytch," 187–88; Daniel, *Recollections of a Rebel Surgeon*, 151.

In addition, the commissary furnished rations: 1,548 pounds beef, 293 pounds bacon, 370 pounds flour, 3,976 pounds corn meal, 294 pounds rice, 88 1/2 pounds coffee, 176 pounds sugar, 132 pounds salt, and 193 pounds lard.[30]

The quality of hospital meals depended to a great degree upon the availability of food. Some seasonal shortages occurred as stored supplies from the previous harvest were exhausted. Hospital gardens did manage to meet some of the needs for vegetables, but success in gardening presupposed that the hospital would not have to be evacuated in the middle of the growing season. In many instances, the area around the hospitals was exhausted of supplies by the hospital's apparently insatiable demands. In other cases, competition between hospital purchasing agents drove up the prices beyond reasonable levels. Physician Robert Battey said the citizens of Rome, Georgia, did not want to sell eggs or chickens for money but would willingly trade for a product like cloth or thread. Later in the war, Stout authorized trading brown earthenware pottery, made specifically for the hospitals, for food supplies. By this time, inflation was such a problem that the citizens wanted some sort of tangible exchange rather than unstable Confederate money. A problem too, in many cases, was the lack of a hospital fund. When the commissary could not provide the money, the hospitals were often unable to buy on credit. Randal M. Lytle, making a "Sanitary Report" for the Direction Hospital in Griffin, Georgia, from January to March, 1865, related that the diet was "inferior." Because the hospital had no hospital fund, the cooks could not get anything but corn bread, sorghum, and beef.[31]

Patient responses to the conditions in the hospitals are much less common than doctor's reports. Patient comments often depended on the particular hospital, the seriousness of the patient's condition, and the soldier's previous hospital experience. A patient who was not seriously ill could find more things to complain about than one who was at death's door. One Robert Banks had an operation in Atlanta to remove a growth from his neck. "Finding things very uninviting at the hospital,"

---

30. C. J. Clark to Stout, October 9, 1864, UTX, box 2G415.
31. Cumming, *Journal*, May 24, 1864, p. 186; J. B. Barnette to Stout, April 11, 1864, Emory, box 2, folder 7; B. M. Wible to Sir, October 25, 1864, Emory, Stout microfilm; Robert Battey to Stout, November 20, 1863, UTX, box 2G420; Stout, "Some Facts," pt. 19, 25 (May 1903): 281; B. M. Wible to Stout, June 23, 1864, UTX, box 2G418; Randal M. Lytle, "Sanitary Report for the Quarter ending March 31, 1865," UTX, box 2G403.

he related, "I obtained permission to stay at" a hotel. "A Confederate Soldier" complained to Stout that a Yankee patient in his hospital was receiving daily visits and delicacies from a Union-sympathizing woman. This Yankee, thought the loyal Confederate, ought to be sent wherever the rest of the "raiders" and "vandals" were. Several former patients of "Grandma" Smith at Tunnel Hill later wrote her letters comparing their present hospital situation unfavorably with their experiences at Tunnel Hill. One did, however, have good things to say about the kindness of the ladies of the town who ministered to the needs of the new patients arriving at the Forsyth, Georgia, railroad depot.[32]

Despite various problems encountered by the hospitals, one group of soldiers thought hospital conditions, whatever they were, were decidedly preferable to being in the field. This group, usually called "malingerers" or "hospital rats," received scant sympathy from doctors and attendants. For example, John M. Johnson, serving in Atlanta, remarked to Stout in May 1862, "I think you have a hard set to deal with [in Chattanooga], judging from the specimens sent down here; these Georgia Cols as well as privates, dont seem to have any just idea of the true character of the War. They all want furloughs to see their families, or if they get a cold, they must go home or never get well, and if there is a battle impending, they take diarrhea, Rheumatism or something of the kind and some dont wait to get sick but run strait [*sic*] off." A year later T. G. Richardson commented, "I presume from what I hear that a great many men have been sent down to hosp within the past few days who have no manner of disease about them except want of heart and as we don't profess to treat cases of this sort they might just as well be in the ranks." Richardson blamed General Hardee's acting or assistant medical director for not examining these spurious patients before they boarded the train. Matron Fannie Beers described a "hospital rat" as one "who at the first rumor of an approaching battle, had experienced 'a powerful

---

32. Robert W. Banks to a sister, "Sunday Night 1864" [probably May 29], in Osborn, ed., "Civil War Letters of Robert W. Banks," 212; "A Confederate Soldier" to Stout, June 29, 1864, Emory, box 3, folder 11; John W. Waynesburg to "Mother Smith," December 11, 1863, W. H. Garrett to Mrs. Susan E. Smith, May 28, 1864, R. D. Compton to [Mrs. Smith], February 24, 1865, and J. E. Ruffin to Mrs. Smith, July 16, 1864, all in Smith, *The Soldier's Friend.* Capt. Thomas Brownrigg, severely wounded in the right arm, commended the hospital in Columbus, Georgia, under Surgeon Carlisle Terry for its discipline, cleanliness, and nutritious food. He also said good things about Dr. Kirksey who was in charge of his ward. Brownrigg to Sir, August 24, 1864, UTX, box 2G395.

misery' at the place where a brave heart should have been, and, flying to the rear, doubled up with rheumatism and out-groaning all the victims of *real* sickness or horrible wounds, had remained huddled up in bed until danger was over." After being deceived several times, Mrs. Beers was able to recognize and ignore such moaning imposters.[33]

Short of purposely shooting oneself in the hand or foot (and a number of soldiers did try this route to the hospital), a wound could not be faked, but many types of diseases could be. The medical *Regulations* specifically warned doctors to beware of "epilepsy, convulsions, chronic rheumatism, derangement of the urinary organs, ophthalmia, ulcers, or any obscure disease, liable to be feigned or purposely produced." This did not mean that anyone complaining of one of these ailments was necessarily untruthful, of course, but simply that these diseases produced less obvious symptoms. The *Regulations* urged doctors to keep such cases, especially ones not originally their own, under observation for a reasonable period of time before issuing a certificate of disability. Many of the malingerers were clever actors and their deception was difficult to detect. Others seem to have been somewhat less ingenious. For example, in November 1863, Pvt. J. R. Mattbie, in the Polk Hospital in Rome, Georgia, complained vigorously to Stout that the medical officers were well fed but that the patients were not. While investigating the complaints, which turned out to be without foundation, Surgeon Battey also investigated Private Mattbie. Mattbie had been in the hospital since August 27 (two and a half months) and the examining board had been unable to find anything wrong with him, despite various professed ailments. Battey believed that they had found a malingerer. Stout suggested, in one of his later writings, that perhaps the Confederate army had fewer malingerers than any army in history. There is no statistical evidence to back up what may be simply a rosy postwar recollection. Whatever Stout thought later, malingering did seem to be a considerable problem at the time and concerned the doctors because each malingerer took the bed, food, and nursing needed by an authentically ill patient.[34]

---

33. John M. Johnson to Stout, May 5, 1862, SHC–UNC, reel 4; T. G. Richardson to Dr. [probably Stout], June 29, 1863, UTX, box 2G423; Beers, *Memories*, 96.
34. *Regulations for the Medical Department*, 11; Daniel, *Recollections of a Rebel Surgeon*, 147; J. R. Mattbie to Stout, November 12, 1863, and Robert Battey to W. L. Nichol, November 14, 1863, both in Emory, box 1, folder 23; Stout, "Reminiscences," 234. An example of feigned deafness can be found in Marcus J. Wright to Stout, September 13, 1864, UTX, box 2G379.

Perhaps the most infamous hospital site that fell within Stout's jurisdiction was the prison camp at Andersonville. Unquestionably conditions at this notorious prison camp were terrible, with impossible overcrowding, abysmal sanitation, and food deficient in quantity and quality. Defenders of the Confederates can legitimately point to shortages of supplies and transportation throughout the Confederacy, even among their own troops, as well as the Federal refusal to exchange prisoners, as mitigating factors. Although Andersonville has a particular infamy, it was certainly not the only prison, North or South, in which conditions were terrible. It was, however, one in which Stout played a role, albeit a small one.[35]

Stout apparently selected the site that became Andersonville prison for a hospital, a factor he used later to combat accusations that the Confederates had deliberately chosen a barren place to mistreat the prisoners. Stout claimed that "there was no better place for a prison or hospital south [of] Macon Ga. on the score of salubrity and abundance of drinking water." When informed that the government wished to place a prison on his chosen site, Stout relinquished his plans for a hospital there. The problem, of course, was that a site suited for a hospital of five hundred to one thousand patients was clearly not suited for an improperly constructed camp with multiplied thousands of prisoners.[36]

In April 1864 Stout visited Richmond, and while there dined frequently with his former commander, General Bragg. Bragg told Stout that he was having the prisoners of war moved to Andersonville where they could be better fed. He specifically asked Stout to take particular care to treat the sick prisoners humanely and to feed them well, if the prison hospital became a part of his jurisdiction. But Stout did not retain much jurisdiction at Andersonville. Stout's associate there, Isaiah H. White, the surgeon in charge of the prison hospital, complained that it took too long to get requisitions filled, because he had to send them to Stout in Atlanta for approval, and then had to get the supplies themselves from Macon. White's problem with getting supplies was not a difficulty unique to the prison camp, of course, as should be evident from

---

35. A good secondary analysis of Andersonville and its problems is Futch, *History of Andersonville Prison*. The testimony used to convict the post commandant can be found in *The Trial of Henry Wirz*. Many survivors of Andersonville also published their recollections of the experience.

36. Stout notes in his copy of Braun, *Andersonville*, [12], 13–14, Emory, box 5, folder 13; Stout, "Address—History," 450.

many examples previously presented. Time lags caused by interruption of the mails, broken-down transportation, suppliers who only filled a portion of the requisition, and recalcitrant quartermasters, could not be charged to Stout or his administration. Responding to White's appeal, however, Richmond made him independent of Stout as chief surgeon of prison hospitals, and thus Stout no longer had any responsibility for White's supplies.[37] In May 1864, before White was removed from Stout's distant supervision, Stout sent his assistant, S. M. Bemiss, to inspect the sanitary conditions at Andersonville. While Bemiss no doubt found these conditions thoroughly deplorable, his report no longer exists.[38]

Stout's main responsibility at Andersonville was to assign doctors to serve in the hospital. While this was often a difficult task at best, the known problems at Andersonville made procuring doctors for the post doubly difficult. Dr. John C. Bates was one such extremely reluctant physician. Long exempted from Confederate service because he was a practicing physician more than thirty years old, Bates, in the fall of 1864, had to become a contract physician for the hospital department to escape conscription into the ranks. Bates claimed, in his testimony at Andersonville Post Commander Henry Wirz's trial, that he was forced to take an oath of allegiance to the Confederacy at bayonet point, and, as a contract physician, he was ordered to Andersonville. J. M. Dossler of Montgomery, Alabama, when assigned to Andersonville, asked for a leave of absence to recover from an illness, and then asked to be assigned elsewhere because he was "opposed upon principle to this duty." Doctors themselves were not the only ones who objected to orders sending them to Andersonville. Several subordinate surgeons and the chief matron of the Asylum Hospital in Augusta, as well as a group of ladies in that town, petitioned Stout not to send Surgeon H. H. Clayton to Andersonville, although eventually he was ordered there anyway.[39]

---

37. Stout notes in Braun, *Andersonville*, 13–14. Isaiah H. White to Capt. Hammond, June 20, 1864, *OR*, series 2, vol. 7, pp. 386–87; White to S. P. Moore, July 1, 1864, ibid., 430. Stout, "Address—History," 450; Testimony of E. A. Flewellen, September 26, 1865, *Trial of Henry Wirz*, 423.

38. Stout to S. M. Bemiss, May 2, 1864, Emory, box 2, folder 8. According to Stout's later recollections, he thought that Bemiss's report was so important that he sent it to the surgeon general without making a copy, certainly a highly unusual procedure for Stout. Stout, "Address—History," 451–52.

39. Stout, "Address—History," 450; Testimony of Dr. John C. Bates, August 24 and 25, 1865, *Trial of Henry Wirz*, 27, 39; J.(?) M. Dossler(?) to Stout, August 2, 1864, UTX, box 2G379. N. F. Howard, J. F. Wooton, and A. M. Turner, September 24,

Perhaps the most important thing to realize about Stout's relationship with the hospital at Andersonville is that it was not typical of the hospital department Stout supervised. Clearly Stout expressed some concern for the well-being of the prisoner patients, in that, while he had any authority over the hospital, he sent an inspector to survey the scene and make recommendations for improvement. That few, if any, of these recommendations were probably carried out was beyond Stout's control, as were most other factors associated with the location. Given Stout's other vast responsibilities during the summer of 1864, he cannot be expected to have focused on the prison hospital at Andersonville.

Stout's primary responsibility was to supervise the hospitals of the Army of Tennessee. While he did not take personal charge of each detail of running the hospitals, Stout maintained as much control over them as circumstances permitted through personal inspections and carefully chosen subordinates who made daily reports. Stout made decisions that would help the hospitals to run smoothly so that the patients would receive adequate care. In July 1864, while conditions were severe at Andersonville, Stout was in charge of sixty-eight hospitals—a huge responsibility because these hospitals were located in twenty-one different towns stretched in a wide band across middle Georgia and Alabama, from Augusta on the east to Montgomery on the west.[40] A representative weekly report, compiled July 21, 1864, showed that 177 physicians, 1,128 nurses, and 1,056 other staff members cared for 14,974 patients in Army of Tennessee hospitals. These ailing soldiers were only a portion of the 49,091 sick and wounded who passed through the hospitals in July as a result of the intensive campaigning in Georgia.[41] These statistics suggest that Stout was in charge of a major operation.

1864, Mus. Confed. ST–9–7; B. H. Washington to Stout, September 28, 1864, and Ladies of Augusta to Stout, October 1, 1864, both in UTX, box 2G389; Sarah F. Livingston to Stout, October 18, 1864, Emory, Stout microfilm, also Duke. Clayton himself asked for a reprieve for a number of good reasons. H. H. Clayton to Stout, September 23, 1864, ibid.

40. "General Summary of the Hospitals of the Army of Tennessee for the month ending July 30/64," UTX, box 2G379.

41. Ibid.; "Weekly Report of Hospitals of the Army of Tenn.," July 21, 1864, UTX, ibid. The patients and attendants were unequally distributed among the various hospital posts.

CHAPTER 6

"WE ARE PACKING UP IN A HURRY TO MOVE"

The major distinction between the behind-the-lines hospitals of the Army of Northern Virginia and those of the Army of Tennessee was the mobility of the latter, which created tremendous differences in the two hospital organizations. By early 1862 Richmond had become the hospital center for the eastern army. The city eventually had twenty hospitals, including the Chimborazo, the largest, with a capacity of 8,000, as well as the Winder (5,000) and the Jackson (2,500). While the Confederacy certainly maintained hospitals in Virginia outside Richmond, it placed most of them in the capital city. Indeed, no hospital post in the west approached Richmond in capacity. Tobias G. Richardson, assistant medical director (field) of the Army of Tennessee under Bragg, who accompanied the general to Richmond as a medical inspector, wrote to Stout in March 1864 comparing Stout's hospitals with those in Richmond. "In my inspections I have gone through the three large establishments here, viz Winder, Jackson, & Chimborazo. They are all upon the plan of the Fair Ground Hosp. at Atlanta and their general management, except that of Jackson, about upon a par with the same. . . . In a domestic point of view none of them surpass your hospitals at Marietta, and in feeding you are infinitely superior. Indeed it is almost impossible for any one to get enough to eat, either outside or inside the hospitals, for the simple reason that it is not to be had at any price." The hospitals established in Richmond remained there and grew until the evacuation of the capital, but in the west, the hospitals began moving almost immediately, as the Army of Tennessee gradually retreated through its extensive territory. While hospitals were being established in Richmond, other hospitals were being vacated in Nashville.[1] The evacuation of these

---

1. Cunningham, *Doctors in Gray*, 51–54. One surgeon who worked at the Chimborazo Hospital recalled that it had one hundred and fifty ward buildings with forty to sixty patients in each ward. J. R. Gildersleeve, "Presidential Address," in "Annual Meeting

Nashville hospitals provoked Stout to devise better ways to "mobilize" the hospitals.

What did Stout mean by mobilizing the hospitals? Upon the departure of the Confederates from Nashville in February 1862, Stout saw the hospitals closed and the medical officers ordered to some other post where they then had to organize new hospitals once again from nothing. Stout had a better idea: "When the exigencies of the services demanded the evacuation of a hospital post, all the hospitals there were removed with their organizations preserved, and their hospital property, cooking utensils, bunks, bedding and medicines too going with them." Although patients often went to other more stable hospitals while the organization moved, the doctors, nurses, and other attendants travelled with the property and set up the facilities in the new location. Moving a hospital was a project easier ordered than done. Some time in late 1864, G. R. Fairbanks, chief quartermaster for the Army of Tennessee Hospital Department, estimated that it would require seventeen four-horse wagons, seventeen two-horse wagons, and six ambulances to move a three hundred patient hospital, leaving the bunks behind as they alone would require fifteen to twenty more wagons. While the railroad was the preferred method of transportation, it was not always available or functioning. It is a tribute to Stout, his subordinates, and even the much-maligned quartermaster department, that the hospitals continued to move until the end of the war.[2]

When Stout took charge of the hospitals in Chattanooga, he worked to see them effectively organized and disciplined. As his responsibilities extended to other posts, he continued to promote hospital excellence as well as to look for sites to which the hospitals could be expanded in case

---

of the Association of Medical Officers of the Army and Navy of the Confederacy," *So. Pract.* 26 (August 1904): 494–95. Lane, "The Winder Hospital," 35–41. It is interesting to note that Lane's account had only good things to say about the hospital. He did not mention a single problem or inadequacy. Richardson to Doctor [Stout], March 10, 1864, Emory, box 2, folder 5; also SHC–UNC, Stout microfilm, reel 2.

2. Stout, "Some Facts," pt. 17, 25 (March 1903): 155–56; Stout, "Outline," 65. G. R. Fairbanks, "Estimate of Transportation required for Moveable Hospital of 300 Beds," no date, UTX, box 2G423. Fairbanks probably made this estimate in the fall of 1864 because he was appointed to supervise all the Army of Tennessee hospital quartermasters on October 11, 1864. Furthermore, with Gen. John Bell Hood's decision in October to lead the army toward Tennessee, the hospitals entered their period of greatest movement. A. R. Lawton to G. R. Fairbanks, October 11, 1864, UTX, box 2G425.

of a sudden influx of many sick and wounded soldiers. It was unusual for the Confederates to be thus prepared, but because of this preparation, Stout was not caught totally off guard when the Federal army appeared outside Chattanooga in August 1863.

On July 1, 1863, Matron Kate Cumming of the Newsom Hospital in Chattanooga reported in her diary: "Great excitement in town. News has come that the enemy is across the river, and intends shelling the place. . . . We are packing up in a hurry to move. Our hospital being near the river, we will be *honored* by the first shot." At this time, Gen. Braxton Bragg and the Army of Tennessee were retreating before the Union forces from Tullahoma, Tennessee, to Chattanooga, where they arrived about July 7. On that date one of Bragg's staff officers ordered Stout not to build any more hospitals in Chattanooga, but to send his building materials to Kingston, "or some suitable place in the rear on the Rail Road." But Stout also seems to have been part of General Bragg's ruse to deceive the citizens and the enemy into thinking that Bragg would not abandon Chattanooga. While Stout moved the patients south, he continued to build a hospital at Camp Direction.[3]

Union forces, under Gen. William S. Rosecrans, did not begin moving close to Chattanooga until August 16, or fire their first shots at the town until August 21. On this latter date Stout moved his office from Chattanooga to Dalton, so that he could communicate with all parts of his hospital command without interruption.[4] Dudley D. Saunders, who had succeeded Stout as surgeon in charge of the hospitals in Chattanooga when Stout became medical director of hospitals in June 1863, wrote a series of letters to Stout describing the evacuation of the hospitals and his attempt to reestablish them in Marietta, Georgia.

On August 23 Saunders reported that, after consultation with Medical Director E. A. Flewellen and Brigadier General Jackson, "it was thought most prudent to abandon the Academy, Gilmer & Foard Hospitals as they were in range of the enemys [sic] guns & got all of their water from the river." The sick at the Foard Hospital moved south that morning, but the Gilmer and Academy patients, who were convalescents, stayed behind to help with the evacuation. The property, supplies, and nurses

---

3. Cumming, *Journal*, July 1 and 21, 1863, pp. 99 and 105; unsigned [probably G. W. Brent], A. A. Gen. to Stout, July 7, 1863, Emory, box 1, folder 18; Stout, "Some Facts," pt. 22, 25 (September 1903): 520–21.

4. Long, with Long, *The Civil War Day by Day* is very useful for establishing the dates of military maneuvers that affected the hospital movements, but are not described in the hospital records. Stout, "Some Facts," pt. 22, 25 (September 1903): 521.

of the Gilmer Hospital went to Stout at Dalton, while men dismantled the bunks for shipping. On the same day Surgeon Frank Hawthorn of the Academy Hospital described his frustration to Stout. "My Agent, Smith, will report to you in charge of the property of this Hosp'l. I can give no estimate of what it consists of. Under orders of all kinds I have packed & unpacked until I am utterly confused. . . . The medicines and instruments are nicely & securely packed up but in the hurry I have had no time to make invoices of them either. Please order the person to whom they are turned over to make the invoices & receipts. Everything has been removed from Camp Direction Hosp'l & I am ordered to re-establish it with a part of the Academy Hospital stores & furniture. I had everything packed in the cars & have had to unpack for this purpose." Saunders gave tents to Hawthorn to use, in addition to the buildings, leaving the single hospital remaining in the Chattanooga area a capacity of about three hundred patients. The primary purpose of this hospital was receiving and shipping sick soldiers to other posts.[5]

During the last few days of August and the early part of September 1863, Stout and his subordinates struggled not only to relocate hospitals but also to prepare for the casualties of an expected battle. Stout ordered all the permanently disabled patients to Rome, Georgia, while he ordered those able to do any sort of duty at all returned to their command. Stout also warned J. P. Logan that all the beds in Atlanta would be needed in case a battle took place before the Chattanooga hospitals reopened in new locations. In the meantime, Medical Director Flewellen planned to talk to Quartermaster McMicken to see whether the hospital buildings on Academy Hill could be dismantled and moved to some other place. Flewellen also gave Stout the responsibility for selecting hospital sites without consulting him, as Flewellen had no information on which to base decisions. He believed that Stout would have no reason to establish hospitals outside the official limits of Bragg's department.[6]

Meanwhile, Saunders was trying to establish his hospitals in Marietta. He believed that Marietta had the best buildings available in the vicinity: stores, a courthouse, a Masonic Hall, and one of the town's

5. D. D. Saunders to Stout, August 23, 1863, UTX, box 2G423. Saunders also had the surgeon at the "Pest House" (smallpox hospital) burn all his tents, bedding, and hospital clothing, and then take his kitchen utensils and nurses to Dalton. Frank Hawthorn to Stout, August 23, 1863, UTX, box 2G392.
6. Stout, Circular No. 5, August 23, 1863, UTX, ledger 4L218; Stout to J. P. Logan, August 29, 1863, ibid; E. A. Flewellen to Stout, August 26, 1863, Mus. Confed., ST–5–5, also TSLA, box 1, folder 4.

two hotels. But he did not think that the buildings could hold more than 850 to 900 patients. What he really wanted, in addition to the other buildings, was the state military institute, a perfect facility that would accommodate 400 to 450 more beds. His objective conflicted with the views of Georgia Governor Joseph E. Brown, however. As Saunders wrote to Stout, "*privately*, I do not like the spirit shown by Gov Brown, there is too much of the demagogue. He is a candidate for Gov, many influential men have their sons, who are now 18, in that Institute to keep them out of the army, as they are exempt, hence Gov Brown's unwillingness to turn the students out as he will lose the influence of their fathers." Whether or not Brown's motivation was as blatantly political as Saunders supposed, Brown continued to refuse the use of the institute buildings for hospital purposes even after Stout paid him a personal visit. Saunders thus resorted to other expedients, such as erecting tents, to try to increase the size of his post, for he estimated that beds would be required for 6,000 wounded plus the usual 4,000 sick. He thought, however, that the entire district only contained about 6,000 beds.[7]

As if relocating the hospitals from Chattanooga did not create enough difficulties, on September 6, Flewellen, in response to further Union movements around Chattanooga, telegraphed Stout to remove all the hospitals north of Resaca to locations south and west of Atlanta, if necessary. Thus, contrary to his earlier supposition, Flewellen gave Stout permission to send them out of the territory assigned to Bragg. This meant the evacuation of the installations at Ringgold, Catoosa Springs, Cherokee Springs, Tunnel Hill, and Dalton, followed by the hospitals at Calhoun and Adairsville which could not be supplied, even though they were south of Dalton.

Kate Cumming described the removal of the hospital from Cherokee Springs. She reported that the hospital authorities received the evacuation order on the afternoon of September 6. The medical staff immediately sent off the sick and began to pack the hospital property, sending it to the depot. Cumming spent the night of September 7 in Dalton, sleeping in cramped quarters on a boxcar floor. She remarked, "At Tunnel

---

7. D. D. Saunders to Stout, August 26, 1863, UTX, box 2G423; August 31, 1863, UTX, box 2G427; September 1, 1863, Mus. Confed., ST–5–6; September 1, 1863 (second letter), UTX, box 2G413; Stout, "Outline," 70–71. Saunders was estimating figures for the whole department of the Army of Tennessee, in contrast to the over 15,500 beds in Richmond alone mentioned earlier.

Hill we saw a number of new hospital buildings; there were so many that they looked like a village. It does seem too bad that we are compelled to leave all of our hard work for the enemy to destroy." Cumming and her hospital settled at Newnan, Georgia. Hospitals from Dalton went to LaGrange; those from Tunnel Hill reopened at Palmetto; and those from Catoosa Springs, Calhoun and Adairsville located in Griffin, where Surgeon R. C. Foster was supposed to prepare for a capacity of 1,000 beds. Stout himself relocated his headquarters to Marietta.[8]

Meanwhile, in preparation for the expected battle, Flewellen asked Stout to establish and control a shipping and receiving hospital at Resaca. "The Sick & Wounded are transported to the Rail Road by the train wagons sent for supplies and as the depot for such supplies is liable to be changed to suit the movements of the army," wrote Flewellen, "you are instructed to order the Medical officer whom you may place on duty at Resaca to change from there to any other place to which it may be necessary to send the wagons for supplies." During the final days before the Battle of Chickamauga Stout and Flewellen lost contact with one another. Though they sent messages to each other, the dispatches seem to have miscarried, contributing to some confusion which could have been avoided.[9]

The Confederates won the Battle of Chickamauga, fought September 19–20, 1863, but they suffered heavy losses. Various sources estimate Confederate casualties at Chickamauga as 18,454–20,950, out of 66,326 troops involved. Of these casualties, 16,000–18,000 were

8.   E. A. Flewellen to Stout, September 6, 1863, NA, chap. 6, vol. 749; Stout to Flewellen, September 17, 1863, Emory, Stout microfilm, also UTX, box 2G427; Cumming, *Journal*, September 6, 8 and 9, 1863, pp. 124–26, 129; Stout to Col. G. William Brent, September 12, 1863, Emory, box 1, folder 18, also SHC–UNC, reel 2; Stout to R. C. Foster, September 13, 1863, TSLA, box 1, folder 20; Stout to Flewellen, September 14, 1863, Emory, box 1, folder 18.
9.   Flewellen to Stout, September 15, 1863, NA, chap. 6, vol. 749, also SHC–UNC, reel 2, and Emory, box 3, folder 10. A shipping and receiving hospital was supposed to receive patients from the field hospitals, give them food and water, and tend their wounds as necessary until they could be put on the train to a more distant hospital where they would receive long-term care. Ideally a wounded soldier should spend only a few hours in such a facility. Stout and Flewellen's communication problems are discussed in Stout to Flewellen, September 17, 1863, Emory, Stout microfilm, also UTX, box 2G427, and Flewellen to Stout, September 22, 1863, Mus. Confed., ST–5–13. Stout noted on the back of Flewellen's letter that the information he sent to Flewellen finally arrived at the latter's headquarters three weeks after the battle! Stout received Flewellen's letter of September 22 on September 30.

wounded (nearly triple the number anticipated by Saunders) who had
to be cared for by the hospital system. These figures do not include an
unknown number of Federal wounded. The masses of new patients seriously strained Stout's hospital system.[10] Of course, many of the problems
were due to the lack of medical officers and transportation. On September 21, W. J. Burt, an assistant surgeon and the only medical officer
at the receiving and shipping hospital at Tunnel Hill, appealed to Stout
for a clerk and other aid. He had already shipped eighty-five men that
morning and was about to send as many more, which was difficult
because the nearest point to which the trains ran was Catoosa Station,
some four miles away. More wounded were expected as soon as they
could be transported from the field. Burt had no cook and had to
impress four "negroes" to prepare food for the patients. Furthermore,
by September 23, Burt was so inundated with wounded that he could
not register them properly. He had shipped 600 the previous evening,
800 that morning, and heard that 10,000 were yet to come. His problems were not over, however, for Burt soon had difficulties with the
quartermaster at the post, Major Horbach, as well. Horbach refused to
furnish a coffin for a dead soldier or fill Burt's requisition for blacks
to help nurse the patients. Burt complained that Horbach "will give no
assistance whatever saying it is none of his business."[11]

Another bottleneck occurred at a "Wood Shed near Burnt Bridge," not
far from Catoosa Station, where twenty to forty carloads of soldiers lay
in a field waiting for transportation, sometimes without sufficient supplies to keep them comfortable. Stout angrily noted on the back of one
letter that it was not until September 27 that Quartermaster McMicken
assumed any responsibility for transporting the wounded. Stout and
other medical officers had procured the transportation previously. By
October 1 Stout reported to Flewellen that all the sick and wounded
had left the Wood Shed and Tunnel Hill. The field hospitals were now
sending patients "able to bear transportation" to a newly opened receiving
and distributing hospital at Ringgold. Stout, however, requested some
clarification of his responsibilities after a battle. If he were to be in
charge of transportation, he wanted an order or a request to that effect
from the commanding general. He protested that if he had known he

10. McDonough, Chattanooga—A Death Grip on the Confederacy, 13, 15.
11. W. J. Burt to Stout, September 21, 1863, Emory, box 1, folder 19, also Mus. Confed.,
    ST–5–12; copy of Burt's request to Major Horbach for a coffin, September 22, 1863,
    SHC–UNC, reel 2; Burt to Stout, September 23, 1863, Emory, Stout microfilm.

was supposed to be in charge of transportation for this battle, he "would have anticipated many of the recent difficulties and prevented them."[12]

The transportation of the sick and wounded during the Civil War was a complex and often problematic procedure. While the army was supposed to have a certain number of spring-equipped ambulances to move the wounded from the field hospitals to the railroad depot, these vehicles were often broken down and, after a battle, were far too few to be effective. Thus, after Chickamauga, wagons hauling supplies from the depot to the army were emptied, filled with pine tops because no straw was available, and then loaded with wounded for the return trip to the depot. Ambulances were also supposed to be available at the hospital posts to take the wounded from the depot to the hospital. Once again, however, the transportation was deficient. An indication of this problem appears in the report of R. D. Gribble, quartermaster at Marietta. When ordered to move with the hospitals from Chattanooga to Marietta he had to leave behind all his transportation except for one two-horse ambulance and one two-horse wagon. In Marietta he had so much trouble hiring wagons that he almost had to use force to get them. Then, the quartermaster ordered these wagons, which Gribble had finally acquired, sent to the front, and Gribble had to borrow wagons from local civilians to move the wounded.[13]

---

12. "Able to bear transportation" is the stock Civil War phrase for those patients who were well enough to travel. Stout to Flewellen, September 23, 1863, Emory, box 1, folder 19; E. Miller to Stout, September 24, 1863, ibid., also Mus. Confed., ST–5–14, and TSLA, box 1, folder 8; E. Miller to Stout, September 25, 1863, Emory, box 1, folder 19; E. Miller to Stout, September 26, 1863, Emory, Stout microfilm, also UTX, box 2G427, and Duke. Stout note on back of W. J. Burt to Stout, September 27, 1863, Emory, Stout microfilm, also Duke; Stout to Flewellen, October 1, 1863, Emory, box 1, folder 20; Stout to S. P. Moore, October 10, 1863, ibid. As late as October 23 Stout complained, "Unless ambulance trains are put upon the road, and run on definite schedule, it is out of my power to prevent such suffering . . . The Director of Hospitals cannot do the duties of the Quartermaster Department and his own. I cannot find a Quartermaster in the rear, who thinks he is at all responsible for the quality of the transportation furnished the sick and wounded." Stout notation forwarding letter to A. A. Genl. of General Bragg, on back of W. J. Sneed to Jno. Patterson, October 23, 1863, Mus. Confed., ST–5–20. M. B. McMicken's performance does not seem to have improved during the course of the war for he received a censure for failing to remove many supplies from Atlanta before the evacuation of the city, even though he had adequate warning. Special Orders, No. 51, A & IGO, Richmond, March 2, 1865, OR, series 1, vol. 38, part 3, pp. 991–92.

13. The ambulances were not very comfortable. Matron Kate Cumming visited a field hospital near Chickamauga and then rode to the railroad in an ambulance. She wrote that

Between their two rides in ambulances or wagons, the sick and wounded usually travelled some distance by railroad. Apparently J. P. Logan prepared the first railroad cars specifically intended for ambulance use by the Army of Tennessee in January 1863. These cars were supposed to run on the Western and Atlantic Railroad between Chattanooga and Atlanta. Frank M. Dennis was the first train surgeon appointed, a capacity in which he continued until his death in a railroad accident on July 18, 1864. Aside from caring for the patients in transit, Dennis and other train surgeons supervised nurses, saw that the cars were kept clean and the bunks "free from vermin," and made accurate reports of the number of patients transported, along with their destinations. Many of these records indicate trips made without incident. Others report men missing upon arrival. Apparently these men were not too sick to desert, which they could easily do since there was no guard on the train. In some cases, the records relate long delays which caused the patients to suffer.[14]

The ambulance cars had berths one above the other, which, as Stout later said, made them undesirable because they were not well ventilated. Even worse for the patients on the upper tier were the severe jolts, caused by starting and stopping or by rough tracks, which sometimes tossed patients out of their bunks. The best means for travelling, in Stout's opinion, were boxcars with several feet of straw and blankets on the floor. Even this arrangement was not totally satisfactory, however. For example, on December 2, 1863, M. W. King reported that the circumstances

---

the wounded must have suffered terribly because the road was very rough and they had to ford two or three deep rivers. Cumming, *Journal*, October 6, 1863, pp. 142–43. Cunningham, *Doctors in Gray*, 118–22. As Cunningham relates, the Army of Northern Virginia had transportation troubles also. Stout, "Transportation of the Sick and Wounded of Armies on Land," 64. R. D. Gribble to Stout, October 21, 1863, Mus. Confed., ST–5–17. Ambulance types and problems with them as experienced by the Union forces are described in Adams, *Doctors in Blue*, throughout, especially 25, 62–63.

14. J. P. Logan to Stout, January 15, 1863, UTX, box 2G387; R. P. Bateman to Stout, July 19, 1864, UTX, box 2G386. After observing Dr. Dennis for several months, Logan recommended him to Stout. "I am fully satisfied that you cannot obtain a more efficient officer for the discharge of the duty in which he has been engaged." Logan to Stout, June 26, 1863, Emory, box 1, folder 17. Flewellen to J. W. Naul and J. E. Wilson, January 28, 1863, N A, chap. 6, vol. 749; Stout, Circular No. 23, November 17, 1863, Emory, Stout microfilm. F. E. B. Stevenson to Stout, May 1, 1864, TSLA, box 1, folder 9; John(?) L. Aulman(?) to J. M. Green, September 1, 1864, UTX, box 2G379; W. J. Sneed to Jno. Patterson, October 23, 1863, Mus. Confed., ST–5–20; Eben Hillyer to M. W. King, December 14, 1863, UTX, box 2G386.

under which he shipped patients that morning were beyond his control, and, thus he had to resort to using cars that "had recently been used in transporting cattle horses &c and had not been cleaned." He added, "I would have cleaned them but Conductor said he could not detain the train [and] could only allow me five minutes to load them. Had not the Hospitals in the city been crowded, and we were expecting more patients from the front, I would have retained them." Unhappily, King lamented, "I was compelled to send them with *filthy transportation*."[15]

As previously noted, the Battle of Chickamauga presented unprecedented problems for Stout's department, for his hospitals in Atlanta, which had 1,800 beds, received 10,000 patients during the month of September 1863. First came the sick being sent south, followed by the wounded from the battle. In a letter to Surgeon General S. P. Moore, Stout described the problems caused by the battle and explained how he handled so many patients in a department with only 7,500 beds. First, Stout reported, he sent many patients out of the department to the hospitals of other commands located in Montgomery, Macon, Columbus, and Augusta. After that, he related, he sent other patients to stay in private homes and to report to the hospital daily for treatment. Soldiers who were incapacitated but who did not need surgical treatment he furloughed, and sent those with slight wounds to convalescent camps.[16]

But some people complained about the treatment of the wounded after Chickamauga, and Stout collected many of the letters previously cited to explain what had happened and why. Much of the blame belonged legitimately to the quartermasters. However, many of the transportation problems resulted from the overuse of the railroad to haul troops, supplies, and refugee citizens, as well as the wounded. Railroad facilities were simply not as extensive, well maintained, or replaceable as the Confederates required, and transportation quality deteriorated during the war. J. P. Logan, however, believed that Stout had done the best he could during the Chickamauga crisis to facilitate transportation and "ameliorate" the suffering of the wounded. "Upon the whole," Logan

---

15. Stout, "Transportation of the Sick and Wounded," 65; M. W. King to J. P. Logan, December 2, 1863, UTX, box 2G386. In November S. M. Bemiss reported lack of water, "frequent and most unreasonable delays," and insensitive engineers who started trains with a jerk. Bemiss to Stout, November 28, 1863, Emory, box 1, folder 24.

16. J. P. Logan to Stout, October 24, 1863, Emory, box 1, folder 21; Stout to S. P. Moore, October 10, 1863, ibid., folder 20; Stout, Circular No. 9, September 25, 1863, ibid., Stout microfilm.

wrote, "you [Stout] have in my judgement great reason to congratulate yourself that so much was accomplished by your corps under the exceedingly adverse, unfortunate and, I have reason to believe so far as you are concerned, unavoidable circumstances in which you were placed . . ."[17]

As a result of the Chickamauga campaign, the locations of some of Stout's hospitals changed. Stout requested permission to establish and control hospitals in towns that had been under Gen. P. G. T. Beauregard's jurisdiction on the railroads to Macon, Columbus, Augusta, and Montgomery. W. L. Nichol inspected Beauregard's hospitals in Augusta in late October to report on the patients from Bragg's army there. He found each of the two hospitals operating independently with "but little system in the conduct of the Hospitals. . . ." While the order granting Stout permission to take over the requested hospital posts was dated October 29, Stout seems to have worked with the organizations already in existence until after the Battle of Chattanooga (November 23–25). Augusta and Montgomery were both on the periphery of Stout's system and, because of their distance from the military action at the time, did not apparently have priority for development as hospital centers. When Stout sent his surgeons to those two cities in December, the men reported unfavorably on the conduct of the hospitals. W. M. Gentry, who had recently become surgeon in charge at Montgomery, wrote, "I am not pleased with the management of the Hospitals of Johnson's Department here—they have neither system or the proper concern for the well doing of their patients. They are not popular Institutions with the Citizens on account of their mismanagement. I hope you will send me Surgeons & Assts. of the 1st order—gentlemen of manners as well as education, so that may [sic] rather get the ascendency & popular favor directed to our Hospitals." As a result of Bragg's defeat at Chattanooga and the withdrawal of the Army of Tennessee to winter quarters at Dalton, Stout

---

17. Stout, "Outline," 72–73. According to this later account, Major McMicken was removed and Major Horbach severely censured for their failure to properly provide transportation for the wounded soldiers, however, other records show McMicken as lieutenant colonel and chief quartermaster for the Army of Tennessee as late as September 5, 1864. Special Orders, No. 51, A & IGO, March 2, 1865, *OR*, series I, vol. 38, part 3, pp. 991–92. A helpful discussion of the railroad problems in general can be found in Black, "The Railroads of Georgia in the Confederate War Effort," 510–34. J. P. Logan to Stout, October 24, 1863, Emory, box 1, folder 21. As Stout complained to Flewellen on November 1, 1863, "My troubles do not arise from want of furniture, but from want of cars, running regularly upon the appropriate schedule, and exclusively set apart for the sick." UTX, box 2G426.

ordered the removal of some of the hospitals from Dalton to Madison and from Rome to Barnesville or Covington.[18]

Until the opening of the spring campaign in 1864, Stout was concerned primarily with tightening the control and efficiency of the hospital system in order to prepare for future battles. In November 1863, as previously discussed, Stout appointed S. M. Bemiss assistant medical director, giving Stout a trustworthy subordinate to whom he could delegate some of the responsibilities of his office. Stout promptly sent Bemiss on an inspection trip to Army of Tennessee headquarters, Dalton, Kingston, and Rome. Stout himself travelled at least to Forsyth and Columbus in mid-December, leaving Bemiss in charge of the office, recently moved from Marietta to Atlanta. Changes occurred in the army leadership during this period as well. Gen. Braxton Bragg was relieved from command and replaced by Gen. Joseph E. Johnston. Meanwhile, in the medical department E. A. Flewellen resigned as field medical director due to ill health and an unwillingness to work under Johnston. A. J. Foard then returned to his previous position.[19]

---

18. Stout to S. P. Moore, October 11, 1863, *OR*, series I, vol. 30, part 4, pp. 736 (text) and 737 (map). W. L. Nichol to Sir [probably Stout], October 23, 1863, Emory, box 1, folder 21; Special Orders No. 259, by Command of Secretary of War, October 29, 1863, N A, chap. 6, vol. 748. W. M. Gentry to Stout, December 8, 1863, TSLA, box 1, folder 6. G. S. West wrote Stout from Augusta on December 7, 1863, "the sooner you commence to organise Hospitals here the better I think, for I am certain you would not be quite satisfied with the conducting of these hospitals, were they in your department." UTX, box 2G386. As the pressure on hospital space decreased when the wounded recovered, Stout apparently decided not to open any hospitals in Augusta, even though he had permission to do so, and ordered Dr. West to send all the Army of Tennessee patients, who could be moved, to Madison, Georgia. S. M. Bemiss to Doctor [Stout], December 18, 1863, TSLA, box 1, folder 3. For the health of the patients it was always better to send them the shortest distance possible. S. Meredith to John W. Glenn, November 28, 1863, Duke; H. V. Miller to Sir [Stout], December 11, 1863, ibid.

19. Stout issued several circulars to reinforce military medical policy: Circular No. 8, March 17, 1864, Emory, Stout microfilm; Circular, March 20, 1864, UTX, ledger 4L215. S. M. Bemiss to Stout, November 6, 1863, Emory, Stout microfilm, also Duke; Bemiss to Stout, November 28, 1863, Emory, box 1, folder 24; Bemiss to Stout, December 15, 1863, SHC–UNC, reel 2; Bemiss to Doctor [Stout], December 18, 1863, TSLA, box 1, folder 3. Bragg ordered Stout to move to Atlanta on December 3, 1863, Stout, Circular No. 29, December 3, 1863, Emory, Stout microfilm. J. P. Logan to Stout, November 25, 1863, UTX, box 2G387, reports on Logan's search for a house for Stout. The "City Military Directory" published in the *Daily Intelligencer* on May 11, 1864 listed Stout's office "on Whitehall Street, below Mitchell," which sounds like the more convenient of the two houses Logan suggested. Garrett, *Atlanta*

During the winter months Stout continued to adjust the assignments of medical officers to place them where their services would be most useful. In so doing he ran afoul of the Ladies Association in Montgomery, Alabama, which sponsored a hospital in the town and wanted to keep particular doctors on duty there. Stout explained that he would do his best to leave those men at the hospital, but he told the ladies that many medical officers, who had spent much time in the field, needed a term of hospital duty to recover from various ailments. Besides, Stout wrote, "We desire to give every young and able-bodied medical officer the privilege of serving in the field. For when this horrible war is over all such will feel that justice has not been done them if medical directors fail to grant them this high privilege."[20]

In preparation for the spring campaign, Stout contemplated increasing hospital accommodations to 12,000. Bemiss also issued a circular in late February 1864, instructing surgeons in charge of hospitals to be sure to have all their wards cleaned, ventilated, and whitewashed. In addition, he ordered the surgeons to keep a stock of emergency supplies and to select one or more surgeons for the reserve surgical corps. Before this order, hospital medical officers were sent to the field in case of a battle; but this was the first attempt to anticipate needs by selecting the medical officers before an emergency arose. Bemiss ordered surgeons in charge of hospitals to choose their most skillful surgeons, at the ratio of one per 500 beds, to be ready to move to the scene of battle or other emergency on a moment's notice, bringing surgical instruments and medical supplies with them. Once the emergency ended, the surgeons would return to their usual posts.[21]

---

and Environs 1: 593. T. G. Richardson to Stout, November 10, 1863, UTX, box 2G379. Flewellen to Stout, January 3, 1864, Emory, box 2, folder 1; Flewellen to Stout, January 31, 1864, ibid., folder 3.

20. A. J. Foard to Stout, January 15, 1864, and Stout to Mrs. Mary J. Bell, January 19, 1864, both in Emory, box 2, folder 2.

21. Flewellen to Stout, January 31, 1864, Emory, box 2, folder 3. Although Flewellen agreed with Stout's desire to increase hospital capacity to 12,000, he suggested that it might be better to stockpile hospital furniture at various places so that capacity could be increased quickly. Then they could use vacant houses and impress other buildings when needed, rather than enlarging the hospitals before the space was required. Bemiss, Circular No. 6, February 23, 1864, UTX, ledger 4L215. Bemiss was, of course, acting for Stout. Flewellen had ordered Stout to send him ten or fifteen medical officers just before Chickamauga. Flewellen to Stout, September 13, 1863, N A, chap. 6, vol. 749.

D. D. Saunders, post surgeon at Marietta, commanded the reserve corps, which received its first test almost immediately. Foard, provoked by enemy movements, dispatched the reserve corps to Dalton on February 25, but he dismissed the surgeons on February 27, since the Federals retreated without a major battle and few soldiers suffered serious wounds in the skirmishing. Foard commended Stout and the corps most enthusiastically.

> Your organization of the Reserve Corps of Surgeons has proven itself a perfect success[.] Within twenty four hours after the call was made on you, the Medical officers of this Corps reported to me from the most distant Hospitals under your control (300 miles) ready for duty with all the appliances, medicines and stimulants necessary for several thousand wounded—with two days cooked rations, of which an abundance of coffee constituted a very important part, for as many patients as would likely have required them. Had a battle taken place the wounded would have received better attention than has ever been given on any of our battlefields[.] Every wound would have been dressed and all necessary operations would have been performed before the wounded were sent to Genl Hospital; the importance of which is so well known to the members of our profession.

The Army of Tennessee reserve surgical corps actually served as intended from the campaign beginning in May 1864 through the rest of the war.[22]

---

22. Both Confederate and Union surgeons found that the sooner a wounded soldier received his amputation or other operation, the better were his chances of survival. Cunningham, *Doctors in Gray*, 222–24; Adams, *Doctors in Blue*, 134. D. D. Saunders to Stout, February 28, 1864, Emory, Stout microfilm, also Duke. Fourteen surgeons, eight assistant surgeons, and some local relief committee members from Atlanta and Griffin comprised the corps, according to Saunders. A. J. Foard to Stout, February 28, 1864, N A, chap. 6, vol. 749, also TSLA, box 1, folder 5. Apparently after this successful trial in the Army of Tennessee, Surgeon General Moore ordered other medical directors of hospitals to set up such a reserve medical corps for their department. S. P. Moore to Medical Directors in Field and of Hospitals, March 15, 1864, N A, chap. 6, vol. 748. W. M. Gentry to Stout, May 11, 1864, Emory, box 2, folder 9; F. H. Evans to Stout, May 16, 1864, ibid., folder 10. Some problems resulted from the surgeons being ordered to the front and then waiting and waiting for a battle to begin, meanwhile depriving the hospitals of their much-needed services. Foard promised not to call up the corps until a battle had actually begun. Foard to Stout, June 4, 1864,

In February 1864, Stout took unusual steps to increase the efficiency of his department. He began by purchasing a printing office. Since he was aware that the hospitals used a multitude of printed forms (twenty-seven were available in October 1864), paid for from the hospital fund, Stout believed that he could save a great deal of money by having all the printing for the department done at one location, rather than by making contracts with local printers. He therefore purchased a complete printing office, formerly used by the Winchester, Tennessee, *Bulletin*, from its refugee owner, at the cost of $16,000. Stout then standardized the various hospital forms and employed a disabled private, T. Marion Barna, to supervise two other printers. Barna arrived in Atlanta on or before May 2, 1864. Just when the press began operation is not clear, but like the rest of the hospital department it suffered severely from the exigencies of war. Since the printing office was part of the medical director's headquarters, it had to move every time the headquarters moved. This was not always an easy task. In one instance when attempting to move to Columbus, Georgia, Barna was unable to find anyone willing to give the press space in a railroad car. Three days later Bemiss decided to "smuggle him in the first hospital which passes to Columbus," and thus the equipment finally arrived at its destination. Stout considered the press a profitable acquisition for the hospital department. By the end of the war, however, the press had moved six times, which destroyed much of the "printing material." In dire financial straits after the war ended, Barna sold the press for $100 and a gold watch and went to South America.[23]

Emory, Stout microfilm, also Duke. Eventually some post surgeons resisted sending away their best doctors when their hospitals were impossibly crowded. They objected to relying on local contract surgeons. James Mercer Green to Stout, July 23, 1864, Mus. Confed., ST–8–18, describes the problems in Macon. Stout described the corps in "Outline," 77.

23. Stout, Circular No. 7, February 27, 1864, UTX, ledger 4L218; T. M. Barna, [list of forms that could be ordered], October 31, 1864, Emory, Stout microfilm; L. T. Blome to Stout, June 15, 1864, UTX, box 2G387; T. M. Barna to Doctor [probably Stout], April 3, 1864, Emory, box 2, folder 7; Stout to G. T. Pursley, May 2, 1864, UTX, box 2G433; Stout, Circular No. 33, August 1, 1864, Emory, Stout microfilm, also UTX, box 2G429. A number of the hospital forms were printed on the backs of blank legal forms. UTX, box 2G406. Stout, Circular Letter, October 1, 1864, UTX, box 2G428; T. M. Barna to Stout, October 8, 1864, and S. M. Bemiss to Stout, October 11, 1864, both UTX, box 2G379. T. M. Barna to Stout, October 29, 1866, Emory, box 3, folder 12. Stout discussed the printing press in two articles: "Some Facts," pt. 19, 25 (May 1903): 281–82, and "Outline," 80. Just how profitable it was is not clear as in "Some Facts" he said that in the first three months the press did $25,000 worth of

On May 7, 1864, after a few days of skirmishing, William T. Sherman's Federal troops advanced on Joseph E. Johnston's Confederate Army of Tennessee. With the onset of this campaign Stout and his department entered the most difficult period of their hospital service. From this point on, the shortage of supplies became more and more acute, and the location of the hospitals became increasingly unstable.

The opening of the spring campaign quickly filled the hospitals in the rear since patients had to be sent away from the field hospitals to free them for fresh battle casualties. In some hospitals a shortage of medical officers complicated the situation. In others the problem was a lack of hospital funds; commissaries had not paid the hospitals, in part because of the confusion caused by the Confederate government switching from old to new-issue treasury notes.[24] As the hospitals evacuated Marietta, Stout and his subordinates made major plans for expansion further south. Fortunately, the onset of warmer weather facilitated quick expansion by permitting the use of tents and rough sheds. In late May various post surgeons explained to Stout how they proposed to expand their facilities. In nearly all cases, however, the doctors said they would need more bedding.[25]

---

printing while "Outline" says $75,000. Undoubtedly this discrepancy is the result of a printer's error. In either case, however, the press quickly did substantially more work than its purchase price. In "Outline" Stout claimed that Barna "sold the press for $650.00 in greenbacks and fled to Buenos Ayers [sic] S.A." I have relied on Barna's October 1866 account of his own activities.

24. W. L. Nichol to Stout, May 18, 1864, Emory, box 2, folder 10; W. M. Gentry to Stout, May 21, 1864, ibid., also SHC–UNC, reel 2; W. L. Nichol to Stout, May 11, 1864, Emory, box 2, folder 9; James Mercer Green to Stout, May 15, 1864, ibid., folder 10, also SHC–UNC, reel 2; U. R. Jones to Capt. M. B. Swanson, May 13, 1864, with Jones to Stout of same date on back, Emory, box 2, folder 9, also SHC–UNC, reel 2; Jno. Patterson to Stout, May 14, 1864, Emory, box 2, folder 9; Lucien L. Saunders to Stout, May 18, 1864, with note from James Mercer Green of same date, Emory, Stout microfilm, also Duke.

25. As the hospital books and papers were packed and at the depot on that date, the Marietta hospitals were obviously moving around May 23. D. D. Saunders to Stout, May 23, 1864, Duke. J. P. Logan (Atlanta), Special Order, May 26, 1864, B. M. Wible (Newnan) to Stout, May 27, 1864, and H. V. Miller (Greensboro) to Sir [probably Stout], May 27, 1864, all in Emory, box 2, folder 11; F. H. Evans (La Grange) to Stout, May 27, 1864, Mus. Confed., ST–8–3; W. L. Nichol (Covington) to Stout, May 28, 1864, TSLA, box 1, folder 8; U. R. Jones (Notasulga, Alabama) to Stout, May 28, 1864, Duke; James Mercer Green (Macon) to Stout, May 30, 1864, Emory, box 2, folder 11, also SHC–UNC, reel 2; Paul DeLacy Baker (Eufaula, Alabama) to Stout, May 30, 1864, Emory, box 2, folder 11.

In some cases the numbers of sick and wounded sent to a particular post prompted post surgeons to protest to Stout. For example, W. L. Nichol in Covington, whose hospital was seven patients over capacity, complained that the surgeon in charge at the shipping and receiving hospital in Atlanta paid no attention to his morning reports. Although these reports showed no empty beds in Covington, the Atlanta surgeon still sent two trains of more than 100 patients each. Even more serious was the situation in Columbus, Georgia, when 700 men arrived within twenty-four hours. G. T. Pursley, the offending surgeon in charge of the receiving and distributing hospital, defended himself against complaints. He never sent 700 patients to Columbus in one day, he said, but some men probably came from Macon, a post over which Pursley had no control. He admitted that he had been sending patients all the time to hospitals reporting no empty beds. But, Pursley asked, what could he do when his own hospital held only 250, and he was receiving up to 600 men daily? In an effort to remedy the problem of overcrowded hospitals, Stout ordered surgeons at posts south of Atlanta not to send patients elsewhere without first contacting Stout's office or the intended receiving hospital to be sure "that Comfortable accommodations can be afforded them."[26]

During June, Stout was concerned both for the safety of the hospitals in Atlanta and for the efficiency of his own office. On June 12 he ordered J. P. Logan to have each hospital staff organize itself as a skeleton military company which convalescent patients could augment in case of a raid on Atlanta. Each hospital was also to fly an identifying flag to protect it from enemy depredations. Probably Atlanta medical officers took advantage of the proximity of Stout's office to run over with any request at any time, and thus made extra work for Stout. At any rate, Stout requested that the Atlanta surgeons organize their paperwork so that all papers coming to Stout's office arrived with the morning reports and requisitions were planned and not excessive. With this cooperation, Stout explained, he would have time to meet his responsibilities for other hospital posts as well.[27]

Meanwhile, on June 6, Foard wrote that he and General Johnston were interested in Stout's consolidated hospital report. "In a short time,"

---

26. W. L. Nichol to Stout, June 1, 1864, TSLA, box 1, folder 8; George B. Douglas to Stout, May 28, 1864 and G. T. Pursley to no addressee but probably Stout, May 31, 1864, both at Duke; Stout to A. Hunter, May 31, 1864, Emory, Stout microfilm.

27. Stout to J. P. Logan, June 12 and 17, 1864, both in UTX, box 2G428.

Foard was confident, "he [Johnston] will fully appreciate the importance of good hospitals and your industry and ability in organizing them with means so limited." It does not appear, however, that Johnston ever matched Bragg in his appreciation of or cooperation with the hospital service. Much conflict in June and July 1864 stemmed from a disagreement over furlough procedures. As Sherman's troops maneuvered Johnston's soldiers closer and closer to Atlanta, many Confederates fell victim to wounds and disease and required hospitalization. Shrinking manpower alarmed Johnston and his subordinate generals, and, for some reason, they chose to place a good deal of blame on the hospitals' furlough policy. Furloughs were necessary, of course, as many recuperating patients required time rather than constant doctor's care before they were well enough for field service again. Such patients should not occupy a bed needed by the seriously ill. But Johnston's subordinates looked upon the furlough policy as the cause of their reduced manpower. Moreover, they seemed to fear that the soldiers would not return to duty. Their constant complaints reached the ear of Johnston, who then harassed Foard, who, in turn, kept asking Bemiss and Stout for detailed information about a system which everyone but Johnston and his generals found satisfactory. Apparently Johnston, among other things, did not understand the hospital figures, and Foard suggested a revision of the Morning Report form to clarify matters for the general. Johnston, however, was removed from command three days later, presumably before the form could be printed. Stout did not say a great deal about Johnston in his published writings, but he was convinced that Johnston never really knew how many troops he had after the Battle of Resaca. In fact, Stout remarked that Johnston's "Med. Director Dr. Foard acknowledged that he [Johnston] could not find out how many casualties had occurred in the campaign." Actually, by 1864 Stout had lost faith in Johnston, and in a private letter to his good friend D. D. Saunders, he poured out his heart about a variety of difficulties with medical officers and other things. Saunders responded, "I am sorry to see you so hard on old Joe Johnston but I do not know that you are far wrong. I hope Hood may be equal to the emergency & give Sherman the devil."[28]

---

28. It is not clear what time period this consolidated report covered. Foard to Stout, June 6, 1864, Emory, Stout microfilm, also Duke. Johnston's Special Field Orders No. 21, June 17, 1864, are given with elaborations on furlough procedure in Stout, Circular No. 19, June 18, 1864, Mus. Confed., ST–8–12. Bemiss to Doctor [Stout], "Sunday noon" [probably July 1864], SHC–UNC, reel 2; Foard to Stout, July 14,

While Johnston was still in command of the Army of Tennessee, he ordered his forces to fall back to the Chattahoochee River. In the context of these movements, which were far too close to Atlanta for comfort, Foard ordered Stout on July 6 to "move every thing to the rear of Atlanta establishing your hospitals at Griffin, Forsyth, and other points on the Atlanta and Macon R. Rd." He also commanded: "Do not increase your accommodations on the West Point or Augusta Roads which may be subject to raids." Stout ordered J. P. Logan to send the Atlanta hospitals to Macon and set them up in tents, leaving only Stout's office and the receiving and distributing hospital in Atlanta. As the military situation deteriorated, Stout himself soon moved to Macon while Bemiss remained in Atlanta to keep his eye on the action from a temporary office.[29]

Soon thereafter, on July 23, 1864, Stout issued a circular that listed his hospitals at Griffin, Milner, Barnesville, Thomaston, Forsyth, Macon, Vineville, Augusta, Greensboro, Madison, Athens, Newnan, LaGrange, West Point, Columbus, and Fort Gaines, Georgia, as well as Auburn, Notasulga, Montgomery, and Eufaula, Alabama. Raiding by Sherman's cavalry, however, quickly made many of these posts untenable. In fact, the day before Stout issued this circular, the Federals raided Covington, completely surprising the staff and giving convalescents and attendants hardly any time to flee to the woods. The Union soldiers destroyed no hospital property, but they captured some Confederates. "Grandma" Susan Smith reported that at her hospital she, a black woman, and one of the nurses who had the presence of mind to jump into a bed and play sick, were all who remained to care for those too ill to flee. Raids of this nature, and threats of raids, set many of Stout's hospitals in motion.[30]

1864, Mus. Confed., ST–8–17; Bemiss to Stout, July 17, 1864, TSLA, box 1, folder 3. Foard's suggestion is in Bemiss to Stout, July 14, 1864, Emory, box 2, folder 14. Stout, "Outline," 81. D. D. Saunders to Stout, July 31, 1864, Emory, box 2, folder 15. It appears that Johnston had problems with medical departments as early as the fall of 1861. He refused to cooperate with medical officials in Virginia, provided only limited transportation for the sick, and suspected a connection between malingering and medical facilities. Lash, *Destroyer of the Iron Horse*, 20–21, 26, 35.

29. A. J. Foard to Stout, July 6, 1864, Mus. Confed., ST–8–15, also UTX, box 2G379; Stout to J. P. Logan, July 6, 1864, Tulane; Bemiss to Stout, July 14, 1864, Emory, box 2, folder 4; Bemiss to Stout, July 20, 1864, UTX, box 2G379.

30. Stout, Circular No. 26, July 23, 1864, Tulane; W. L. Nichol to Stout, July 27, 1864, Emory, box 2, folder 15; Smith, *The Soldier's Friend*, 129. The hospitals in LaGrange, for example, were moving on August 11. F. H. Evans to Stout, August 11, 1864, UTX, box 2G407.

The fall of Atlanta on September 1 was, in some respects, a blessing in disguise for the hospitals, as the decreased action for the rest of the month afforded some opportunities to recoup. The Foard Hospital had moved from Newnan to Americus in mid-August, and was promptly destroyed by a fire on August 30. Kate Cumming described the process of "getting the hospital put to rights again. On the square where the fire was new buildings are being erected. The latter is one of the things I do not like to see; for. . . the sight of new lumber gives me an unpleasant feeling, as it is always a sure sign of our exodus. We are having a fine bakery built—I believe the eighth one our baker has had to put up since the war."[31]

When E. N. Covey, medical inspector for the district of Virginia, Tennessee, and Georgia, visited the Army of Tennessee hospitals in early September, he reported: "Nearly ever since I began my tour, of Inspection, the Hospitals of this Department have been in a migratory state, and I have been fully able to appreciate both the trials of the Med. Officer and the hardships of the sick soldier; both of which have been trying in the extreme." Indeed, his observation was apt, for all the hospitals on the line from Augusta to West Point, as well as farther north, were no longer usable because they were either within the enemy lines or too close to them. As Covey noted, "This has necessitated the still greater scattering of, the already too much scattered, Hospitals, and squatting them in little towns, where every available house from a common Grocery to the town church has been taken for their purposes, and in most instances building [sic] so taken have been entirely unfit for the treatment of the sick and wounded, I am perfectly satisfied that, the Service has lost immensely from the want of adequate Hospital accommodations." Much of this problem was caused by a lack of tents, which Covey blamed on "Maj. Cunningham's tardiness in furnishing the cloth for their manufacture and want of appreciation of their necessity. This Officer, I think, has either too many duties to perform or lacks ability to perform them, probably both." Once again the quartermaster department could be held responsible for the less than optimal conditions. Covey did not believe that the situation was hopeless, however, and so he made several suggestions. First, he recommended that

---

31. B. M. Wible to Stout, August 31, 1864, UTX, box 2G381; Cumming, *Journal*, September 1 and 21, 1864, pp. 214–15, 217–18 respectively. Cumming's prognostications came true as on November 26 the hospital was ordered to Gainesville, Alabama, November 26, 1864, p. 223.

command of the hospital department be given to a general who would be able to supervise the quartermasters and commissaries as well as the medical directors. Then he suggested that the department should order 4,000 hospital tents and stockpile enough lumber near the railroads so that during the winter 400 carpenters could erect consolidated accommodations for 12,000 patients. Consolidation in fewer locations, he argued, would also help to keep the western hospital department in better communication with the medical department at Richmond. Given the state of the Confederacy in the fall of 1864, Covey's suggestions were extremely optimistic, if not incredibly idealistic. Because of the movements of the Army of Tennessee, which began soon after Covey made his recommendations, however, the ideas proved to be hopelessly unrealistic.[32]

Realizing after the battles around Atlanta that maneuver might succeed against Sherman where direct attacks had failed, Gen. John Bell Hood, commander of the Army of Tennessee since July 17, proposed in September to attack Sherman's lengthy supply line. Then, in mid-October, Hood decided to go north into Tennessee, and hopefully further, in an attempt to draw Sherman back out of Georgia. Sherman refused to be drawn and was soon "marching through Georgia" with his troops. Hood, in the midst of administrative chaos, continued toward Tennessee and disaster. Historians have discussed the wisdom or foolishness of Hood's endeavor, but to continue that discussion is not the point here. The issue is the effect of Hood's actions on Stout's hospitals.[33]

As Hood moved toward Tennessee his hospitals could not remain in south Georgia where they would be too far from the troops and, therefore, comparatively useless. Thus began a period of unprecedented hospital movement, complicated by competition for the limited and deteriorating transportation facilities. By October 9, D. D. Saunders was preparing to move his hospitals from Forsyth, Georgia, to Auburn, Alabama. On October 26 Saunders was in Auburn, where his hospitals arrived the next day, but he wrote Stout that he would not "hurry my preparations here very much as I do not expect to remain long." General Hood had announced plans to move toward Nashville and, Saunders

---

32. E. N. Covey to Sir, September 8, 1864, Emory, box 2, folder 17, also SHC–UNC, reel 2.

33. A study of Hood, which is sympathetic but also properly critical of Hood's fitness for high command, is McMurry, *John Bell Hood.* See also Connelly, *Autumn of Glory,* chaps. 15–17.

reminded Stout, "Remember that I am to lead the advance northward of the hospital Dept." Numerous examples could be given of hospitals packed and waiting for days for transportation, of destruction of hospital property through carelessness, and of hospitals sent from one point to another without ever opening, in a procedure one doctor called "*inspecting* the railroad."[34] It would, however, be more instructive to observe the effects of these excursions through the experience of one hospital.

This institution, the Flewellen Hospital, began in Cleveland, Tennessee, on August 5, 1863, as the "Reception Hospital." It was not, however, prepared to receive patients before the Army of Tennessee withdrew from the post. On August 24 the hospital moved to Cassville, Georgia, where it was reorganized and named for the field medical director, Flewellen. Surgeon Miles H. Nash, a Floridian who had served in the Catoosa Springs Hospital since December 1862, took charge of the new facilities. In December 1863, Nash and one assistant surgeon found their hospital crowded with 212 patients, which gave them considerably more work than the official ratio of seventy patients per doctor. On May 18, 1864, in response to Sherman's movements above Marietta, Stout ordered the hospital to be removed south of Atlanta to Barnesville, where it remained during the summer of 1864. There, in July, B. W. Avent, newly in charge of all the hospitals at Barnesville, inspected the Flewellen Hospital. He found it clean and well arranged, but crowded due to "the late call for beds in the Department." Two hundred and fifty beds were stuffed into four houses of varying quality and ten four-patient tents, all of which, Avent thought, should only hold 150 persons. With more tents the capacity of the hospital could be increased.

In early October Stout ordered the Flewellen Hospital to Columbus, Georgia, from which, on October 13, General Hood ordered the hospital to Opelika, Alabama. On November 18, Nash received instructions to move his hospital to Tuscumbia, Alabama. Thus began his adventure in moving. The transportation promised for November 24 never arrived, and Nash finally had to take matters into his own hands. First, he seized several railroad cars after they unloaded supplies at Opelika and five days later he finally got them attached to a passing train. The hospital staff and supplies arrived in Montgomery that evening.

Transportation troubles were by no means over once the hospital arrived in Montgomery, however. The quartermaster, Major Harris, tried

---

34. D. D. Saunders to Stout, October 9, 1864, UTX, box 2G401; October 26 and 27, 1864, both in Emory, box 2, folder 18. Cumming, *Journal*, March 9, 1865, p. 245.

MAP 2—THE MOVEMENTS OF THE FLEWELLEN HOSPITAL

The route of the Flewellen Hospital from its foundation in Cleveland, Tennessee, on August 5, 1863 to its return to Opelika, Alabama, on January 23, 1865. The dates indicate the arrival of the hospital at that point, if known, or else the date the hospital was ordered to that point.

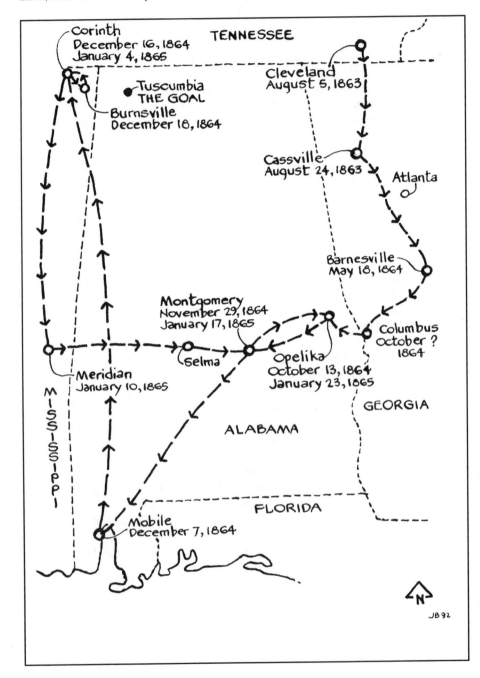

to force Nash to take the route through Selma, but Nash refused because he knew that it was a very difficult road where the hospital supplies might easily sustain severe damage. Like most other people, Nash preferred the water route to Mobile. He finally gained passage on the steamer *Jeff Davis*, left Montgomery on December 4, and arrived in Mobile on December 7. A leak in the boat damaged some of the hospital bedding slightly, but the problems were worse in Mobile, where Nash found several other hospitals ahead of him awaiting transportation to Corinth, Mississippi. The delay resulted from shipping priorities which sent supplies for the troops first. Nash finally left Mobile on December 13 and arrived in Corinth on December 16, where he had to unload his material in the middle of a heavy rainstorm, which soaked the hospital supplies.

In Corinth Nash found orders from B. W. Avent to select a spot on the railroad to store his material until the railroad was finished to Tuscumbia, since no wagon transportation was available. On December 18, Nash reached Burnsville, Mississippi, fifteen miles from Corinth, where he was able to unpack and dry his hospital supplies to keep them from being ruined. Although Nash was ordered by Avent to Corinth on December 27, he was unable to leave Burnsville because he could not get transportation. Ordered by A. J. Foard to Meridian, Mississippi, for further orders, Nash went to Corinth on January 4, where he received directions to return to Opelika, Alabama. On January 8 he left Corinth, abandoning his bunks and tables as ordered by General Cheatham, and arrived in Meridian on January 10. There he discovered that the chief quartermaster had forbidden hospitals travelling east of Meridian to go by way of Mobile. Nash was thus forced to travel from Meridian to Montgomery by the difficult Selma route, and he lost some hospital supplies as a result of much loading and unloading. Leaving Meridian on January 13, Nash arrived in Montgomery on January 17, where, due to troop movements, he was delayed until January 23.

Thus, on January 23, Nash returned to Opelika, Alabama. In two months he had done nothing except travel, wait, and lose supplies— through no fault of his own. He had returned to his starting point, never having even come close to his original destination. In a letter to Stout of February 9, 1865, Nash blamed quartermaster situations— transportation and lack of facilities—for his problems in transit and delay in reopening the hospital. He was unable to say whether these difficulties were avoidable or unavoidable. Nash and the Flewellen Hospital were not alone in their problems, however. Their frustration, useless movement, transportation difficulties, and loss of supplies must be multiplied forty or fifty times to achieve a realistic picture of the chaos that struck the Army of Tennessee hospital department as a result of Hood's operations in the fall of 1864.[35]

Only a general idea of Stout's activities during this period is possible, because only a small number of sources survive. On October 28, A. J. Foard, who was with Hood and the army at Decatur, Alabama, told Stout, "You must watch our movements and base yours upon them." He also warned Stout, "All our sick will be sent to Miss[issippi]." At this time, Stout did not have any hospitals as far west as Mississippi. The hospitals in that department were headed by Preston B. Scott. Scott, willing to cooperate with Stout as necessary, suggested, "In truth I think the best thing to be done is for you to take chg of all the Hospitals here & there, & you can make such changes as the military movements require." Stout followed Scott's suggestion and took charge temporarily. Thus, the postwar sources that indicate Stout directed hospitals from the Savannah River to the Mississippi River and supervised nearly 500 medical officers

---

35. Most of the information on the Flewellen Hospital can be found in its Order Book at Emory on the Stout microfilm. Nash gave the basic hospital history in a letter to Stout of March 21, 1865. He detailed his experiences in hospital moving in Nash to Stout, February 9, 1865. Other useful documents are Robert C. Foster, "Return of Officers," December 8, 1862, and A. Hunter to S. M. Bemiss, December 15, 1863, both on Emory, Stout microfilm, but not in the Order Book. B. W. Avent to Stout, July 15, 1864, TSLA, box 1, folder 3. All of the following are in the Order Book: Stout to B. W. Avent, October 1, 1864; B. W. Avent to Miles H. Nash, October 13, 1864; S. M. Bemiss to B. W. Avent, November 18 and December 26, 1864; A. J. Foard to Miles H. Nash, January 3, 1865; B. W. Avent to Miles H. Nash, January 8 and 25, 1865. On March 21, 1865 Nash summarized the patient record of the Flewellen Hospital. From September 8, 1863 to March 1, 1865 the hospital received 2,041 patients, 581 of them suffering from gunshot wounds. One hundred and twenty-eight patients died, thirty-seven from wounds. About thirteen percent of the deaths resulted from pneumonia, which took a greater toll than any other disease. The problems of moving other hospitals can be seen, among many other sources, in F. H. Evans to Bemiss, November 13, 1864, UTX, box 2G426; D. D. Saunders to Bemiss, November 14, 1864, UTX, box 2G427; L. W. Tuttle to Stout, November 19, 1864, UTX, box 2G379; D. D. Saunders to Bemiss, November 23, 1864, UTX, box 2G404. Saunders did actually get some hospitals set up and operating in Iuka, Mississippi. Although he received orders to move these three hospitals to Decatur, Alabama, in mid-December, he was unable to procure transportation. As the army vacated Tennessee, Saunders moved back to Auburn, Alabama. Saunders to Bemiss, December 8, 11, 15, 21, and 30, 1864, also Saunders to Captain Reid, December 20, 1864, all UTX, box 2G404; Saunders to Stout, February 2, 1865, Emory, box 3, folder 12.

in that region, refer only to this period. Stout's increased responsibilities were limited to the time of Hood's Tennessee campaign.[36]

Since he was ordered by Foard to establish hospitals in Mississippi at Iuka, Corinth, and other places on the Mobile and Ohio Railroad, Stout spent the early part of November travelling in Mississippi to locate suitable hospital sites. By November 12, Stout was in Decatur, Alabama, preparing to cross the Tennessee River with Hood's troops. He left the office under Bemiss's direction and encouraged him to select a capable surgeon as an assistant if necessary.

Stout did not give many clues to explain why he went along on the Tennessee campaign, leaving what would ordinarily seem to have been his responsibilities. In his postwar "Outline," Stout does note that he went along as "a guest" of Dr. Foard. While Stout no doubt went under Foard's auspices, he was hardly going on a pleasure trip or on one in which he had no active role. In fact, he likely went because the trip gave him an opportunity to see his family. Although Stout wrote Bemiss that he had "but little hopes of seeing my home," clearly he did have some hope. Probably Stout had not been home since March 1862, and during the intervening period his family had endured a good deal of trauma. Should the Confederates be able to push their way into Tennessee, Stout might well be able to visit his home, as it was not far from the Alabama border.

A second reason for Stout's participation in the Tennessee campaign may well have been related to matters of communication. Hood was apparently a terrible administrator. Stout may have hoped that by being present himself at the scene of activity he would be able to give more accurate, appropriate, and timely directions to his subordinates. In fact, he wrote to Bemiss on the eve of his departure for Tennessee, "I shall go on with Hd. Qrs. and do the best, that can be done. I fear all of my dept. will be left so far in the rear as to be of but little service, to this army." Stout telegraphed directions and asked for a number of doctors and hospitals to care for the wounded from the Battle of Franklin, but as Stout had feared, snarled in the web of transportation breakdown, most of his hospitals were of little use.[37]

---

36. A. J. Foard to Stout, October 28, 1864, Emory, Stout microfilm; Preston B. Scott to Stout, October 28, 1864, UTX, box 2G425; Secretary of War, Special Order No. 245, November 7, 1864 and S. M. Bemiss, Circular No. 42, November 17, 1864, Emory, Stout microfilm. Stout, "Some Facts," pt. 1, 22 (November 1900): 522–23.

37. Foard to Stout, October 31, 1864, Duke; Stout to Doctor [Bemiss], November 8, 1864, Emory, box 2, folder 19. A number of telegrams from Stout to Bemiss during

As Hood's army withdrew from Tennessee, Stout's hospitals returned to posts in eastern Alabama and Georgia. Stout's good friend D. D. Saunders, back in Auburn, Alabama, in early February 1865, said he was sorry to have missed seeing Stout, "for I wanted to know how you stood the campaign & whether you were as badly whipped as many men I meet since our reverses. I have almost lost my religion cursing croakers & weak kneed souls since we commenced falling back. . . . I see no good reason for *throwing up the sponge yet.*" Saunders then indicated that he was concerned to carry on hospital business as usual, by asking Stout if the hospital would be there long enough for him to plant a garden.[38]

The hospitals were not in very good condition in early 1865. Kate Cumming reported, for example, that her hospital in Griffin had little wood to combat the bitter cold, and no candles or other lights. As a result, Cumming and the staff had to go to bed at dark. Fortunately the hospital had no patients. As the Union troops moved into Alabama, W. M. Gentry reported from Montgomery that the citizens were very much afraid that the Yankees were coming, and he wondered if he should send as many sick as possible to Georgia, especially because an attack on Mobile would produce a flood of patients from the hospitals there. Experiencing similar fears, on March 16, D. D. Saunders informed Stout that he had organized the hospital post at Auburn, Alabama, into a battalion.[39]

Disaster approached in the eastern Confederacy as well, and on April 2, 1865, Richmond fell. The hospitals there had never been mobilized and were not prepared to travel in support of Robert E. Lee's Army of Northern Virginia as it moved toward Appomattox. Surgeon General S. P. Moore telegraphed and wrote to Stout for help on April 6. He ordered Stout to select his "most efficient medical officers" (naming specifically D. D. Saunders, B. W. Avent, Alexander Hunter, W. M. Gentry, R. C. Foster, F. H. Evans, and J. C. Mullins) and to report to Charlotte, North Carolina, with them and all of the hospital stores, furniture, bedding, and tents for which he could find transportation. The remainder of Stout's

---

early November are at Duke. Stout to Bemiss, November 12, 1864, Emory, box 2, folder 19. Stout, "Outline," 78. The problems experienced by Stout's family are discussed in chapter 4. McMurry, *John Bell Hood*, 158–59. Stout to Bemiss, December 7 and 8, 1864, both at Duke.

38. D. D. Saunders to Stout, February 2, 1865, Emory, box 3, folder 12.

39. Cumming, *Journal*, March 10 and 13, 1865, p. 248. W. M. Gentry to Stout, March 9, 1865 and D. D. Saunders to Stout, March 16, 1865, both at Emory, box 2, folder 22.

hospital department Moore entrusted to Bemiss. Communications were slow in the disintegrating Confederacy, however, and Stout apparently did not receive Moore's message until April 12, as it was on that date that he issued orders to his subordinates to organize skeleton hospitals and report to Atlanta. Stout wrote to Moore on April 16 that he had received his superior's order and was then in Macon on his way to Charlotte. "I am doing the best I can under the circumstances and the present transportation facilities. Without positive orders from the War Department to transport the material it will be a month before I can get one hospital through. I will proceed tomorrow to Atlanta to await the arrival of the officers with their property and to render them all the aid in my power." He added that he believed that Surgeon Gentry and his hospital property had already been captured in Montgomery. Two days later Stout wrote to Moore, "We are almost surrounded by the enemy's Cavalry and there is a strong probability that I and my entire Corps of medical officers and hospital property will be captured. Much property has already been destroyed by them for want of transportation to remove it out of their reach."[40]

As April progressed, surgeons from various posts reported that they had had to surrender to the Federals. On April 22 Stout wrote Bemiss to stop further hospital movements in light of the unstable situation, and several days later Stout, as the highest ranking medical officer in Atlanta, ordered Medical Purveyor J. F. Young not to try to take his supplies to Charlotte because transportation was so bad and the citizens were so "demoralized."

Later, in his "Outline," Stout wrote, "To the final surrender Dr. Stout's department was well in hand, and all under his direction could be accounted for if required." To some extent, at least, Stout expressed the truth, for despite shortages and losses, many of Stout's hospitals were still functioning at the end of the war and even helped to meet the needs

---

40. S. P. Moore to Stout, April 6, 1865, UTX, 2G432, also Mus. Confed., ST–10–4, and quoted in Stout, "Address," 453. The request was reiterated by Medical Inspector E. N. Covey who wrote that since most of the other hospitals were now "in the enemie's [sic] hands, so much will be expected of yourself and staff." Covey also wanted Stout to bring a particularly skilled dentist and the printing press. Covey to Doctor [Stout], April 6, 1865, Duke. Stout to A. Hunter, April 12, 1865, and similar letters of the same date to B. M. Wible, B. W. Avent, D. D. Saunders, R. C. Foster, G. B. Douglas, and C. B. Gamble, all in UTX, box 2G432. Stout to S. P. Moore, April 16 and 18, 1865, UTX, box 2G432.

of parolees returning home.[41] Considering the upheaval experienced by most of the hospitals in the last stages of the war, it is probable that these institutions would have ceased to function without the discipline and accountability, combined with delegation of responsibility, developed by Stout in the Army of Tennessee hospitals.

Stout's achievements in keeping his hospitals functioning are only magnified when compared with the situations which prevailed in most of the Confederate departments during the last days of the war. As already discussed, the problems of the quartermaster department were evident in the department's inability to supply such basic needs as wood and candles, let alone transportation by rail and wagon. Commissary General Lucius B. Northrop, long anathema to most of the Confederate populace, was finally removed from leadership in February 1865 and replaced by Isaac M. St. John, efficient head of the successful Nitre and Mining Bureau. While St. John brought new energy and optimism to the department, he had little time to make substantial changes, nor did he have more transportation resources than his predecessor. Virtually the only bureau still achieving relatively positive results at the close of the war was the Ordnance Bureau (and its adjunct Nitre and Mining Bureau), success due in large measure to Josiah Gorgas's wise delegation of responsibility.[42] In short, Stout's ability to keep his hospitals functioning is certainly worthy of notice.

Stout continued to transact what hospital business he could as long as he could. But the end had clearly come. In early May Stout surrendered to the Federal forces and went home to Tennessee.[43]

---

41. Carlisle Terry to Bemiss, April 22, 1865, UTX, box 2G394; Charles E. Michel to Stout, April 29, 1865, UTX, box 2G388. Stout to Bemiss, April 22, 1865, and Stout to J. F. Young, April 24, 1865, both in UTX, box 2G432. Stout, "Outline," p. 81. J. W. Oslin to Stout, April 25, 1865, UTX, box 2G423.

42. Goff, Confederate Supply, 231–35; Vandiver, Ploughshares Into Swords, 268.

43. On April 30 Stout relieved hospital steward W. W. Grace from duty in Atlanta and ordered him to report to Washington, Georgia. UTX, box 2G432. This is Stout's last known business for the Confederate medical department.

CHAPTER 7

"MORAL HEROISM" IS TO GO ON AFTER DEFEAT

When Samuel H. Stout signed his parole in Atlanta on May 6, 1865, the former medical director of hospitals for the Army and Department of Tennessee promised not to bear arms, not to "do any military duty," and not to encourage anyone else in opposition to the United States. Receiving a pass, Stout made his way back to Pulaski, Tennessee, and his home "Midbridge," arriving four years after he first left with such high hopes for the new Confederacy.[1] Suddenly the intensive medical battles were over. Stout was no longer an administrator with widespread responsibilities for hundreds of medical officers and numerous hospitals. Instead, he was a civilian who had to pick up the pieces of a devastated career. He had to find a position where his life and actions had a purpose and significance such as he had experienced during the war. In this new postwar battle Stout again had a major enemy—poverty.

No doubt Stout was pleased to be reunited with his family at the conclusion of the war. He might even have been relieved to be rid of the hospital responsibilities that became more and more onerous as the Confederacy collapsed. But the situation to which Stout returned was by no means an easy one, for the Federal and Confederate armies had fought on, and plundered, Stout's land several times. His prewar wealth was gone. His slaves were free. To Stout's disgust, the Federals visited "peculiar hardships upon the immediate neighborhood," by giving the two nearby Brown family plantations to the Freedmen's Bureau. One plantation was occupied by poor white refugees, but the other housed former slave refugees from Mississippi, Georgia, and Alabama. Stout remarked, "It was not until the inauguration of the Ku-Klux Klan after the war that order was restored, and the negroes [sic] deterred from intrusion upon the white people's rights." Stout clearly seemed to approve

---

1. Parole, May 6, 1865, Mus. Confed., ST–17–5; Pass, May 4, 1865, ibid., ST–17–4; Daniell, *Types of Successful Men*, 311.

the achievements of the Ku Klux Klan. In one of his last published articles he commended Thomas Dixon's The Leopard's Spots as "among the historical novels that ought to be found in every Southern family," a "truthful unveiling of the oppressions and insults endured by the Southern people" during Reconstruction. He added, "The organization of the Kuklux [sic] Klan saved Christian civilization in the rural sections of the South." Although the Klan originated in Pulaski, Tennessee, near Stout's home, in 1866, there is no indication that Stout actually was a member. Evidence from this period of Stout's life, however, is very sparse, much too sparse to speculate on his possible involvement with such an infamous group as the Klan.[2]

Stout's situation was not completely bleak, however. He had a "good physique," and "survived the privations of war, without any noticeable impairment of vitality," which was certainly more than many Civil War medical officers could say. In addition, it appears that Stout's wife and sons were able to raise some cotton in 1864. Four bales was a small amount, but perhaps it gave some reason for hope. Also, with the exception of his baby daughter Mollie, who was born and had died during the war, and his mother, Catherine Tannehill Stout, who had died in Nashville in 1863, the rest of Stout's immediate family had survived the conflict. Hindsight may well make these factors look brighter than Stout himself saw them, for in other respects his prospects were indeed grim, as he took the oath to receive amnesty in June 1865, and attempted to pick up the pieces of his life and career.[3]

Stout never indicated what led him to accept a position on the faculty of the Atlanta Medical College in the fall of 1865, but he may have

---

2. "Samuel Hollingsworth Stout, A.M., M.D., LL.D.," 212; Stout, "Some Facts," pt. 13, 24 (November 1902): 622–23. The contraband camp at Pulaski allegedly was an exemplary place where the blacks "moved toward self-sufficiency" through farming, practicing trades, and attending school. Ash, Middle Tennessee Society Transformed, 135. Stout, "Confederate History," 462. The origins of the Klan are discussed in Trelease, White Terror, chap. 1.

3. Stout, "Some Facts," pt. 23, 25 (October 1903): 573. Account for Mrs. Martha Stout, by C. N. Ordway(?), January 25–June 29, 1865, Emory, box 4, folder 3. This account indicates various amounts of cash loaned, fees for drayage, depot, and ginning of cotton in April 1865, and credit for four bales of cotton. Thomas E. Abernathy to Stout, June 22, 1864, Emory, box 2, folder 12. Genealogical material in TSLA, box 2, folder 11. R. W. Johnson, June 12, 1865, Mus. Confed., ST–17–7. Brevet Major General Johnson, of the Sixth Division of the Cavalry Corps, gave Stout permission to keep a gun and pistol, protection for his provisions and forage, and the right to make business arrangements. Stout was to report to Johnson to take the oath within ten days.

done so for a number of reasons. It was probably obvious to Stout that his land was not going to provide more than a bare subsistence for his family for some time to come, especially with the uncertain labor situation as both former masters and former slaves adjusted to freedom. Furthermore, Stout's neighbors were in similar straits and unlikely to provide him with a very remunerative private medical practice. It is also quite possible that Stout felt some restlessness after a few months in Giles County, a rural, provincial locality. It would seem particularly small and restricted since he had just spent four years seeing wider areas of the country and making larger medical and administrative contributions. While Stout might have liked a new position as a hospital administrator or physician, this was not a possibility open to him, given the nature of mid-nineteenth-century hospitals. Nonmedical laymen invariably administered these civilian institutions. Furthermore, the position of hospital physician paid in prestige rather than money, giving the established doctor a place to train his medical students and a reputation that would increase his elite, paying clientele. Thus, a hospital position was not a viable alternative for Stout, as he was not already well-established in a city with a hospital.[4] However, the idea of teaching in a medical school surely appealed to Stout since it combined his two major interests— medicine and education. Stout had spent a good deal of time in Atlanta during the war, and the city was hastening to rebuild after its wartime destruction, making Atlanta a reasonable location for Stout to choose. But certainly his potential faculty colleagues would also have been particularly appealing. Four of them—Joseph P. Logan, Daniel C. O'Keefe, George G. Crawford, and Willis F. Westmoreland—had served under Stout during the war, and he had probably had some contact with two or three of the remaining four. Thus, Stout probably accepted the proffered chair of professor of pathological anatomy at the Atlanta Medical College with fairly high expectations.

The medical college was a relatively new institution, incorporated by the state legislature in 1854. At least two of the founding faculty, the brothers John G. Westmoreland, dean and professor of materia medica and therapeutics, and Willis F. Westmoreland, professor of surgery, were still part of the faculty in 1865. The cornerstone of the college building on Butler Street was laid on June 21, 1855, but the first session of the school met in rented quarters from May to September of

---

4. Rosenberg, *The Care of Strangers*, 20, 58–59.

that year. Thirty-one students, who had already attended a course of lectures elsewhere, graduated on September 1. Since the school did not hold classes during the war, its facilities were used as a hospital. The building sustained some damage but P. P. Noel D'Alvigny, a doctor at the hospital, managed to save the building from destruction as Sherman's troops prepared to vacate Atlanta. He dressed some hospital attendants as wounded patients and placed them in an attic room, claiming that Sherman was about to commit the atrocity of burning a hospital with patients inside. While these "wounded" were being removed, Sherman's troops were leaving the city and the building was saved.[5] The remnants of the prewar faculty, including J. P. Logan and Thomas S. Powell, met on August 16, 1865, accepted the resignation of one of their number, and then, on September 17, announced the new faculty members.[6] With this announcement were sown the seeds of a great quarrel which soon followed.

It is a little difficult to determine exactly what caused the intrafaculty quarrel that rent the medical college because the only remaining source is a decidedly partisan booklet assembled by one side to justify its position.[7] Certainly at the root of the difficulty, however, was an amendment to the school's charter passed by the legislature in 1858. The charter of 1854 gave the trustees of the college permission to organize the school but did not specify who would appoint new faculty members once the school was in operation. The amendment in 1858 allowed the professors to fill vacancies by faculty vote. This would seem to have been a wise move since the trustees did not meet between early 1858 and September 1866. The school could hardly have reopened in 1865 without faculty action. Faculty members did not suppose that they

---

5. "An Act to Incorporate the Atlanta Medical College," Emory University Archives, box 16a, folder 1. Garrett, *Atlanta and Environs* 1: 375–76, 509, 651–52. Calhoun, "The Founding and the Early History of the Atlanta Medical College," 35–54. Calhoun's information came from the faculty minute book.

6. The returning faculty included the Westmoreland brothers in their prewar positions, Alexander Means, professor of chemistry; Joseph P. Logan, professor of medicine; and Thomas S. Powell, professor of obstetrics. Besides Stout as professor of pathological anatomy, the new faculty members were Eben Hillyer, professor of physiology; Daniel C. O'Keefe, professor of anatomy; and George G. Crawford, demonstrator of anatomy. Garrett, *Atlanta and Environs*, 1: 684.

7. Fulton Co., *Report of the Delegate*. It takes the side of Thomas S. Powell. As the report consists of a number of sometimes repetitive documents, information on any aspect of the quarrel can often be found in more than one place.

were doing anything irregular, for other medical school faculties filled vacancies at their own institutions. It was not until their meeting on October 29, 1866, that the trustees rejected the amendment of 1858, saying that it had been railroaded through the legislature by John G. Westmoreland when the trustees did not know anything about the bill. The trustees eventually declared the four new appointments to be void. Clearly the trustees were jealous for their own powers and claimed that the faculty had usurped some of them.[8] But something provoked the trustees to oppose the amendment in late 1866 after they had ignored it for years. It would appear that Thomas S. Powell was the provocateur.

Apparently there were no problems when the Atlanta Medical College's first postwar session, the winter course, began on November 7, 1865, with approximately forty students. Specific information about Stout's particular classes is not available, but he did tell the students in 1866 that the faculty intended not only to teach with "didactic lectures," but also to employ "frequent, thorough and searching examinations to stimulate thought and investigation," and show the faculty how the students were doing. Thomas Powell reported that he visited Stout's office some time during the winter term "and discovered that Dr. Stout was not well satisfied with his chair—spoke of it as unnecessary, and like a fifth wheel to a wagon." Stout apparently felt that this chair, which the faculty had activated for him because "It was deemed advantageous to the Institution to secure the services of this distinguished gentleman and hence it was thought proper to fill this chair at this time," overlapped too much with some of the other professorships. He hoped that either Dr. Means or Dr. Logan would resign, as they seemed to be contemplating, and then he wished to assume one of their chairs. Powell relayed this information to another member of the faculty and, in his account, seemed indignant that Stout was not satisfied with his position.[9]

The faculty took the then relatively unusual step of deciding to offer both a winter and a summer course, that is, two sessions per year rather than the usual one. As Stout put it in May 1866, when he was chosen to deliver the introductory lecture to the summer course, the faculty believed it was in accord with the "spirit of the times" to keep "the halls devoted to science" always open. He also provided general encouragement for the medical students. Although defeated, the South

---

8. Ibid., 20–21, 24–29, 32.
9. Stout, "Address—Eighth," 18. Fulton Co., *Report of the Delegate*, 45, 59.

was attempting to recover. Because of certain "ethnological" peculiarities which Southerners could best understand, he urged Southerners to remain in the South, be educated there, and attempt to contribute to the improvement of Southern society. Stout called it "moral heroism" to pick up the pieces and go on after the defeat. "We would be dishonest to profess that we regret not our loss. We are honest in accepting the situation and rejoicing that bloodshed has ceased, and that we are again permitted to cultivate the arts of peace. Of the resurection of the dead cause, men of common sense have no hope. For the age of miracles has passed, and the stern realities of the situation forbid the vain indulgence of the imagination. . . . Having accepted the situation, yet ignoring none of the nobler impulses of our nature, with the realities of the present we are now engaged."[10]

Apparently early in the summer course serious problems began to arise. Even before the war Thomas S. Powell had disagreed with the Westmoreland brothers over the way Dean J. G. Westmoreland managed the college's finances. The disagreements may have originated because Powell felt that his influence in procuring the $15,000 legislative appropriation in 1857 ought to allow him to have some influence on the budget. Several other incidents provoked prewar hostility as well. Then, some time during the spring of 1866, Powell, as he claimed, single-handedly and of his own accord, persuaded the Atlanta City Council to issue $5,000 worth of bonds to give the college money to repair the wartime damage to the building so that the funds would not have to be subtracted from faculty salaries. In July, J. G. Westmoreland reported that a certain amount had been spent for repairs. The faculty then divided the remainder of the money among some of the chairs. But, Powell said, when he asked for some of the funds for his chair, the others disagreed and said that there should be a contingency fund in case the cost of repairs exceeded the amount allotted. Powell soon uncovered, as he claimed, the disgusting financial mismanagement of J. G. Westmoreland, who not only spent much more money than was necessary on shoddily made repairs but also kept poor records.[11]

Over the course of the summer, relations worsened between Powell and the members of the faculty, including Stout, who supported the Westmorelands. At a faculty meeting on August 31, Eben Hillyer,

---

10. Ibid., 59. Stout, "Address—Eighth," 6–7, 17.
11. Fulton Co., *Report of the Delegate*, 37–40, 44–47, 50–52.

professor of physiology, introduced a resolution, seconded by Stout, to ask Powell to resign. The main reason given was Powell's management of a literary magazine called the *Ladies' Home*, which was supposed to raise funds to build a women's hospital in Atlanta. Powell claimed that the real problem was not the management of the magazine, but rather his complaints about the college financial management, as well as the desire of someone else (Powell suspected Stout) for Powell's chair. The majority of the faculty voted to ask for Powell's resignation. It seems to have been during this squabble that Powell involved the trustees. The amendment of 1858 enabled the faculty to ask Powell to resign and to appoint the person Powell believed wanted his chair. Thus, the amendment became the focus of the dispute.[12]

Beginning, then, in the fall of 1866, the quarrel was no longer simply between faculty factions but also between some of the faculty and the trustees. The trustees insisted that they recognized only the faculty members who remained from the prewar period, and they declared the other seats vacant. Moreover, they wanted Powell reinstated and the amendment of 1858 repealed. Then the disagreement spread to the rest of the Atlanta medical community, and widened a preexisting split between the Atlanta Medical Society and its splinter group, the Fulton County Medical Society. The Fulton County group took the medical college problem to the Georgia Medical Association (GMA) meeting in 1868, claiming that they believed they were bound by the Code of Medical Ethics to report the attempts of the faculty to "usurp" the rights of the trustees. Matters became even more complex as the GMA refused to recognize graduates of the Atlanta Medical College as regular, degreed physicians. In 1870, over a matter primarily of pride, the GMA expelled the college faculty from the association, even though the legislature had repealed the offending amendment in 1868, because the faculty refused to apologize publicly for criticizing the 1868 association meeting. At the association meeting in 1871, a group, led by members of the Atlanta Academy of Medicine, who were now rivals of the Fulton County Medical Society and supporters of the medical college, managed to outvote a movement to expel them from the meeting and to pass a

---

12. Ibid., 22, 46–50, 52, 60. Powell claimed that the accusations against him were made by only four faculty members: the Westmorelands, Stout, and Hillyer. Ibid., 36–37. A letter from Powell to the board of trustees stated that "he was at the disposal of the Board as they might think best for the interest and honor of the institution." This is apparently a paraphrase of Powell's letter. Ibid., 23.

resolution, proposed by J. P. Logan and seconded by Stout, to expunge all the rulings against the Atlanta Medical College passed between 1868 and 1870. It was in response to this supposedly unjust resolution that the material contained in the pro-Powell *Report of the Delegate of the Fulton County Medical Society* was compiled and printed.[13]

Clearly the situation at the Atlanta Medical College was an example of the worst type of academic bickering. And certainly Thomas Powell was very much involved in making the situation as bad as it became. Powell claimed that his position was vindicated by the documents in the *Report of the Delegate*. But a few things can be determined about Powell from this report that clarify his less-than-innocent role. Unquestionably Powell was very self-righteous. *He* was the only one standing up for principles and ethics, and thus he was ousted for his stand. Powell may well have been rather obnoxious in his stand for principles, since he apparently alienated some doctors who had initially been his friends. It also appears that Powell was a gossip. Whenever he found out some information from one person, he generally told it to another faculty member. This was hardly behavior that promoted harmony and trust. In addition, there may be some truth to the Atlanta Medical College faculty charge that the 1868 GMA meeting, which ruled against the college, was dominated by a Powell clique, since Powell was vice president of the association at that time. By 1871 Powell was extremely bitter at his former faculty colleagues and had unkind things to say about nearly every one of them. O'Keefe he called a "Judas" for seeking his own interest rather than defending Powell. Powell had little respect for Stout, and repeatedly called him a "*probationer*," because he had not been approved by the Board of Trustees. But Powell's use of the epithet "probationer," as well as the term "fifth wheel," implied that Stout had no reputation, no knowledge, no position, and certainly no right to express an opinion. Powell seemed to consider Stout to be the root of the problem, a manipulative schemer trying to steal Powell's position, who should never have been hired in the first place.[14]

---

13. Ibid., 3–15, 23–24, 30–31, 65–66, 72–77, 80–81. The delegate of the Fulton County Medical Society was Dr. W. T. Goldsmith. Ibid., 3. Actually the booklet contains many other documents besides Goldsmith's report.

14. Powell claimed vindication in ibid., 68–71. Instances of his gossiping tendencies can be found on 45 and 47. The charge against the 1868 meeting is on 74. Powell is listed as vice president on 79. The "Judas," O'Keefe, had formerly been one of Powell's best friends, he claimed, 47–49. Powell's greatest vituperation against Stout is on 45–48.

Stout indeed played a role in the upheaval at the Atlanta Medical College; however, no account gives his perspective on the situation. Certainly Stout had no idea that his appointment was merely probationary. Based on the sample letter of notification to Daniel O'Keefe printed in the *Report of the Delegate*, the trustees' approval was expected to be perfunctory. No doubt Stout was dissatisfied with his position since it seemed to infringe on other chairs. But Powell's speculations about Stout's motives and his accounts of Stout's manipulations are suspect because Powell's presentation is so bitterly self-serving. Stout apparently seconded the resolution to ask for Powell's resignation, which probably helps to explain Powell's hatred. The extent to which Stout manipulated any part of the situation for his own personal gain cannot be known. But striving for some sort of control or supervisory responsibilities, perhaps unconsciously, while probably supposing that he could be helpful to the struggling school, would have been quite natural for Stout since he had only recently ceased his supervisory labors as medical director of hospitals. In this position he had supervised a number of these same faculty colleagues, and he seems to have had no conflict with them. However, Stout had had little, if any, wartime contact with Powell, which might, perhaps, have contributed in some way to Powell's resentment.[15]

While Stout was a professor at the medical college, he had an opportunity to begin using the medical papers that he had collected during the Civil War. He decided to publish a complete list of the Confederate dead of the Army of Tennessee by name, rank, and regiment, as well as statistical tables summarizing the causes of death. Stout wished to honor the memory of the dead, and also to provide useful scientific information. He began with the earliest figures he had, some relating to the troops under Braxton Bragg at Pensacola, Florida, during the second half of 1861. These records actually belonged to A. J. Foard, who had left a box

---

15. Ibid., 59–60. The Atlanta Medical College survived the faculty splits, the battle with the trustees, and the alienation from the several medical societies. In 1879 Powell founded his own rival Southern Medical College, and competition between the two institutions continued until Powell's death in 1895. The two schools joined in 1898 as the Atlanta College of Physicians and Surgeons, and in 1915 became part of Emory University Medical School. Garrett, *Atlanta and Environs*, 1: 955–56; 2: 332. Apparently only one article has been published about the Atlanta Medical College controversy. Its author attempted to vindicate Powell, trying to show that he did nothing unprofessional or unethical. The documentation is not thorough and the article does not give any real indication of how vituperative the *Report of the Delegate* actually was. Murphy, "The Controversy Between Dr. T. S. Powell," 236–52.

of early war papers at Stout's office and never reclaimed them. Stout had a ready vehicle for his articles in the *Atlanta Medical and Surgical Journal*, which was published by the Westmoreland brothers, but Stout published only two installments of the list before he left the school.[16] Unfortunately, this unfinished project became typical of his attempts to write about the Civil War medical experience.

In his later writings Stout barely mentioned his medical college stint, merely stating that he taught at the school for two terms and then returned home to Tennessee because he needed to take care of his affairs there. Many personal factors probably contributed to Stout's desire to escape an increasingly unpleasant situation at the medical college. Certainly his financial situation was precarious, and the job at the medical college seemed to be no help. As he complained to a correspondent, "My income from my chair in the Atlanta Medical College has been so small that the position rather adds to my pecuniary embarassments." Family matters also made it difficult for Stout to be away from home for eight months of the year. In March 1866, a new daughter, Katherine Tannehill, joined Stout's family. Also by mid-1866 Stout's son, Burwell, then about twelve, was ill with something his uncle called "white swelling," which may have been rheumatic fever.[17]

---

16. These lists do not give the cause of death for each individual. Stout, "List of Confederate Dead," 381–84; "Statement of Deaths of Confederate Soldiers," 429–32. A. J. Foard to Stout, October 25, 1866, Emory, box 2, folder 24.

17. Stout to Hon. Richard Coke, January 26, 189[3], TSLA, box 1, folder 12; Daniell, *Types of Successful Men*, 311. Stout to [Joseph Jones?], undated but 1865 or 1866, Tulane. Katherine's birth month and year are found in the 1900 Census, Texas, Dallas County, Dallas, roll 1625, vol. 27, E. D. 122, sheet 5, line 14. In a letter written to his nephew, Thomas James Paine, on August 27, 1866, Burwell Abernathy, Stout's brother-in-law, giving the family news, said that Burwell Stout "is suffering very much with white swelling." TSLA, box 1, folder 16. According to an 1872 medical dictionary, "white swelling" was the popular name for "hydrarthrosis," defined in a modern dictionary as "an accumulation of watery fluid in the cavity of a joint." J. Thomas, *A Comprehensive Medical Dictionary* (Philadelphia: J. B. Lippincott & Co., 1872); *Dorland's Illustrated Medical Dictionary* 26th ed. (Philadelphia: W. B. Saunders, 1981), 621. Based on Burwell's age, his uncle's remark that he was "fearful he [Burwell Stout] will never get over it," and the fact that by about 1890 Burwell was listed in Daniell's *Types of Successful Men* (among Stout's children) as a "permanent invalid" (314), he probably had rheumatic fever, and consequently, rheumatic heart disease. Darleen Powars, M.D., interview with Glenna R. Schroeder, June 30, 1989. Burwell apparently died between 1900, when the census indicated that Martha Stout had five living children, and 1904, when her obituary listed only three surviving children, and Burwell was not among them. "Obituary" from Giles County, Tennessee,

Therefore, when Stout returned to Tennessee, he apparently determined that he had to do more to earn money than rely on the produce of his farm. A seemingly ideal opportunity for Stout to use his administrative skills presented itself when several people asked him to become general superintendent for the Confederate Orphan Asylum in Clarksville, Tennessee. Stout accepted the position but resigned after less than six months on the job because of the financial instability of the institution.[18] Then, by mid-1868, Stout lost his farm, probably because of debt.[19] So, in 1869, Stout chose to return to Atlanta, this time taking his family and planning to set up a private medical practice. In an article, written in the 1890s, he explained what he considered to be a fact of postwar southern life, which probably helped to induce him to leave Giles County after the loss of his property: "Since the abolition of slavery, in those regions of the South where the negroes form a very large moiety of the population, the practice of medicine offers little inducement for educated physicians to settle therein, and nearly all such who formerly lived there have abandoned the country to live in the towns, or have ceased to practice and engaged in other pursuits, or are deceased." Like most of his fellow Southerners, Stout did not have a very positive view of the freedmen, and he certainly did not consider it worth the while of any "educated" physician to work among them. The poverty of local whites and the preponderance of blacks likely convinced Stout that appropriate financial rewards could only be found elsewhere.[20]

In 1869 Stout's five children ranged in age from twenty to three, and Stout was particularly concerned about the education of the three youngest. Probably because he had few funds to devote to private

---

paper, TSLA, box 2, folder 11. From 1871 to 1883 Burwell is listed in the Atlanta City Directory, beginning in 1874 as a post office clerk. He does not appear in the directory again, nor with any family members in the 1900 Texas or Georgia census.

18. J. H. Bufton [or Buffon] to Stout, January 26, 1867, Emory, box 2, folder 25; Mrs. G. A. Henry and Mrs. E. Galbraith to Stout, June 10, 1867, Emory, box 3, folder 12.

19. John C. Brown to Stout, July 3, 1867, Emory, box 2, folder 25, indicates that some of Stout's land was about to be sold for the benefit of his creditors. A receipt dated May 26, 1868, shows that Stout deposited $100 "under Bankrupt Act," TSLA, box 2, folder 3. Other than this, nothing is known about the loss of Stout's land.

20. Stout, "Reminiscences," 235. Medical historian John Duffy also suggests that while the public image of physicians improved after the Civil War, "the average physician enjoyed neither money nor social position." Because there were so many doctors, Stout was part of the majority who had to do something else on the side to make ends meet. *The Healers*, 233–34.

schooling, Stout became one of the leading actors in the movement to establish a public school system in Atlanta. Stout's former colleague D. C. O'Keefe, since called the "Father of Atlanta's Public Schools," was on the city council, and proposed that the council establish a committee to investigate the possibility of opening public schools in Atlanta. This committee included O'Keefe, J. P. Logan, and Stout, who served as secretary. The committee examined reports from a number of public school systems, and concluded that the first thing to do was to appoint a board of education.[21]

The city council promptly elected twelve board members and the board organized itself on December 23, 1869. Former Governor Joseph E. Brown became president, J. P. Logan, vice president, and Stout, secretary. As secretary for the board, Stout was in charge of keeping records, reminding members of meetings, notifying instructors of appointment, sending diplomas to schools, examining bills, and similar functions. It is safe to say that Stout never performed some of these proposed tasks as his secretarial tenure preceded the actual opening of any of the schools. The board, while awaiting an amendment of the city charter permitting the establishment of public schools, did not meet between January and October 1870. In October, Brown appointed a number of standing committees. Stout served on those for salaries and supplies; grievances; sanitary affairs; and examinations, course of study, and textbooks, of which he was chairman. At the board meeting on May 8, 1871, Stout submitted his letter of resignation, having served less than his two-year appointment.[22]

Stout was not disillusioned with public schools, nor did he resign because the school system did not develop instantly. Rather, in one of his numerous short-term efforts to improve his precarious financial status, Stout had accepted a contract "as Agent for the Introduction of the Educational Works of Harper & Brothers of New York." Even had his contract not forbidden him to hold any board of education position,

---

21. Garrett, *Atlanta and Environs*, 1: 822; *Report of the Committee on Public Schools*. Stout also attended the 1869 and 1871 annual meetings of the Georgia Teacher's Association, participating in the discussion in 1871. Orr, *A History of Education in Georgia*, 190–91, 200.

22. *Hanleiter's Atlanta City Directory, 1871*, 46. Atlanta Board of Education Minutes, December 23, 1869, January 8, October 4, and October 13, 1870, May 8, 1871, Atlanta Public School Archives. Construction of three elementary school houses began in September 1871 and finished in January 1872, when school opened. *Hanleiter's Atlanta City Directory, 1872*, 146.

Stout would still have had to resign because he would have had a clear conflict of interest as chairman of the textbook committee. Instead of giving up on education, he probably saw his new position as a way to encourage education and still gain some financial remuneration for himself. In the city directory for 1872 Stout placed a large advertisement that listed numerous Harper textbooks available on a variety of subjects. Stout continued his book sales at least into 1874, but by 1875 he once again found his situation changing.[23]

Both Thomas and Burwell, Stout's two oldest sons, had acquired clerking jobs by 1871. While they still lived with their parents, they were becoming more independent, as well as contributing to the family finances. By 1874 the third son, Samuel V. D., joined the work force. About 1875, Thomas apparently moved to Chattanooga, where he lived and worked until 1897. Stout, his wife, and two daughters moved to Roswell, Georgia, then outside metropolitan Atlanta, in November 1874. While Stout lived in Roswell, he became interested in the diseases which afflicted the women factory workers in the neighborhood, and concluded, as he treated them, that the frequently used Battey's operation (ovariotomy), as a solution to female problems, was unnecessary in most cases. While Stout continued as a general practitioner, he did, after this point, take an increased interest in gynecological cases, and published several articles on the subject.[24]

---

23. Atlanta Board of Education Minutes, May 8, 1871. *Hanleiter's Atlanta City Directory, 1872*, 109; *Beasley's Atlanta City Directory, 1874*, 220.
24. Atlanta City Directories, under various names, for: 1871, p. 225; 1874, p. 220; 1875, p. 216; 1876, p. 226; 1877, pp. 318–19. Burwell and S. V. D. Stout are both listed through 1883, but from 1884 to 1896, S. V. D. seems to be the only Stout son in Atlanta. 1883, p. 428; 1884, p. 324; 1896, p. 1190; 1897, p. 1217. Both Thomas and S. V. D. married. Thomas's wife, the former Clara C. Allen, whom he married in 1880, probably died about 1900, as she is listed in the city directory of that year, but not in the 1900 census. In the census, Thomas and his three daughters, Rane, Martha, and Margaret, lived with S. V. D., his wife Fannie, and their two children, Erskine and Clara. [Obituary] "Thomas Edward Stout," *Confederate Veteran* 28 (November 1920): 429. *Atlanta City Directory, 1900*, p. 1254; 1900 Census, Georgia, Fulton County, roll 198, vol. 29, E. D. 50, sheet 4, line 47. About 1890 Thomas is listed as a teller at the Fourth National Bank in Chattanooga. Daniell, *Types of Representative Men*, 314. Daniell discusses Stout's interest in gynecology. Ibid., 311–12. Atkinson, ed., *Physicians and Surgeons*, 306. Stout's articles were: "Dysmenorrhoea," 166–72; "Puerperal Convulsions," 172–90; and "Report of the Section on Gynecology for the Seventh Congressional District," 151–90. This last article seems to have included his two other articles.

In September 1876 the death of his former commander, Braxton Bragg, in Galveston, Texas, reminded Stout of his Civil War experiences. In December of that year Stout wrote his recollections of Bragg. "Now that he [Bragg] has passed beyond reach of the sound of flattering tongues, which could never turn him from the lines of duty, nor induce him to evade or permit others under his command to evade responsibility, and cannot longer be stung by the venom of defamation, the time has arrived for his friends and all who admire self-denying nobility of character to place upon record truthful reminiscences of this remarkable man, whose career of fortune and misfortune, must fill a large space in the history of the warfare of the late Confederate Government against the United States."[25]

Stout had noticed that in the eleven years since the end of the Civil War some of the wartime leaders had been glorified while others had been ignored. He felt that "American citizens of every section and phase of political or sectarian opinion, are or should be interested in the study of American manhood. Personal dislike should not be permitted to obstruct the exercise of strict impartiality in judging of the merits or demerits of any character public or private." If historians merely pay attention to what is printed in the press by men who have their own favorites, Stout continued, these historians will not have a proper view of the characters involved in the Civil War.[26] Stout realized that Bragg had made a number of enemies, but he blamed this on Bragg's influence with Jefferson Davis, his refusal to praise or flatter, and his strict enforcement of discipline. According to Stout, however, Bragg had an excellent relationship with the medical department and was very supportive. Bragg expressed great concern for the sick and wounded, actually weeping at the thought of leaving some of the wounded behind

---

25. Stout, Reminiscences of General Braxton Bragg (published version), 6, 23. The original, as well as the published pamphlet, is in UTX, box 2G379.

26. Ibid., 5. While Stout himself was hardly an impartial observer of Bragg, he realized the problem of partisanship which has been discussed by late twentieth-century historians in such works as: Thomas L. Connelly, The Marble Man: Robert E. Lee and His Image in American Society (Baton Rouge: Louisiana State University Press, 1977); Gaines M. Foster, Ghosts of the Confederacy: Defeat, the Lost Cause, and the Emergence of the New South, 1865–1913 (New York: Oxford University Press, 1987); and William Garrett Piston, Lee's Tarnished Lieutenant: James Longstreet and His Place in Southern History (Athens: University of Georgia Press, 1987). Stout's contact with Bragg was primarily professional, rarely social. They last saw one another in 1874. Stout, Reminiscences of General Braxton Bragg, 6, 21.

when the army evacuated a portion of Tennessee after the battle of Murfreesboro. This was a side of Bragg the public never saw, and Stout believed that people would have had more sympathy for Bragg had they observed his tenderness.[27]

Soon after writing his recollections, Stout attempted to publish them. He tried the *Century Magazine*, the Philadelphia *Times*, and the St. Louis *Republic*, all without success, not, he later said, because his recollections lacked historical value, but because the papers did not wish to devote equal space to any opponents of Stout's perspective in a debate about the controversial Bragg. Even the Tennessee Historical Society declined to publish Stout's recollections in 1895. Stout's work was not in vain, however, as he later managed to incorporate a good bit of his material into his other writings and thus spread his opinions about Bragg.[28]

As usual, short of funds, Stout in April 1877 attempted to gain pecuniary aid by writing to the surgeon general of the United States. After explaining something about his career and his collection of Confederate medical records, Stout, "encouraged by the signs now perceptible of a cordial restoration of good feeling between the two sections of our country," and "believing I am in possession of facts of great interest to humanity," suggested that funds might be provided to support him and his family while he got the papers together. "I am becoming alarmed," he wrote, "(after nearly 12 years have transpired since the war closed,) lest my life may close ere my work is done."[29]

Having no success with the surgeon general, Stout tried another tack in 1878. Just about this time Confederate General Marcus J. Wright, with whom Stout had worked during the war, became involved as an agent or liaison for the collection of Confederate papers for the project that became *The War of the Rebellion: A Compilation of the Official Records of the Union and Confederate Armies*, usually called the *Official*

27. Ibid., 6, 8, 12, 21–22.
28. Stout to Officers and Members of Tennessee Historical Society, January 11, 1895, TSLA, box 1, folder 12. Information on Bragg appeared more than once in Stout's series "Some Facts," pt. 2, 22 (December 1900): 567; pt. 14, 24 (December 1902): 667; pt. 23, 25 (October 1903): 570. Stout had a substantial section on Bragg in his address to the Association of Medical Officers of the Army and Navy of the Confederacy at their Dallas reunion in 1902, which was printed as "Address—History," 445–47. Stout also wrote about Bragg for Tennessee Governor Porter in his 1897 account which was later published as "Outline," 73–75. In 1895 Stout published excerpts in "Tributes to Braxton Bragg," 132–33.
29. Stout to Surgeon General, April 9, 1877, Emory, box 2, folder 27.

Records. Stout wrote to Wright on July 18, 1878, with a proposition about his papers. Eventually, Stout decided that he was willing to accept $10,000 for the papers. Wright explained that "The appropriation for this Bureau is very limited and no such price as you ask I am informed has ever been paid for papers (except in the case of the Pickett papers)." Although Wright wanted to help Stout in any way he could, he informed him that "the only compensation you need expect would fall far short of the sum you name." In a final letter, Wright suggested that Stout make a catalogue of his papers and determine the lowest price he would accept to send the papers to Wright's office for copying, with the originals then to be returned to Stout. Since "many" Confederate surgeons had donated their papers to the project, Wright felt that Stout could not expect to receive much money, "but if the catalogue shows yours to be valuable, I think a reasonable price will be paid you."[30] Once again Stout was disappointed. No satisfactory settlement could be made, so Stout retained his papers, and deprived the scholarly world of the inclusion of important documents in the *Official Records.*

In late 1879 Stout suffered a severe illness. While removing a tumor from the shoulder of a patient, Stout scraped the middle finger of his right hand rather severely with his operating instrument (surgeons did not wear gloves in those days). Two days later the wound had become extremely painful, and by the fourth day the inflammation gave him a chill, high fever, and dry skin. No medication he tried seemed to combat what was obviously a case of blood poisoning, as Stout developed gangrene in his wounded finger and swelling in his arm up to the shoulder. Finally, after taking massive doses of salicylate of soda, a compound similar to aspirin, Stout began to recover, aided by lancing the infection

---

30. If Stout kept copies of his letters, they have not been found. Marcus J. Wright to Stout, July 25, August 14, and August 22, 1878, all in Emory, box 2, folder 27. The "Pickett papers" were Confederate State papers that had come into the hands of Colonel John T. Pickett, which he sold to the United States government in 1872 for $75,000. Bragg, "Charles C. Jones, Jr., and the Mystery of Lee's Lost Dispatches," 437–38. It is quite likely that Stout knew about the Pickett purchase and thus did not consider his price too high. It must be remembered that most of the records of the Confederate surgeon general's office were destroyed in the fire which accompanied the evacuation of Richmond, so that Stout could rightly consider such a large cache of records as he held to be valuable for the study of Confederate medicine. Perhaps, however, there was less interest in Washington in medical rather than military or political records, possibly combined with less interest in the western than the eastern theater of war. In any case, Stout's papers remained in his own hands.

and applying poultices. Recovery was a slow process, however, as it was four months before he was able to ride horseback again.[31]

Little else survives about Stout's life in Georgia. The census of 1880 listed him as a physician residing in Roswell with his wife, who was keeping house, and his daughters, twenty-year-old Margaret, a school-teacher, and fourteen-year-old Katherine, a student. In 1881 Stout decided to leave Roswell. A number of friends, neighbors, and patients presented him with a gift "to show their appreciation of your skill as a Physician and your worth as a friend, neighbor and citizen." While Stout may have developed some good relationships in Roswell, he had once again failed to gain financial success, and, once again, his pursuit of fiscal stability apparently took him and his family elsewhere, this time to Chattanooga. There he remained for only six to eight months. The family may have stayed with the oldest son, Thomas, who was probably living there, while Stout investigated the local opportunities and found them wanting.[32]

Stout's next move took him west to Texas. At this point Texas appeared to be a land of opportunity, and Stout was not alone in moving to that vast state to start again. He may have been encouraged to move by relatives or friends already in the state. In any case, in May 1882 Stout, his wife, and two daughters settled in Cisco, Eastland County, Texas. Cisco was certainly a place for a new beginning as the town was very young. At the junction of the Texas Pacific and Texas Central

31. Stout, "Salicylate of Soda in Septic Poisoning," 11–13. Probably Stout contracted a virulent bacterial infection because it developed so rapidly, but it is quite probable that the scrape became infected from some other cause than the tumor on which he was operating. Stout took ten grains of salicylate of soda, or about 650 milligrams, every half hour for two hours. The salicylate of soda reduced Stout's fever, decreased his chills, acted as an anti-inflammatory, and generally made Stout feel better. The lancing and poultices were then the best way to cure his condition. With twentieth-century antibiotics, Stout would have been out of the hospital and nearly recovered in a week. Darleen Powars, M.D., interview with Glenna R. Schroeder, June 30, 1989.

32. Apparently during his Roswell period, Stout attempted to earn money doing physicals for life insurance companies, but he ceased to perform examinations in the early 1880s because the companies refused to pay the physicians the real worth of their services in saving the business from bad risks. Stout, "Ethical Relationship of the Medical Profession and Life Insurance Companies," 493–97. 1880 Census, Georgia, Cobb County, Roswell, Roll 9, E. D. 33, p. 5 (p. 128). Archibald Smith, et al., to Stout, June 21, 1881, Emory, box 2, folder 27. Nineteen individuals and seven families signed the letter which accompanied the gift. Henry W. Morgan to Stout, January 3, 1882, ibid., indicates that Stout was in Chattanooga.

railroads, Cisco was situated in a location expected to prosper, when
it was founded in 1880–81 and named for a millionaire rancher who
provided financing for the Texas Central. In the early days the Texas
Pacific circulated promotional brochures advertising the advantages of
Cisco and encouraging settlement with a special "immigrant coach,"
half-price fare, and a pledge to haul two hundred pounds of baggage
free per person. Stout may well have taken advantage of this offer.
He seems to have hoped that the railroads would establish a company
hospital in the crossroads town. Naturally, Stout wanted to administer
this prospective facility, which, as a company institution, would be as
similar as possible to a military hospital. But the railroads never built it.[33]

Stout began practicing medicine and discovered that the inhabitants
of Cisco and the surrounding area were relatively healthy, except in
winter when drastic climatic changes caused many people to contract
severe colds. The other major health problem was a tendency "to become
scorbutic to an extent I have never seen elsewhere, except in badly fed
armies," Stout wrote. This condition developed because the residents
generally lived on bread, meat, and coffee, rarely eating vegetables. Once
again, Stout's patients seem to have been impoverished, which helped
to account for the lack of variety in their diet, and also provided Stout
with insufficient income.[34]

So, once more Stout turned to his other interest—education. In January 1883, Stout wrote a revealing letter to his friend Anson Nelson
in Nashville, Tennessee, explaining that he had become involved in
education again because it "offered immediate remuneration." Yet Stout
also had more altruistic motives. He believed that the nature and quality
of the public schools in the area depended very much on the types of

---

33. Daniell, *Types of Successful Men*, 313; Ghormley, *Eastland County, Texas*, 253–55;
    John C. Brown to Stout, May 19, 1883 and February 4, 1886, both in Emory, box 2,
    folder 27. It is possible that Stout briefly lived in Comanche, a town in the county of
    the same name just southeast of Eastland County, as he mentioned "that editing a
    newspaper in Comanche and practicing medicine in a thinly settled country" did not
    produce financial success. Stout to Anson Nelson, January 27, 1883, TSLA, box 1,
    folder 12. John C. Brown, Stout's good friend and former commander, moved to Texas
    and may have encouraged Stout to do the same. Enough former residents of Giles
    County, Tennessee, had moved to the Ellis County area south of Dallas to hold a
    reunion in 1894. Stout, "Days of Long Ago," *Pulaski Citizen*, August 9 and 16, 1894
    (originally delivered as a speech at the reunion on July 1).
34. Scorbutic is related to scurvy. The dry climate also contributed to some skin diseases.
    Stout, "Observations of the Influence of the Climate," 98, 100, 102–11. Stout,
    "Address—History," 443.

local laws passed, and Stout wanted to use his previous experience to help shape the school system. Stout lamented the fact that the quality of education was much worse in the rural South and in small Southern towns like Cisco than it had been before the Civil War. He explained that because of his views on education, "and having a hearty sympathy for our rural fathers and mothers—having spent most of my active manhood among such,—having had much to do with the shaping of public educational enterprises every where I have lived—fond of teaching and thoroughly posted by observation and experience in the practical working of public schools and the most improved methods of instruction, I became desirous of experimenting in the establishment and management of graded schools, in this small, far western town, of Cisco, and making a practical demonstration as to what can be done with the graded school system in a frontier locality, in a poorly constructed and poorly furnished school house." So, in October 1882, Stout became superintendent and principal of the new public schools. He joined with an "enlightened" but educationally inexperienced politician, who was head of the school Board of Trustees and had local influence, as well as his older daughter Maggie, an experienced teacher, in the educational endeavor. Four months later Stout wrote that it had "succeeded beyond my most sanguine expectations."

But Stout also had other purposes for his letter to Nelson than simply to tell his friend how successful his new school system was. Despite the school's success, Stout felt that "such daily labor as I undergo will, if persisted in, soon break down one of my age (60 yrs), and after the expiration of another four months of experiment in that line, I ought to be in a position wherein I would have opportunities of giving my experiences to the world—not only in the educational but also in the medical line, in civil and military life. And this brings me back to the principal topic of my former letter. . . ." It is evident that this "principal topic" was the 1,500 pounds of hospital records Stout had saved. Stout wanted Nelson to help him procure an "academic or other literary position," or to convince Tennessee Governor Bate to "recommend an appropriation adequate to enable me to collate them [the papers] and place them in the archive of the State." What Stout actually wanted was to retire from his school organization to a position, preferably in Nashville, or at least somewhere in Tennessee, where he would be paid to work on his papers for the literary and historical benefit of the state, if not the nation.

Stout had one further request to make: "In my last letter to you, I alluded to a desire to receive some recognition of [honorable?] service in the cause of humanity and education from my native state. Even the degree of LL.D. empty as the title generally is, would gratify me and if sent to me away out here, where I am exerting myself in the cause of education and progress, would now greatly enhance my usefulness."[35] Stout most likely felt isolated in Cisco. Probably he still experienced the culture shock, stress, and homesickness that most people feel when they move to a new place, especially a place that was such a contrast from Atlanta, or Stout's various Tennessee homes. Stout had been in Cisco for less than a year and could not be expected to adjust to his new environment sufficiently in such a brief period. Stout's requests suggest that his own solution to his situation was recognition from the outside world. Some affirmation of his contributions, preferably monetary, but even symbolic, would bolster his self-esteem, as well as give him more prestige in the eyes of his neighbors. Whatever else Stout's requests may show, they belie the statements of one biographical sketch writer: "Whatever honors he wears were thrust upon him. . . . Retiring and modest in his disposition, his friends have often expressed surprise at his lack of self-assertion."[36]

Since a position with an assured salary was, as usual for Stout, not forthcoming, he remained involved with education and medicine. On July 24, 1884, Stout spoke to a group of summer "normal school" students. "Teaching[,] like the practice of medicine," he told them, "is a great art, founded upon principles derived from observation of the laws of nature applied with judgment and skill to meet the indications for the treatment of the untrained mind and body of the subject of it." As in medicine, so in teaching, the prescription should fit the case; one technique could not work for all students. Stout also discussed problems peculiar to rural schools, which he hoped these teachers would help to solve. Among the solutions he recommended was the employment of educated female teachers. According to Stout they were "better qualified to teach objectively than men," and they were naturally more sensitive and affectionate to young children. He did not see any objection to female teachers since most educational endeavors fit quite nicely within "woman's sphere" or "woman's mission."[37] Certainly Stout practiced what he preached as his own two daughters spent their careers as teachers.

---

35. Stout to Anson Nelson, January 27, 1883, TSLA, box 1, folder 12.
36. Daniell, *Types of Successful Men*, 134.
37. Stout, "A Lecture on the Educational Outlook in Rural and Sparsely Settled Districts in the South," unpublished, unpaged, UTX, box 2G379.

During his early years in Texas, Stout also practiced medical education through publishing a series titled "Clinical Lectures from the Standpoint of the Private Practitioner" in the *Texas Courier—Record of Medicine*, edited by his friend Ferdinand Daniel. Through these articles, which dealt with various diseases such as influenza and Asiatic Cholera, Stout intended to aid younger doctors who had not had the benefit of much clinical experience.[38]

In 1885 Stout received at least a part of the recognition for which he was looking—an honorary LL.D. from his alma mater, the University of Nashville.[39] Unfortunately for Stout, this recognition had little practical value. The main benefit of the degree was that he could add the title to the A.B. and M.D. behind his name when he published articles. From the early 1880s until the early 1890s, Stout wrote a number of articles on medical and historical subjects. The historical pieces generally remained unpublished, although a series on Davy Crockett appeared in the *Ellis County Mirror* in 1894. An undated and unpublished seven-chapter draft, entitled "Life and Times of General Sam Houston, For the Use of Juvenile Readers," is a good example of Stout's writings at this time. Very little of his work pertained to the Civil War. In 1887 Stout apparently attended the Ninth International Medical Congress, held in Washington, D.C., where he presented two papers on hospital construction and transportation of patients, which were published in the *Transactions* of the meeting. His only other article on the Civil War, published at this time, was his "Reminiscences of the Services of Medical Officers of the Confederate Army and Department of Tennessee," requested by the *St. Louis Medical and Surgical Journal* to help celebrate its fiftieth year of publication.[40]

In the fall of 1892 Grover Cleveland, the only Democrat elected president between James Buchanan and Woodrow Wilson, won reelection after the four-year term of Republican Benjamin Harrison. Stout, who

---

38. For a listing see the bibliography of Stout's works.
39. Edward D. Hicks to Stout, May 25, 1885, Emory, box 2, folder 27.
40. Stout, "David Crockett, The Pioneer, Statesman, Hero and Martyr," published in five parts in the *Ellis County Mirror*, Waxahachie, Texas, beginning February 27, 1894, TSLA, box 2, folder 12, also UTX, box 2G380; "Life and Times of General Sam Houston, For the Use of Juvenile Readers," UTX, box 2G379. "On the Best Models and Most Easily Constructed Military Hospital Wards for Temporary Use in the War," 88–91; "Transportation of the Sick and Wounded of Armies on Land," 64–65. Based on the recommendation of Ferdinand Daniel, Stout was invited to write the *St. Louis* article in Frank L. James to Stout, January 14, 1893, Emory, box 3, folder 1.

had never previously sought or held political office of any sort, applied for the position of commissioner of education, a national position but not, at that time, a cabinet post. The circumstances that led Stout to seek office are not clear beyond Stout's general desire for recognition and the annual salary of $3,000 paid to the commissioner. Texas Senator Richard Coke supported Stout's case, as did most of the top state officials in Texas, the Texas congressional delegation, and a few friends in Tennessee and Georgia. Stout's supporters submitted their recommendations to the secretary of the interior, Hoke Smith, by February 1893. As with many job applications, months elapsed and Stout received no word about the status of the position. In June 1893, Senator Coke wrote to Judge J. V. Cockrell in Anson, Texas, "I filed a great many testimonials for Dr. Stout with the Secretary of the Interior, and have urged him very warmly in person. It seems to have done no good, and I feel disinclined to continue to write letters which I presume from the silence attending their receipt have been thrown into the wastebasket. I believe Dr. Stout to be the best man that is applying for the place by long odds, and would gladly do anything for him that I can. The course of the administration in making appointments is so very erratic that I do not know what to do on the subject. The first thing Mr. Cleveland knows, if he does not mind, he will produce such a feeling of indifference towards the administration among the Democrats that he will get into the same fix he was in when he was President before."[41]

Apparently the unsuccessful applicants for commissioner of education never received notification that a commissioner had been appointed or, more accurately, retained. William T. Harris of Massachusetts, Benjamin Harrison's appointee, who took the oath of office on September 12, 1889, continued in the position through successive administrations until June 30, 1906. What Stout could not know was that despite a good educational background and varying experience, his largely political recommendations could hardly compete with Harris's letters from the presidents of Harvard, the University of Texas, Johns Hopkins University, Gallaudet College, and several normal schools, as well as from the

---

41. *Official Register of the United States*, 1: 776. Stout to Richard Coke, January 26, 189[3], TSLA, box 1, folder 12; S. W. T. Lanham to Stout, February 13, 1893, Emory, box 3, folders 1 and 13; William S. Scruggs to Richard Coke, February 13, 1893, Emory, box 3, folder 1. Other letters can be found in TSLA, box 1, folder 17, some of which are duplicated in Emory, box 3, folder 13. Richard Coke to J. V. Cockrell, June 3, 1893, ibid.

superintendents of education of most of the southern states, including Texas, Tennessee, and Georgia, where Stout drew his support. Stout never had a chance. In July 1894, he wrote to Cleveland, asking to have his recommendations returned to him. "I do not now desire the appointment," Stout explained, "and it would not now be my interest or pleasure to accept it, if appointed."[42]

While Stout was in the midst of his unsuccessful application for commissioner, he found his life disturbed in a drastic way. On the evening of April 28, 1893, after three stormy days, a cyclone struck Cisco, destroying a good deal of property and killing twenty-eight people. The Stout family escaped unscathed and their home became a temporary hospital for the injured. However, apparently the economy of the town was so devastated that Stout was not prepared to wait for its recovery, and he soon moved his family to Dallas, where he continued to practice medicine, at least to some extent.[43]

Despite his move and his advancing age, Stout still had his 1,500 pounds of Confederate hospital records and still hoped to do something with them, but he realized he could not hope to complete such a massive task without assistance. In 1895, Stout, then nearly seventy-three years old, wrote to the Tennessee Historical Society, which he had helped to found in the 1840s, suggesting that if the society would agree to pay him a salary and provide him with a clerk, he would move to Nashville, dividing his time between working for the society and preparing his reminiscences. Once again, Stout found no support for his endeavor and he had to remain in Texas.[44]

Yet Stout did not give up hope. In 1897 he wrote a brief "Outline of the History of the Services of the Medical Officers of the Army and

42. N A, Record Group 48, Secretary of the Interior, No. 14 Central Office Appointment Papers, William T. Harris envelopes; ibid., S. H. Stout envelope, Stout to Grover Cleveland, July 11, 1894. This is the only document in Stout's envelope, but it explains why the original letters of recommendation are in Stout's collection.

43. Ghormley, *Eastland County, Texas*, 260–63; Stout, "Some Facts," pt. 3, 23 (February 1901): 99. "Dr. S. H. Stout," *Ellis County Mirror*, January 24, 1894, Atlanta Public School Archives. A good many of Stout's fiscal frustrations in Cisco may have resulted from the fact that he was one of five physicians in a town of 1,500. When the town was partially destroyed and the railroads provided free transportation for anyone who wanted to leave, it was too much for Stout's practice. *Medical and Surgical Register of the United States* 2nd ed. (Detroit: R. L. Polk & Co., 1890), 1073.

44. Stout to Officers and Members of Tennessee Historical Society, January 11, 1895, TSLA, box 1, folder 12; Moore, "The Tennessee Historical Society, 1849–1918," 207.

Department of Tennessee (Confederate)," at the request of Tennessee Governor James D. Porter, a manuscript that ended up at the Tennessee Historical Society and was not published until 1956. Stout made it quite clear that the "Outline" was just that, a mere sketch in preparation for his proposed *magnum opus* of three volumes, which he had decided to prepare in manuscript even if he could not find a publisher. According to Stout the projected volumes were to contain:

> I. A full history of the organization and services of the medical department of the Confederate Army and Department of Tennessee. II. A Roster of the Surgeons, Asst. Surgeons, and Contract Physicians, Hospital Stewards, Detailed men, and matrons who served in the hospitals, giving date, length of service, and where services were rendered, with an Appendix containing name, rank, company and Regt. of every soldier or officer who died in the hospitals, from original reports in possession of the author. III. Recollections of the Confederate War, its causes, the battles fought by the Army of Tennessee, the Generals in Chief and their strategy, etc. The cooperation of the citizens especially the Noble Women of the South in comforting with clothing and supplies, the soldiers at the front and in nursing the sick and wounded in the hospitals.[45]

Although he had major writing plans, Stout was as yet unable to carry them out. He was still involved in earning a living. The year 1898 marked his fiftieth anniversary as a doctor, and the Dallas medical community honored him. Stout also participated in the organization of a medical college in Dallas. By 1900 the city of 42,638 inhabitants had 146 medical doctors, at least some of whom thought a medical college would be an asset to the city. At a meeting of physicians on August 16, 1900, the majority did not want a school and forced the meeting to adjourn. Stout was among the fifteen who thought otherwise and prepared to organize a school anyway. They named the institution the University of Dallas Medical Department, even though there was no University of Dallas, and elected Stout president of the Board of Trustees. Quickly organized, the school opened on November 19, 1900, with eleven faculty members

---

45. Stout, "Address—History," 443; "Outline," 55–56.

and eighty-one students. Stout apparently never actually taught in this school, but he became emeritus professor of obstetrics in 1901. The young institution struggled somewhat, coping first with the rebellion of three faculty members and then with the results of a destructive fire. In 1902 the school adopted a four-year curriculum and the next year, realizing the need for affiliation, joined with Baylor University, to become the Baylor University College of Medicine. Stout's involvement was probably limited to the initial organization of the medical school, and decreased as the problems of his age made themselves increasingly felt.[46]

After Stout retired from the active practice of medicine about 1900, he finally did manage to write something about his Civil War medical experiences, but not what he had intended. His greater amount of leisure coincided with an added stimulus to write and an opportunity to publish. That stimulus to write was provided in 1900 by the death of Dr. Preston B. Scott, former medical director of hospitals for the Department of Mississippi, with whom Stout had cooperated in 1864 and 1865 when a number of Stout's hospitals moved into Scott's area while remaining under Stout's control. As Scott had held a position similar to Stout's and was ten years younger than Stout, his death was a strong reminder of Stout's own mortality.[47]

The publication opportunity came from the *Southern Practitioner*, a monthly medical journal edited and published in Nashville by Deering J. Roberts. Although Roberts had been publishing for some time, he took on a new responsibility in 1900. At the United Confederate Veterans reunion in Louisville, Kentucky, that spring, the Association of Medical Officers of the Army and Navy of the Confederacy held their third annual meeting and elected Roberts secretary of the organization. During the course of the meeting, the doctors realized once again how many of their colleagues had already died. In view of the destruction of the materials in the surgeon general's office at the time Richmond was evacuated, they felt that if any Confederate medical information were to survive them, they had better make haste to get their memories down in writing. Roberts offered the *Southern Practitioner* as the "official organ"

---

46. Stout, "Address—History," 443; Charles B. Smith to Stout, April 11, 1898, Emory, box 3, folder 2; Moursund, *A History of Baylor University College of Medicine*, 7–27.
47. Stout, "Address—History," 443; "Some Facts," pt. 1, 22 (November 1900): 521; "Death of Dr. Preston B. Scott," *So. Pract.* 22 (October 1900): 463–65.

of the association and volunteered to add sixteen pages to each issue for recollections and reminiscences, an offer that the medical veterans unanimously accepted.[48]

By 1900, then, Stout gave up hope of financial remuneration for anything he might write and began a race with death to record his memories about the Confederate medical department for the benefit of "the future Historian" and to honor those who faithfully worked with him to tend the sick and wounded. Instead of his projected three volumes, Stout ultimately managed to publish only twenty-three installments in the *Southern Practitioner*. These reminiscences, while they have their value, are by no means as helpful as might be hoped. Stout tended to write about whatever came to mind, not necessarily chronologically, resulting in a fragmented account. Rather than using his records, Stout seems to have elaborated on material he wrote in 1893 for the *St. Louis Medical and Surgical Journal*, as well as the account written for Governor Porter in 1897. Thus, all Stout's published accounts tend to cover the same subjects and to have the same major weakness—they focus on the earlier part of the war and do not address his activities as medical director in any detail. In his twenty-third installment Stout proposed "to enter upon the task of recording the practical operation of the system" in number twenty-four, but his death prevented him from carrying out this proposal.[49]

In 1893, when Stout applied for the position of commissioner of education, he wrote to Richard Coke that although he was seventy years old, "I am as active bodily as I was 30 years ago. I find my memory as good as it ever was, and I have not arrived at that period in the age of minds, when many men, my juniors in years, find themselves losing interest in the present, and zeal in self-improvement." But by 1900 he found that he "experienced evidences of the physical debility usual in one of my age." In the spring of 1901 Stout suffered an attack of "la grippe" which kept him flat on his back for two months and forced him to miss the Memphis

---

48. "Annual Meeting of the Association of Surgeons of the Confederate States, United Confederate Veterans," *So. Pract.* 22 (July 1900): 302–3; "The Reunion of Confederate Veterans at Louisville," *So. Pract.* 22 (July 1900): 278–79.

49. Stout, "Address—History," 443; "Some Facts," pt. 1, 22 (November 1900): 523; pt. 3, 23 (February 1901): 98–99; pt. 8, 24 (January 1902): 51; pt. 20, 25 (June 1903): 350. These installments are the articles noted as "Some Facts," and published intermittently from November 1900 to October 1903. There was an error in numbering, the number 21 being omitted, so there are actually only twenty-two articles. The quotation is from "Some Facts," pt. 23, 25 (October 1903): 573.

reunion of the United Confederate Veterans and the Association of Medical Officers of the Army and Navy of the Confederacy.[50] Although Stout recovered sufficiently to write more installments of his series for the *Southern Practitioner*, he never completely regained his strength. When the veterans organizations met in Dallas in 1902, Stout attended and invited the doctors to visit him at his house, but he was not strong enough to accept the presidency of the Association of Medical Officers nor to deliver his address to them. His daughter Katie read the speech for him.[51]

In August 1902 Stout's son Samuel V. D. died in Atlanta, apparently while Maggie and Katie were there to visit and perhaps help during his illness. Stout evidently did not expect the case to be fatal since only two days before the son's death he had encouraged "Sammy" and his wife, Fanny, to move their family to Texas. In June 1903, Stout and his wife, who by this time had been married for fifty-five years, moved with their daughters to Clarendon, Texas, in the panhandle, not far from Amarillo, where the daughters had school teaching jobs. Stout was pleased with his new location. "I am more satisfactorily situated here in Clarendon than I have ever been anywhere in Texas . . . ," Stout wrote to Deering J. Roberts, the editor of the *Southern Practitioner*. "I decline to visit patients, and I now have nothing to do save to work upon my Records, write my 'Narrative,' and to take care of myself. My wife and I have greatly improved in strength and health since we have been here."[52]

But Stout's improvement was only temporary. In mid-August he became ill. While conscious to the end, he gradually weakened to such an extent that he could not read the proofsheets for what became his final *Southern Practitioner* installment. The family realized that the end was near and called Thomas to come from Atlanta to be with his failing father. Samuel Hollingsworth Stout died at 5:30 A.M. on September 18,

50. Stout to Richard Coke, January 26, 189[3], TSLA, box 1, folder 12; Stout, "Some Facts," pt. 3, 23 (February 1901): 99; pt. 6, 23 (June 1901): 294–95.

51. The delegates unanimously elected Stout president but he declined. "Annual Meeting of the Association of Medical Officers of the Army and Navy of the Confederacy," *So. Pract.* 24 (June 1902): 340; (July 1902): 398–99.

52. Stout to Maggie and Katie Stout, August 25, 1902, Lester Fitzhugh Collection, now at Emory. S. V. D. Stout died August 27, 1902, according to the *Atlanta City Directory, 1903*, p. 1154. Stout, "Some Facts," pt. 22, 25 (September 1903): 526; pt. 23 (October 1903): 566; "Obituary: Samuel Hollingsworth Stout, A.M., M.D., LL.D." *So. Pract.* 25 (October 1903): 587, quotes Stout's letter to Roberts.

1903. His family shipped his remains to Dallas where his funeral, with Masonic honors, took place at the First Presbyterian Church at 3:00 P.M. on Sunday, September 20. During the service, representatives of the United Confederate Veterans and the Dallas medical profession delivered tributes to their departed colleague who was then buried in Oakland Cemetery in Dallas.[53]

53. Ibid., p. 586; J.(?) W. Phillips to Mrs. Stout, Maggie, and Katie, September 23, 1903, Emory, box 3, folder 3; "Information for Matriculate Catalogue of the Medical Department of the University of Pennsylvania," filled out by Katie Stout, University of Pennsylvania Archives; unidentified Dallas newspaper clipping, [September 19, 1903], TSLA, box 2, folder 11; [Ferdinand E. Daniel], "Obituary," *Texas Medical Journal* 19 (1903–04): 132; Biographical sketch, probably by Katie Stout, Emory, box 5, folder 2.

EPILOGUE

STOUT'S LEGACY

In the obituary composed for his friend and former superior, Dr. Ferdinand Daniel wrote: "As a man he [Stout] was immensely popular and greatly beloved by all who knew him. A scholar, whose conversation was at all times entertaining and instructive, an optimist who never knew the meaning of the word 'fail,' a companion whose society was a delight and whose geniality and eternal youth were stimulating and inspiring. As father, husband, friend, citizen, physician, teacher,—in every relation of life, he was admirable." D. D. Saunders, in a letter of condolence to Stout's daughter Maggie, remarked that he shared the family's grief because Stout was "one of the finest [purest?], noblest, & most loveable characters it has ever been my good fortune to know. He was honest, earnest, true, intelligent, efficient, and untiring in his official duties as a Confederate officer, loyal & loving as a gentleman & friend."[1] While funerary tributes can tend to be overly effusive, it does seem that Stout retained the respect and appreciation of his colleagues until the end.

Stout accomplished several things in his long and sometimes eventful life. Although a wealthy and well-educated but obscure gentleman farmer and doctor before the war, Stout became one of the Confederacy's premier administrators. He took charge of what, based on the size, the number of hospitals involved, and the continual movement of these hospitals, was undoubtedly the most complex hospital department in the Confederacy. Stout not only took charge of this hospital department but he also demonstrated considerable skill in carrying out his responsibilities. He was particularly adept at personnel management: selecting and assigning subordinates, delegating responsibilities, and handling personal problems and interpersonal relationships. Stout also played the crucial role of an organized middleman, troubleshooter, and contact point between the multitude of hospitals he supervised, which helped to keep these facilities functioning or moving, as necessary. In short, in the

---

1. [Ferdinand E. Daniel], "Obituary," *Texas Medical Journal* 19 (1903–04): 128–30; D. D. Saunders to Margaret Stout, September 28, 1903, Emory, box 3, folder 3.

areas over which Stout had control, his administration of the hospitals was exemplary. True, individual hospitals had problems of various sorts caused by their own particular situations, but solving such problems was an important part of Stout's supervisory task. Stout's excellent management skills could not prevent the collapse of other departments of the Confederacy, however. Difficulties beyond his control in the quartermaster and commissary departments, which led to communication and transportation breakdowns and shortages of supplies, combined to render some of Stout's work ineffective. But the fact remains that in April 1865 Stout's hospitals *could* have moved again, *if* they could have gotten transportation. It is safe to say that without the administrative competence of Stout, or someone like him, in a central role, the hospitals of the Army of Tennessee would have been much less able to care for the floods of patients which inundated their facilities.

With the end of the war Stout lost not only his wealth, but also his position. Tragically for Stout, his administrative skills were no longer necessary anywhere. No organization was large enough to require Stout's ability to manage on a massive scale. In this respect he was ahead of his time.[2] As described by Charles E. Rosenberg, hospitals were relatively small civilian-controlled institutions, unconcerned with treating sudden influxes of patients or moving on short notice. As before the war, hospitals were a place for the indigent or the traveller who became ill. Their goal was to provide a healing environment for persons who could not be cared for at home. Until the early twentieth century, little specialized medical equipment was necessary or available, and the place of choice for medical treatment was the home. The Civil War was an anomaly. Most of the soldiers who crowded into the military hospitals never went near a hospital again. Furthermore, civilian hospitals were not remunerative institutions. Doctors who served in them were poorly paid or not paid at all. They simply used the post to increase their prestige and private patient load or to provide teaching examples for their medical students. There was no place for a nearly destitute Stout in this situation.[3]

---

2. Stout was not alone among former Confederates in his inability to find a satisfactory administrative job. The excellent administrator Josiah Gorgas, head of the Confederate ordnance bureau, also was largely unsuccessful in his postwar business and educational endeavors. Vandiver, *Ploughshares into Swords*, chaps. 20–22.

3. Hospitals, both before and after the Civil War, are described in Rosenberg, *The Care of Strangers*. In this period, trustees, who were not physicians, generally controlled the hospitals.

Given the positions available in the postwar South, a medical school post would probably have utilized Stout's skills best. But, as has been seen, his involvement with the Atlanta Medical College proved to be a dismal failure as a result of personality conflicts in this particular institution. Unfortunately for Stout, he probably had no other medical school option either, because he had no prewar southern medical school connections. While the University of Pennsylvania Medical School provided one of the best medical educations available in the 1840s, it did not give Stout any advantage over young men with southern medical school educations and contacts in the postwar south. Even if Stout had received another medical school offer, he might still have declined it because, as he found in Atlanta, sufficient remuneration for faculty members was not assured.

The major theme of the last thirty-eight years of Stout's life was his constant search for financial security and job satisfaction. Frequently restless, changing occupations and moving several times, Stout still was unable to meet these goals. Often straitened circumstances forced Stout to try some other opportunity before giving his first choice a fair chance because he needed instant funds to support his family and could not wait for potential long-term gains. This incessant search for funds is clearly evident in Stout's brief involvements with the medical school, the Confederate orphan asylum, the textbook sales, and the public schools in Cisco, Texas, among other examples. The only valuable possession Stout had after the war was the 1,500 pounds of hospital records that he had saved. But he seems to have been the only person, at the time, who thought the records of value. Despite all his valiant efforts to find a financially secure position in which he could edit and publish them, he could locate no one willing to fund a medical records project. Ultimately, in his later years, when he wrote about the Civil War, Stout relied on his memory and a few readily available papers, not touching the body of his massive collection.

Stout made major contributions at two points. During the Civil War his administrative skills kept the hospitals of the Army of Tennessee functioning in the midst of situations that would have caused a less determined or competent man to request a transfer to a less responsible position. Stout also realized that, whether the Confederacy won or lost, the records of his post would have historical value, and so he retained these papers past the point of their immediate usefulness. Stout's second contribution, after the war, was to preserve his papers, despite years of frustration and disappointment. In addition, he so imbued his daughters with a sense of the value of the manuscripts that when they could no longer feasibly care for the records, they sold them to collectors and repositories that would preserve the papers, rather than simply throwing them in the trash.

Stout has been briefly mentioned in several works on medical history. John Duffy compares his "initiative and executive ability" to that of Jonathan Letterman, field medical director in the Union Army of the Potomac. Horace Cunningham in *Doctors in Gray* calls Stout "one of the most remarkable medical men of the Civil War." Yet Stout is not mentioned in such basic Civil War reference works as *The Civil War Dictionary* or the *Historical Times Illustrated Encyclopedia of the Civil War*, an omission that may be partly due to a low priority for medical as opposed to military figures, since Confederate Surgeon General Samuel Preston Moore is not included either. Part of Stout's obscurity may be a result, as Richard Harwell suggests, of the defeat of the Confederacy.[4] But part of the problem must be blamed on Stout himself since he refused to permit his papers to be published in the *Official Records* and he was never able to publish the papers himself. Stout does not deserve this obscurity, however, for his administrative activities, as revealed in his papers, made a significant contribution to the Confederate war effort.

---

4. Duffy, *The Healers*, 216; Cunningham, *Doctors in Gray*, 55; Boatner, *The Civil War Dictionary*; Faust, ed., *Historical Times Illustrated Encyclopedia of the Civil War*; Cumming, *Journal*, 71, n. 3.

APPENDIX A

THE DISPERSAL OF STOUT'S PAPERS

Samuel Hollingsworth Stout collected roughly 1,500 pounds of hospital records while serving as a Confederate medical officer. During the remaining thirty-eight years of his life he repeatedly tried to find a job where he would be remunerated for cataloging his papers and writing several sizeable volumes on the medical history of the Army of Tennessee. These attempts all failed. Ultimately Stout used just a few of his papers when he wrote his articles for the *Southern Practitioner*, leaving his huge stash largely untouched when he died in 1903.

Martha Stout did not long survive her husband for she died of typhoid fever in 1904, leaving the papers in the hands of the couple's two youngest children. Margaret (Maggie), born in 1859, and Katherine (Katie), born in 1866, were both unmarried and teaching school in Clarendon, and eventually other small towns, in Texas. They wanted to carry out their father's wishes for the publication and preservation of his records. To that end they corresponded with some of his former associates who were yet members of the Association of Medical Officers of the Army and Navy of the Confederacy, particularly Deering J. Roberts, editor of the *Southern Practitioner*, as well as Samuel E. Lewis and Edwin D. Newton. While all these men wanted to see the papers published and frequently brought the idea up during the annual meetings of the association, no one wished to undertake the massive project personally, nor could any of them afford to underwrite the publication price. The longer publication was deferred, the fewer medical officers were left alive to buy the finished product, and they would, naturally, be its primary audience.[1]

---

1. Obituary from unidentified Giles County, Tennessee, newspaper, TSLA, box 2, folder 11; 1900 Census, Texas, Dallas County, Dallas, roll 1625, vol. 27, E.D. 122, sheet 5, line 14. Deering J. Roberts to Margaret J. Stout, October 18, 1903, Emory, box 3, folder 3; Roberts to Miss Stout, January 20, 1905, Edwin D. Newton to M. Stout,

At last the sisters, seeing that publication was unlikely, were more concerned to relieve themselves of a great burden of space and effort and to put the papers in a safe place. As they also had to support themselves, the sisters proposed to make what money they could from their father's records as well. In 1916 they sold the bulk of the papers to the University of Texas at Austin for $750. Before they gave up the papers, however, the sisters carefully weeded them, removing much of the correspondence, especially of a personal or potentially controversial nature. Although Miss Katie, some years later, suggested that the university had been cheated and did not know it, the persons acquiring the collection were, at the time, aware that the Stouts had removed material from it. While the sisters may indeed have hoped to sell these letters individually at a later time, keeping them as a sort of nest egg perhaps, it is also likely that the sisters had been warned by their father not to allow anything to appear in public that might damage someone's reputation, a concern Stout himself had, at one point, voiced.[2]

Although the Stout sisters did sell some duplicates and other things to private parties during roughly the same period as their transaction with the University of Texas, the next major activity with the papers seems to have begun after the death of Miss Maggie in 1942.[3] Miss Katie had far more material than she could store comfortably in her various residences

---

April 24, 1914, Roberts to M. Stout, May 2, 1914, Samuel E. Lewis to M. and K. Stout, July 8, 1915, Lewis to M. Stout, September 23, 1915, and Roberts to Miss Stout, July 11, 1916, all in Emory, box 3, folder 4; M. Stout to Lewis, September 28, 1915, Va. Hist. Soc.

2. A series of letters pertaining to the sale of the materials, written by Katherine Stout to Dr. E. C. Barker, dated June 12, June 25, July 13, July 28, and August 27, 1914, can be found in UTX, Stout Collection accession file. The account book for the Littlefield Fund for Southern History ("For the full and impartial study of the South and its part in American History," as its special bookplate states) indicates that on July 11, 1916, $750 was paid to Margaret Stout for the "S. H. Stout Collection of Manuscripts." Ralph L. Elder to Glenna R. Schroeder, July 11, 1988. A notation on an envelope in Emory, box 4, folder 14, indicates that the Stout sisters used the money to buy a small house in Lancaster, Texas, the place where Lester Fitzhugh later found the remnants of the Stout Collection. Fitzhugh to Seale Johnson, August 28, 1955, Emory, box 3, folder 6. Stout, "Some Facts," pt. 20, 25 (June 1903): 352; K. Stout to W. E. Thomas, July 28, 1945, Emory, Stout microfilm.

3. K. Stout to Barker, June 25, 1914, UTX, accession file; M. Stout to Lewis, September 28, 1915, Va. Hist. Soc.; K. Stout to President of the State Historical Society [Tennessee], July 6, 1918, TSLA, box 1, folder 1. Until the beginning of World War I, Katie was selling autographs for one dollar each and orders for fifteen or twenty-five cents apiece. K. Stout to Barker, August 27, 1914.

(she moved a good deal, having rented her home in Lancaster), and she was also pinched financially. Having long since ceased to teach, she was subsisting on her earnings from tutoring and selling little articles she had written. She proposed to supplement her meagre income by the sale of her father's remaining papers. Not only did she attempt to sell more items to the University of Texas, particularly manuscripts of her father's writings, but she also developed a regular clientele of collectors across the country. These frequent buyers included W. E. Thomas in Medford, Oregon; Richard D. Steuart in Baltimore, Maryland; Forrest Sweet, a dealer in Michigan; Stanley Horn in Tennessee; and Thomas Spencer of Atlanta, Georgia. Spencer was apparently Miss Katie's largest purchaser. At one point he was sending ten dollars a week for documents. Spencer eventually encountered financial difficulties and sent at least nine hundred items from his collection to John R. Peacock in North Carolina who had the materials microfilmed at Duke University and then sold them to the Abraham Lincoln Bookshop in Chicago. The materials returned south when Emory University Library bought them.[4]

Miss Katie's selling tactics can be traced through her correspondence with W. E. Thomas. Just how she became acquainted with him is not known, but letters survive from August 1942 to April 1950, showing that she sent materials anywhere from three to seven times per year, accompanied by such notes as "I am sending you several papers. Do not hesitate to return any you do not care for. I do not want to impose on good nature." On occasion she would include personal comments about health problems, often as an excuse for not looking up papers for him sooner, and probably also as a none-too-subtle hint that she could use money. Certainly she used illness as a direct plea for money in her correspondence with the University of Texas during the 1950s. As time went on, Miss Katie's eyesight weakened and she found some of the documents, which were written on blue paper, to be illegible. She had to trust Thomas to return anything that might reflect adversely on someone's character. In the end, however, Miss Katie was willing

---

4. Fitzhugh to Johnson, August 28, 1955, Emory, box 3, folder 6; K. Stout to E. W. Winkler, July 8, 1943, UTX, accession file; John R. Peacock to Fitzhugh, October 12, 1955, Fitzhugh Collection; Seale Johnson to Fitzhugh, September 6, 1955, Fitzhugh Collection; Emory, Stout Collection accession file. The persons to whom Miss Katie sold letters were listed in her notebooks which were found by Fitzhugh. Fitzhugh to Bell I. Wiley, September 7, 1955, Emory, box 3, folder 6. Correspondence with W. E. Thomas can be found in Emory, Stout microfilm; with Stanley Horn in TSLA, box 1, folder 1; and with Forrest Sweet in Emory, box 3, folder 5.

to sell anything, and she labeled numerous letters that even hinted that all aspects of the Confederacy did not run smoothly with "Not for publication K.S.M." in shaky blue fountain pen.[5]

Perhaps the most astonishing thing about Miss Katie's later years was her marriage, for the first time, in 1948 at the age of eighty-two. Her husband, Herman Moore, somewhat younger than she, had apparently been a first-grade student of hers in Cisco, Texas, about 1890. She continued to sell her father's papers, apparently without involving her husband in the process. Mr. Moore was quite willing to allow Lester Fitzhugh to go through whatever was left of the papers after her death. Fitzhugh found fourteen letters or fragments of letters that Miss Katie either considered too confidential to sell or was unable to find in the midst of her mess, as well as newspaper clippings, personal letters, memoranda, and a few manuscripts, relating to Stout but not pertaining to the Civil War or anything that Fitzhugh felt was of particular interest.[6]

While Fitzhugh did not find as much material as he had hoped, he was nonetheless excited about the rediscovery of Stout. He corresponded extensively with his friend Seale Johnson, president of McCowat-Mercer Press, Inc. in Jackson, Tennessee, publisher of southern historical materials, and Bell I. Wiley, noted Civil War scholar and Emory University historian, who was also editor for McCowat-Mercer. Fitzhugh hoped to see some work of Stout's published, perhaps an edited reprint of the *Southern Practitioner* series, and wanted to be involved in whatever it might be. By 1956, a year later, Fitzhugh had spent a good deal of time on the Stout project and was beginning to have some doubts. In April 1957, Fitzhugh gave up the endeavor. With considerable effort, involving removing repetitions and rearranging the material to make it

---

5. There are thirty-one letters from K. Stout to Thomas on Emory, Stout microfilm. Specific letters cited are November 4, 1943 and February 27, 1945. K. Stout to Winnie Allen, December 5, 1953 and February 1, 1954, UTX, accession file. K. Stout to Thomas, July 28, 1945 and October 27, 1947, Emory, Stout microfilm. Numerous letters with such markings can be found at TSLA and Emory.
6. Unidentified newspaper clipping attached to K. S. Moore to Thomas, March 30, 1949, also Moore to Thomas, April 4, 1950, both in Emory, Stout microfilm; Fitzhugh to Johnson, August 28, 1955, Emory, box 3, folder 6; Fitzhugh to Peacock, October 14, 1955, Fitzhugh Collection; Fitzhugh to Bell I. Wiley, September 13, 1955, Emory, box 3, folder 6. Some of this miscellaneous material survived in Fitzhugh's possession. He graciously allowed the author to use it, as well as some of his personal correspondence. The Stout material has been donated to Emory and is presently filed as a separate addition to the Stout papers.

more chronological, Fitzhugh had managed to combine the *Southern Practitioner* series and the "Outline" written for Governor Porter into a single account. But he was not satisfied that the production had serious potential as a publication, and he dropped the project.[7]

Over the course of the 1950s, and occasionally later, Stout's papers, which Katie had broadcast, came to rest in various libraries across the country. Most of Thomas Spencer's purchases, as already mentioned, ended up at Emory, with microfilms of much of the material in the Southern Historical Collection at the University of North Carolina at Chapel Hill and at Duke University. The material purchased by Forrest Sweet, or in some cases, a microfilm of it, also entered the Emory collection. At least some of the letters and hospital registers owned by W. E. Thomas were purchased by the University of Texas, Austin. Stanley Horn donated his collection to the Tennessee Historical Society, whose materials are housed at the Tennessee State Library and Archives. Richard D. Steuart apparently died before 1955 and his materials may well be those added to the Museum of the Confederacy's holdings in Richmond, Virginia, in 1952.[8]

While it was commendable that Stout's daughters sold his papers to institutions or persons who would find them of historical or at least collectable interest, the consequent dispersion of the documents has made it difficult for scholars to study the Army of Tennessee hospitals. Because many of the papers were sold as individual pieces, parts of the same story ended up in different repositories, only compounding the researcher's problems. As a result, Stout has received much less credit than he deserves for his important administrative contributions which helped the Confederacy to survive as long as it did.

---

7. Fitzhugh to Johnson, August 25, 1955; letterhead, Johnson to Fitzhugh, May 24, 1955; Fitzhugh to Johnson, September 6, 1956, April 29, 1957, all in Fitzhugh Collection; Fitzhugh to Johnson, August 28, 1955, Emory, box 3, folder 6.

8. The microfilming record at the beginning of the microfilms held by SHC–UNC indicates that the filming was done at Duke. SHC–UNC, reel 4. Records in Emory, Stout accession file dated February 1, 1956 and September 20, 1956 indicate material received from Sweet. The University of Texas purchased a folder of correspondence and some hospital registers from W. E. Thomas in 1959. UTX accession file. Johnson to Fitzhugh, September 1, 1955, quoting a letter from Stanley Horn to Johnson of August 1955. Fitzhugh Collection. The Museum of the Confederacy claims that their accession files are confidential and they refuse to divulge the source of their purchase. Guy R. Swanson to Glenna R. Schroeder, January 24, 1989. The Stout Collection at the Western Reserve Historical Society mainly consists of duplicate materials sold by the Stout sisters in the early twentieth century.

APPENDIX B

BIOGRAPHIES OF SELECTED PHYSICIANS AND MATRONS

Avent, Benjamin W.

Benjamin W. Avent (1813–78) of Murfreesboro, Tennessee, was a well-established practitioner who, despite his previous supervisory position as surgeon general of the Provisional Army of Tennessee, was willing to subordinate himself to Stout. He served as post surgeon at Kingston and elsewhere. Hamer, *The Centennial History of the Tennessee State Medical Association*, 136–38; Stout, "Some Facts," pt. 18, 25 (April 1903): 220; ibid., "Outline," 57, 67–68.

Battey, Robert

An 1857 graduate of the Jefferson Medical College in Philadelphia, Robert Battey (1828–95), a noted doctor of obstetrics and gynecology, was famous for inventing an operation to remove the ovaries. Before heading some of Stout's hospitals Battey had served as a field surgeon. By 1878 he and his wife, the former Martha B. Smith whom he had married in 1849, had had fourteen children. Emory has a Battey Collection (361). Atkinson, ed., *Physicians and Surgeons*, 54–55.

Beers, Fannie

Beers (1840?–*fl* 1888), although Northern-born, became an ardent Southern sympathizer after she married Augustus P. Beers and they moved to New Orleans. When her husband joined the Confederate military, she became a nurse in a Richmond hospital. After recuperation from a serious illness, she became a hospital matron at the Buckner Hospital in the Army of Tennessee and moved with it to a number of locations. During the last winter of the war she nursed soldiers through a smallpox epidemic at a primitive tent hospital in Lauderdale Springs, Mississippi. In 1888 she published her *Memories*.

Bemiss, Samuel Merrifield

Bemiss (1821–84), an 1846 graduate of the medical department of the University of New York, was from Louisville, Kentucky, where he had been a professor of materia medica at the University. According to Ferdinand Daniel, Bemiss joined the Confederate troops when Bragg made his foray into Kentucky, which seems to be supported by two letters of recommendation dated October 11, 1862. Bemiss became a contract surgeon at Tunnel Hill and eventually was invited to appear before the examining board, which he passed as a surgeon. Both matrons Fannie Beers and Kate Cumming worked under Bemiss in the hospitals at Newnan and lauded his character. According to Beers, he "was a general favorite . . . Invariably the whole party brightened up at his coming. He was so genial, so witty, so sympathetic, so entirely *en rapport* with everybody," and a great storyteller besides. Cumming reported that Bemiss was very kind to the patients and constantly concerned that they got enough to eat. Everyone in Newnan was sorry to see Bemiss, a "devoted patriot," as well as "a gentleman and a scholar," leave to take the position as Stout's assistant medical director. Stout had proposed the idea to Bemiss already in August 1863, pending the approval of the surgeon general, but it was not until November that Stout was able to make the offer and Bemiss accepted it. (Stout had offered the position to D. D. Saunders first, as they had worked together at Chattanooga, but Saunders could not accept it for family reasons.) Bemiss remained in this position until the close of the war and afterwards became a professor at the New Orleans Medical School. Atkinson, ed., *Physicians and Surgeons*, 39; Daniel, *Recollections*, 75–77; Robert C. Foster to Stout, B. M. Wible to Stout, both October 11, 1862, Emory, box 1, folder 6; B. M. Wible to D. D. Saunders, December 6, 1862, ibid., folder 8; Beers, *Memories*, 119; Cumming, *Journal*, October 18 and November 13, 1863, 139–40, 153; Stout to Bemiss, August 9, 1863, Va. Hist. Soc., Mss 1D4255d71.

Crawford, George G.

Crawford, a graduate of the Jefferson Medical College in Philadelphia, after a brief stint as a brigade surgeon, transferred to the hospital service in the fall of 1862, due to ill health. He served in Atlanta, as well as Vineville, Georgia; Corinth, Mississippi; and Montgomery, Alabama. After the war he became demonstrator of anatomy at the Atlanta Medical College. Fulton Co., *Report of the Delegate*, 97; Garrett, *Atlanta and Environs*, 1:684.

Cumming, Kate

Although born in Scotland, Kate Cumming (1835–1909) immigrated with her family to Mobile, Alabama, when she was quite young. Despite the objections of family and friends, Cumming became involved in nursing wounded Confederates in the spring of 1862 after the Battle of Shiloh. By that fall she was serving as a hospital matron with the Army of Tennessee. Over the course of the war she migrated a great deal with the hospitals. After the war she published her *Journal* in 1866 and a watered down version, *Gleanings from Southland*, in 1895. Cumming, *Journal*; Faust, ed., *Historical Times Illustrated Encyclopedia of the Civil War*.

Daniel, Ferdinand Eugene

The surgeon who helped Stout a great deal with his administrative setup, although not actually until after the Battle of Perryville (October 8, 1862), was Ferdinand Eugene Daniel (1839–1914). A medical student who had not yet finished his coursework when the war broke out, Daniel joined the Eighteenth Mississippi Infantry as a private and was present at First Manassas. Thanks to Jefferson Davis's proclamation releasing all medical students from the ranks, Daniel was able to graduate from the New Orleans School of Medicine just before the Federals captured the city. On July 8, 1862, Daniel appeared before the examining board at Tupelo, Mississippi, with unusual results for a recent graduate who was not quite twenty-three. The board passed Daniel as a surgeon, not an assistant surgeon, and, because he had beautiful penmanship, assigned him to serve as secretary of the board. Daniel then worked with Stout in Chattanooga. He wanted more experience with sick and wounded soldiers, however, and so he served in hospitals in Resaca, Marietta, Kingston, Covington, and Macon, Georgia, as well as Lauderdale Springs, Mississippi. After the war Daniel moved to Texas where he helped to found and taught at the state's first medical school. He also edited two publications, the *Texas Courier—Record of Medicine* and the

Texas Medical Journal, for which Stout wrote a number of articles. Daniel and Stout remained friends until Stout's death. In 1899 Daniel published his war reminiscences, *Recollections of a Rebel Surgeon*, which recounts a number of amusing stories as well as useful information about his career and the hospital service. See also "Obituary" [Ferdinand Eugene Daniel], *So. Pract.* 36 (July 1914): 306–8; Stout, "Some Facts," pt. 20, 25 (June 1903): 354–55; Daniel to Stout, February 11, 1903, TSLA, no box and folder number.

Flewellen, Edward Archelaus

Flewellen (1819–1911), a Georgia native, graduated from the Jefferson Medical College in Philadelphia in 1851. He received his commission as surgeon of the Fifth Georgia Regiment and from there moved to hospital administration in LaGrange, Tennessee, in April 1862. In June 1862, Flewellen became Foard's assistant medical director and he spent most of 1863 as medical director for Bragg's army. Later in the war Flewellen again assisted Foard and also served as a hospital inspector. In this role he inspected the hospital at Andersonville, but no report seems to survive. After the war he was active in railroad and state and local government positions. "E. A. Flewellen, M.D.," *So. Pract.* 24 (April 1902): 207, 209; [Obituary] "Dr. E. A. Flewellen," *Confederate Veteran* 20 (January 1912): 33; Special Orders No. 45, by Beauregard, April 29, 1862, N A, Flewellen file; Special Orders No. 97, T. H. Jordan, June 28, 1862, UTX, box 2G421; Flewellen to S. P. Moore, January 9, 1863, N A, chap. 6, vol. 748; Flewellen to Stout, August 16, 1864, Emory, box 2, folder 16; E. A. Flewellen to W. J. W. Kerr, June 4, 1903 in *So. Pract.* 25 (July 1903): 420; *The Trial of Henry Wirz*. Flewellen testified on September 26 and 28, 1865, pp. 422–23, 471–78.

Foard, Andrew Jackson

Andrew Jackson Foard was born in Milledgeville, Georgia, about 1829. He graduated from the Jefferson Medical College in Philadelphia, and served as an assistant surgeon in the United States Army from May 11, 1853 until he resigned on April 1, 1861, to become a Confederate surgeon. Foard's first assignment was that of medical director for General Braxton Bragg's troops near Pensacola, Florida. In this position he seems to have thoroughly organized Bragg's medical department. When Bragg became commander of the Army of Tennessee, he appointed Foard his medical director, a position Foard held until December 1862 when he became medical director for General Joseph E. Johnston's new and rather anomalous Department of the West which was supposed to supervise Bragg's army as well as that of General John C. Pemberton near Vicksburg. Most of Foard's duties here pertained to hospital inspection. In November 1863 Foard was again named medical director of the Army of Tennessee, a position he assumed in February 1864 and held until the end of the war, serving under Johnston and also John Bell Hood. After the surrender, Foard, as the result of long-term urging by one of his medical colleagues, unsuccessfully attempted to set up a private practice in Columbus, Georgia. Ill health cut short Foard's next endeavor as professor of anatomy at Washington University in Baltimore. He died, apparently of tuberculosis, in Charleston, South Carolina, on March 8, 1868. Stout, "Some Facts," pt. 9, 24 (February 1902): 106–8; William H. Powell, comp., *List of Officers of the Army of the United States from 1779–1900* (New York: L. R. Hamersly and Co., 1900), 312; "The Late Dr. A. J. Foard," undated clipping with notation by Katherine Stout Moore that it was from a Nashville paper of May 18, 1868, TSLA, box 1, folder 14; Braxton Bragg, "Report on Bombardment of Pensacola," December 4, 1861, *OR*, series 1, v. 6: 489–93; Braxton Bragg, General Orders No. 159, December 23, 1862, Emory, Stout microfilm; Braxton Bragg, Special Orders No. 1, January 6, 1863, TSLA, box 2, folder 4 and A. J. Foard military service file, N A; John Withers, A. A. Genl. by command of Secretary of War, Special Orders No. 282, November 17, 1863, ch. 6, vol. 748, N A; Foard to Stout, October 25, 1866, Emory, box 2, folder 24, also SHC–UNC, Stout microfilm, reel 2.

Hawthorn, Frank

Frank Hawthorn (1835-76), a native of Alabama, graduated with a medical degree from the University of Louisiana shortly before the Civil War. Enlisted as a private in the Tenth Alabama Infantry, serving at Pensacola, Hawthorn performed a skillful emergency operation on the foot of a wounded private while all the regimental surgeons were away fishing. Foard immediately appointed Hawthorn assistant surgeon, and he soon passed the board as a surgeon. Once in charge of the Academy Hospital, Hawthorn moved with it to Marietta, Georgia, and then Auburn, Alabama. While with his hospital following Hood's march into Tennessee in the fall of 1864, Hawthorn suffered a physical breakdown

from overwork and scurvy, which threatened his eyesight and made him
a patient of Bolling A. Pope in the eye ward in Americus. Stout called
him a "rigid disciplinarian" who was sympathetic to the common soldier,
but Cumming thought that he was "not a humane man" when she
heard about the harsh punishments, such as bucking and gagging, that
Hawthorn meted out to offenders. After the war Hawthorn taught at the
University of Louisiana and died of Bright's Disease. Donald, "Alabama
Confederate Hospitals," (pt. 2), 73; Register of Medical Officers, TSLA,
box 2, folder 1; Daniel, *Recollections of a Rebel Surgeon*, 254–55; D. D.
Saunders to S. M. Bemiss, December 8, 1864, UTX, box 2G404; Stout,
"Some Facts," pt. 22, 25 (September 1903): 524–26; pt. 23, 25 (October
1903): 566–67; Cumming, *Journal*, 93–94.

Hillyer, Eben

Hillyer (b. 1832), a general practitioner and eye specialist in Rome,
Georgia, who had graduated from the Jefferson Medical College in
Philadelphia, seems to have served in Stout's hospitals temporarily as
a contract surgeon in early 1864 and then been commissioned and sent
to the field where he served with Mississippi regiments in Cleburne's
division. After the war he taught at the Atlanta Medical College. Eben
Hillyer to Stout, January 24, 1864, UTX, box 2G402; Jones, "Roster of
the Medical Officers," 214; Atkinson, ed., *Physicians and Surgeons*, 397.

Logan, Joseph Payne

Virginia-born Joseph Payne Logan (1820–91) became one of Stout's
most trusted subordinates. He graduated from the University of Pennsylvania medical school in 1841 and practiced in Virginia and Baltimore,
Maryland, before he moved to Atlanta in 1854, where he supplemented
his medical practice with involvement in antebellum politics. He was one
of the five Atlanta delegates elected to attend the Confederate Congress
in January 1861 to press Atlanta's claim as a potential Confederate capital. With his Atlanta background, Logan was a good choice for surgeon
in charge of the city's hospitals, a position to which he was assigned in
June 1862. In February 1863 Logan received orders to report to Stout.
Logan's position was no sinecure. In November 1863, for example, he
was supervising thirty-nine medical officers who were working in ten
hospitals. With the evacuation of Atlanta, Logan took charge of hospitals

in Augusta. After the war Logan taught at the Atlanta Medical College, helped organize the Atlanta public school system, and served on the City Board of Health. Atkinson, ed., *Physicians and Surgeons*, 685; Garrett, "Historic Oakland Cemetery," 52; Garrett, *Atlanta and Environs*, vol. 1: 510, 684, 859, vol. 2: 246; Special Order No. 133, A&IGO, Richmond, June 10, 1862, UTX, box 2G380; E. A. Flewellen to Logan, February 17, 1863, NA, chap. 6, vol. 749; L. T. Pim, [Report on inspection of hospitals at Atlanta, November 8, 1863], November 24, 1863, Mus. Confed. ST–6–1; Logan to Stout, August 17, 1864, Emory, box 2, folder 16; *Hanleiter's Atlanta City Directory for 1871*, 46; Atlanta Board of Education Minutes, December 23, 1869, Atlanta Public Schools Archives; Fulton Co., *Report of the Delegate*.

Moore, Samuel Preston

Charleston, South Carolina, native Samuel P. Moore (1813–89) graduated from the Medical College of South Carolina in 1834. He was commissioned an assistant surgeon in the United States Army in 1835 and promoted to surgeon in 1849. During his military career Moore served at posts in Missouri, Kansas, Florida, Texas, Wyoming Territory, New York, Mexico, and Louisiana. When the latter state seceded, Moore resigned his assignment as medical purveyor in New Orleans and moved to Little Rock, Arkansas, where he intended to establish a private practice. Moore accepted the appointment as Confederate surgeon general with reluctance, and held the post from July 31, 1861, until the end of the war. His personal papers were apparently destroyed when Richmond burned. After the war he remained in the city but became involved with education, rather than returning to the practice of medicine. Lewis, "Samuel Preston Moore, M.D.," 380–86; Cunningham, *Doctors in Gray*, 30–31, 271.

O'Keefe, Daniel C.

Daniel C. O'Keefe (1827–71), a native of Ireland and graduate of the Medical College of Georgia (Augusta), had practiced in Georgia and Tennessee before moving to Atlanta about 1857 or 1858. During the war O'Keefe served hospitals in Atlanta and elsewhere. Logan characterized O'Keefe as "A very reliable physician & Surgeon. Unassuming and of

Sterling Merit, good business talent. His hospital not so neat as desirable." After the war O'Keefe taught at the Atlanta Medical College and helped to found the Atlanta public school system. Logan, "Confidential Report," Mus. Confed., no number; Garrett, *Atlanta and Environs*, 1: 684, 822.

Powell, Thomas Spencer

Thomas S. Powell (1824–95), a native of Virginia, practiced in Sparta, Georgia. His influence was instrumental in persuading the state legislature to pass a bill giving the new Atlanta Medical College $15,000. In September 1857 Powell spoke at the school's graduation on "The Moral Duties of a Physician," so impressing the faculty and trustees that they invited him to join the faculty. During the war, Powell remained in Atlanta and in 1864 he volunteered his services temporarily, without desiring compensation. No record indicates whether Stout accepted his services. After his controversy with the Atlanta Medical College, Powell founded his own rival Southern Medical College in 1879. Garrett, *Atlanta and Environs*, 1: 431–32, 955–56; Fulton Co., *Report of the Delegate*, 19–20; J. P. Logan to Stout, August 4, 1864, Emory, box 2, folder 15.

Richardson, Tobias G.

Richardson (1827–92) was formerly assistant (field) medical director of the Army of Tennessee, in which capacity he amputated Gen. John Bell Hood's leg at Chickamauga. He went to Richmond with Bragg, when the general was assigned there, and became a medical inspector. After the war Richardson had a successful career as a professor at the University of Louisiana Medical School, beginning in late 1865. Jones, "Roster of the Medical Officers," 251–52; E. A. Flewellen to S. P. Moore, May 2, 1863, NA, chap. 6, vol. 748; Richardson to Doctor [probably Stout], December 3, 1863, UTX, box 2G398; University of Louisiana Medical School advertisement, *New Orleans Daily Picayune*, December 21, 1865; Gross and Gross, eds., *Autobiography*, 2: 110.

Saunders, Dudley Dunn

Saunders (1835–1908) was a native of Alabama who read medicine in Mobile and then graduated in medicine from both the University of New

York and the University of Pennsylvania in 1856. After interning in New York and spending three years in European hospitals, Saunders joined the faculty of the Memphis Medical College. Commissioned a Confederate surgeon in April 1862, Saunders was one of the best prepared medical officers in the Army of Tennessee. Saunders began working with Stout October 30, 1862. Although they had never met before that date, Stout reminisced that Saunders "never failed in helpfulness to me officially or personally; I, from the beginning of our official intercourse, regarded him as almost my *alter ego*, in whose presence I did not hesitate to speak, and, as it were, to think aloud." Stout put Saunders in many responsible positions during the war, including surgeon in charge of hospitals at Marietta after the evacuation of Chattanooga, and the head of the reserve surgical corps of hospital surgeons who rushed to the field during a battle. After the war Saunders returned to Memphis where he was active in the Tennessee Medical Association and later the Association of Medical Officers of the Army and Navy of the Confederacy. Stout, "Some Facts," pt. 20, 25 (June 1903): 356–59; "Dr. D. D. Saunders," *So. Pract.* 23 (July 1901): 333; Hamer, *The Centennial History of the Tennessee State Medical Association*, 195.

Smith, S. A.

Medical director for Edmund Kirby Smith and the troops of the Department of East Tennessee in 1862, Smith had been a wealthy planter in Alexandria, Louisiana, and made many financial sacrifices for the Confederacy, according to Stout. By the fall of 1864, S. A. Smith was a medical director of hospitals, headquartered in Alexandria, Louisiana. Stout, "Some Facts," pt. 13, 24 (November 1902): 625; Cunningham, *Doctors in Gray*, 285.

Thornton, Francis

Thornton seems to have been post surgeon at Ringgold July-December 1862. In this position he apparently had difficulties with some of the citizens of the town, which may have led to his assignment to Chattanooga where he became surgeon in charge at the Newsom Hospital and then at the Foard Hospital. On May 30, 1863, Dr. Thornton was murdered by two drunken attendants ("Irishmen," says Cumming) from the Newsom Hospital, either because he refused to give them whiskey or because one nursed a grudge after being punished for insubordination. This is the only case of this nature so far discovered. Register of Medical Officers, TSLA, box 2, folder 1; William L. McAllister to Foard, December 30, 1862, and Frank Hawthorn to Stout, January 5, 1863, Emory, box 1, folder 10, also SHC–UNC, reel 2; Thornton to Stout, March 14, 1863, TSLA, box 1, folder 9; Cumming, *Journal*, May 31, 1863, p. 95; Beers, *Memories*, 86–87.

Westmoreland, John G.

John G. Westmoreland (1816–87) received his degree from the Medical College of Georgia and practiced in several small communities in the state before moving to Atlanta. In 1857–58 he served in the Georgia House of Representatives. He was not a member of the Confederate medical corps, but was apparently a private in the army. Garrett, *Atlanta and Environs*, 1: 376–77; Atkinson, ed., *Physicians and Surgeons*, 542.

Westmoreland, Willis F.

W. F. Westmoreland (1828–90), an 1850 graduate of the Jefferson Medical College in Philadelphia, also studied medicine in Europe. He served in the Medical College Hospital in Atlanta and other places to which it migrated during the war. J. P. Logan described him as an "eminently skilful Surgeon—utterly regardless of regulations but faithful and attentive to his patients. The most provokingly careless man I *ever* knew." Atkinson, ed., *Physicians and Surgeons*, 467; Jones, "Roster of the Medical Officers," 268; J. P. Logan, "Confidential Report in Regard to Merits of Medical Officers, Atlanta April 1864," Mus. Confed., no number; Garrett, *Atlanta and Environs*, 2: 224.

Yandell, David Wendel

Yandell (1826–98) was a part of the third generation of a family that ultimately had six generations of physicians. His father, Lunsford Pitts Yandell, was one of the founders of the Louisville Medical Institute, where David was educated. He was particularly influenced by the professor of surgery, Samuel David Gross, apparently a "fanatic" for cleanliness because he held the belief, unusual at the time, that there was something yet unknown on a surgeon's hands and instruments that spread infections and caused many surgical patients to die. Yandell was interested in medical education and taught in Louisville both before and after the war. His first wartime position was on the staff of Gen. Simon Bolivar Buckner, a former Louisville neighbor, at Bowling Green. In mid-October 1861 he assumed his position with Gen. Albert Sidney Johnston. Although Yandell had been with Johnston on the battlefield at Shiloh, the general had left his medical director behind to care for some unattended wounded. Ironically, Yandell had given tourniquets to all the members of Johnston's staff and the general had one in his pocket when he died, but no one knew how to use it. After Johnston's death, Yandell became medical director of Gen. Hardee's corps since Gen. Braxton Bragg brought his own medical director, A. J. Foard, when he assumed command of the Army of Tennessee. Stout suggests that if Yandell had had as much time to organize the hospitals as his successor Foard did, he might have been equally successful. Eventually, Yandell became medical director for Joseph E. Johnston during the Vicksburg campaign. Unfortunately, some private correspondence of Yandell's, in which he defended Johnston and criticized Jefferson Davis, was published and the irate Davis "banished" Yandell to the Trans-Mississippi Department in November 1863, to keep him from causing further trouble. After the war Yandell returned to teaching in Louisville and edited a medical journal. In his later years he suffered from arteriosclerosis and a stroke. Baird, *David Wendel Yandell*, 1–2, 4, 12–13, 25–26, 30, 35–37, 48, 50–56, 85–86, 103–4; Stout, "Some Facts," pt. 7, 23 (December 1901): 587–88; pt. 8, 24 (January 1902): 53–54; "Outline," 61.

APPENDIX C

THE LOCATIONS OF STOUT'S HOSPITALS

Four sample lists show the changing locations of Stout's hospitals.

November 17, 1862

    Chattanooga, Tennessee
    Cleveland
    Tunnel Hill, Georgia
    Catoosa Springs
    Ringgold
    Dalton
(Stout to Sir, November 17, 1862, Emory, box 1, folder 7)

October 5, 1863 (after Chickamauga)

    Ringgold, Georgia—receiving and distributing only
    Dalton—receiving and distributing only
    Kingston
    Rome
    Cassville
    Marietta
    Atlanta
    Newnan
    LaGrange
    Griffin
    Forsyth
(OR, series 1, vol. 30, pt. 4, pp. 736–38)

July 1864 (during the Atlanta Campaign)

Macon, Georgia
Vineville
Columbus
Augusta
Griffin
Forsyth
Barnesville
Thomaston
LaGrange
Newnan
Covington
West Point
Fort Gaines
Greensboro
Athens
Milledgeville
Atlanta
Montgomery, Alabama
Auburn
Eufaula
Notasulga
(List, July 1864, UTX, box 2G379)

February 24, 1865 (after Sherman's troops had left Georgia and Hood's remaining troops had returned from Tennessee)

Milledgeville, Georgia
Macon
Columbus
Albany
Americus
Cuthbert
West Point
Geneva
Atlanta
Fort Valley
Auburn, Alabama

Montgomery
Opelika
Eufaula
Notasulga
(Consolidated morning report, February 24, 1865, UTX, box 2G395)

BIBLIOGRAPHY

PUBLISHED WORKS BY STOUT (chronological)

An Address, Introductory to the Eighth Regular Summer Course of Lectures in the Atlanta Medical College. Atlanta: J. J. Toon, 1866.

"List of Confederate Dead, Dept. of Alabama and West Florida, for Quarter Ending Sept 30, 1861." *Atlanta Medical and Surgical Journal* 7 (October 1866): 381–84.

"Statement of Deaths of Confederate Soldiers at and Near Pensacola, Florida, for Quarter Ending Dec. 31, 1861." *Atlanta Medical and Surgical Journal* 7 (November 1866): 429–32.

"Letter." *Richmond and Louisville Medical Journal* 14 (September 1872): 360–61.

"Psoriasis: Non-Syphilitica, Popularly Known in a Variety of forms as Tetter." *Transactions of the Medical Association of Georgia,* n.d.; reprint ed., Atlanta: Jas. P. Harrison & Co., n.d. [probably 1870s as Stout was living in Roswell].

"Report of the Section on Gynecology for the Seventh Congressional District." *Transactions of the Medical Association of Georgia* 32 (1881): 151–90.

"Dysmenorrhoea." *Transactions of the Medical Association of Georgia* 32 (1881): 166–72.

"Puerperal Convulsions." *Transactions of the Medical Association of Georgia* 32 (1881): 172–90.

"The Clinical Importance of Abnormities of the Mucous Membrane." *Texas Courier—Record of Medicine* 1 (December 1883): 5–12.

"Continued fevers." *Transactions of the Texas Medical Association* 16 (1884): 66–84.

"Salicylate of Soda in Septic Poisoning." *Texas Courier—Record of Medicine* 1 (January 1884): 11–13.

"Catarrhal fever." *Texas Courier—Record of Medicine* 1 (February 1884): 5–11.

"Clinical Lectures from the Standpoint of the Private Practitioner: Prefatory and Influenza." *Texas Courier—Record of Medicine* 1 (March 1884): 26–31.

"Correction." *Texas Courier—Record of Medicine* 1 (March 1884): 61–62.

"Iodide of Potassium in Syphilitic Epilepsy and Paralysis." *Texas Courier—Record of Medicine* 1 (April 1884): 27–29.

"Clinical Lectures from the Standpoint of the Private Practitioner: Influenza." [continued] *Texas Courier—Record of Medicine* 1 (May 1884): 23–28.

"Clinical Lectures from the Standpoint of the Private Practitioner: Sayre's Plaster of Paris Jacket." *Texas Courier—Record of Medicine* 1 (July 1884): 7–12.

"Clinical Lectures from the Standpoint of the Private Practitioner: Asiatic Cholera." *Texas Courier—Record of Medicine* 2 (October 1884): 89–96.

"Clinical Lectures from the Standpoint of the Private Practitioner: Treatment of Influenza and Bad Colds, etc." *Texas Courier—Record of Medicine* 2 (December 1884): 206–14.

"Observations of the Influence of the Climate, and Modes of Living of the People of Northwestern Texas, in the Production and Modification of Disease." *Transactions of the Texas Medical Association* 17 (1885): 95–111.

"Infantile Diarrhoea." *Texas Courier—Record of Medicine* 3 (September 1885): 691–701.

"A Case of Abnormal Reproduction." *Texas Courier—Record of Medicine* 3 (December 1885): 133–35.

"The Prophylaxis of Smallpox." *Transactions of the Texas State Medical Association* 18 (1886): 100–115.

"Abortion; From the Stand-point of Personal Experience." *Daniel's Texas Medical Journal* 2 (1886–87): 221–26.

"The Management of the Third Stage of Labor; From the Standpoint of Personal Experience." *Transactions of the Texas State Medical Association* 19 (1887): 213–22.

"On the Best Models and Most Easily Constructed Military Hospital Wards for Temporary Use in the War." *Transactions of the International Medical Congress* 9th session, vol. 2 (1887): 88–91.

"Transportation of the Sick and Wounded of Armies on Land." *Transactions of the International Medical Congress* 9th session, vol. 2 (1887): 64–65.

"Puerperal Convulsions." *Daniel's Texas Medical Journal* 5 (April 1890): 365–76.

"Reminiscences of the Services of Medical Officers of the Confederate Army and Department of Tennessee." *St. Louis Medical and Surgical Journal* 64 (April 1893): 225–36.

"Ethical Relationship of the Medical Profession and Life Insurance Companies." *Texas Medical Journal* 9 (1893–94): 493–97.

"David Crockett: The Pioneer Statesman, Hero and Martyr." *Ellis County Mirror* (Waxahachie, Tex.), beginning February 27, 1894, running four or five weeks.

"Days of Long Ago." *Pulaski Citizen,* August 9 and 16, 1894.

"Tributes to Gen. Braxton Bragg." *Confederate Veteran* 3 (May 1895): 132–33.

"Buttons Made in the Confederacy." *Confederate Veteran* 5 (June 1897): 246.

["An Incident of the War."] *Confederate Veteran* 6 (January 1898): 18.

[Two funny stories.] *Confederate Veteran* 6 (January 1898): 37–38.

"Small-pox; Its Successful Abortion and Treatment as Originally Suggested and Adopted by Dr. Thomas Crutcher Osborn, of Cleburne, Texas." *Southern Practitioner* 22 (April 1900): 146–56.

"Some Facts of the History of the Organization of the Medical Service of the Confederate Armies and Hospitals." Parts 1–23 *Southern Practitioner* 22–25 (November 1900–October 1903).

"Small pox—the Osborn Treatment—Biographical Sketch of the Author, Thomas Crutcher Osborn, M. D." *Southern Practitioner* 23 (January 1901): 7–17.

"An Address: Concerning the History of the Medical Service in the Field and Hospitals of the Army and Department of Tennessee." *Southern Practitioner* 24 (August 1902): 434–54.

[Book Review of *Two Wars: An Autobiography* by Gen. S. G. French.] *Confederate Veteran* 11 (May 1903): 235–36.

"Confederate History." *Confederate Veteran* 11 (October 1903): 462–63.

Reminiscences of General Braxton Bragg. Hattiesburg, Miss.: The Book Farm, 1942.

"Outline of the Organization of the Medical Department of the Confederate Army and Department of Tennessee." Edited by Sam L. Clark and H. D. Riley, Jr. *Tennessee Historical Quarterly* 16 (March 1957): 55–82.

MANUSCRIPT COLLECTIONS

Atlanta, Ga. Atlanta Historical Society.
  Samuel H. Stout Papers. Collection 342f.
Atlanta, Ga. Atlanta Public Schools Archives.
  Atlanta Board of Education Minutes.
Atlanta, Ga. Special Collections. Robert W. Woodruff Library, Emory University.
  Emory University Archives.
  Samuel H. Stout Papers. Collection 274.
Austin, Tex. Eugene C. Barker Texas History Center. University of Texas.
  Samuel H. Stout Papers.
Chapel Hill, N. C. Southern Historical Collection. University of North Carolina.
  Samuel H. Stout microfilm collection.
Cleveland, Ohio. Western Reserve Historical Society.
  Samuel H. Stout Papers.
Durham, N. C. William R. Perkins Library. Duke University.
  Samuel H. Stout Papers.
Lancaster, Tex. Lester N. Fitzhugh Private Collection.
Nashville, Tenn. Tennessee State Library and Archives.
  Samuel H. Stout Papers. Collection THS 39. (Also available on microfilm)
New Orleans, La. Howard-Tilton Memorial Library. Tulane University.
  Joseph Jones Collection.
Philadelphia, Pa. University of Pennsylvania Archives.
  Samuel H. Stout biographical file.
Richmond, Va. Virginia Historical Society.
  Samuel H. Stout Papers.
Richmond, Va. Eleanor S. Brockenbrough Library, Museum of the Confederacy.
  Samuel H. Stout Papers.
Savannah, Ga. Georgia Historical Society.
  Samuel H. Stout Papers. Collection 764.

Washington, D. C. National Archives.
  Record Group 48. Office of Secretary of the Interior.
  Record Group 109. War Department Collection of Confederate Records.

PUBLISHED PRIMARY OR CONTEMPORARY SOURCES

Alcott, Louisa May. *Hospital Sketches*. 1869. Reprint. Boston: Applewood Books, 1986.
"Annual Meeting of the Association of Surgeons of the Confederate States, United Confederate Veterans." *Southern Practitioner* 22 (July 1900): 289–312.
"Annual Meeting of the Association of Medical Officers of the Army and Navy of the Confederacy." *Southern Practitioner* 24 (June 1902): 333–42; (July 1902): 397–403.
"Annual Meeting of the Association of Medical Officers of the Army and Navy of the Confederacy." *Southern Practitioner* 26 (August 1904): 483–507; (September 1904): 550–68.
Atkinson, William B., ed. *The Physicians and Surgeons of the United States*. Philadelphia: Charles Robson, 1878.
Atlanta City Directory. 1870–1918. Various publishers.
Beers, Fannie A. *Memories: A Recollection of Personal Experiences During Four Years of War*. Philadelphia: J. B. Lippincott, 1889.
Bratton, J. R. "Letter of a Confederate Surgeon on Sherman's Occupation of Milledgeville." *Georgia Historical Quarterly* 32 (September 1948): 231–32.
Braun, Herman A. *Andersonville, An Object Lesson on Protection*. Milwaukee: C. D. Fahsel, 1892.
Chancellor, Charles W. "A Memoir of the Late Samuel Preston Moore, M.D., Surgeon General of the Confederate States Army." *Southern Practitioner* 25 (November 1903): 634–42.
Confederate States Medical and Surgical Journal. Richmond, Va., 1864–65. Reprint. Metuchen, N.J.: Scarecrow Press, 1976.
Cumming, Kate. *The Journal of Kate Cumming, A Confederate Nurse, 1862–1865*. Edited by Richard Harwell. Baton Rouge: Louisiana State University Press, 1959. Reprint. Savannah: Beehive Press, 1975. Originally published as *A Journal of Hospital Life in the Confederate Army of Tennessee from the Battle of Shiloh to the End of the War: With Sketches of Life and Character, and Brief Notices of Current Events During That Period*. Louisville: John P. Morton & Co., 1866.
Cummings, C. C. "Story of R. E. Lee Camp, Fort Worth, Texas." *Confederate Veteran* 17 (December 1909): 585–86.
The Cyclopaedia of Practical Medicine. Philadelphia: Lea and Blanchard, 1848.
[Daniel, Ferdinand E.] "Obituary" [Samuel Hollingsworth Stout.] *Texas Medical Journal* 19 (1903–4): 128–32.

Daniel, F[erdinand] E. *Recollections of a Rebel Surgeon*. Austin: von Boeckmann, Schutze & Co., 1899.

Daniell, Lewis E. *Types of Successful Men*. Austin: E. von Boeckmann, 1890.

"Death of Dr. Preston B. Scott." *Southern Practitioner* 22 (October 1900): 463–66.

"Dr. D. D. Saunders." *Southern Practitioner* 23 (July 1901): 332–33.

"Dr. S. H. Stout." *Ellis County Mirror* (Waxahachie, Tex.), January 24, 1894.

"E. A. Flewellen." *Southern Practitioner* 24 (April 1902): 207–9.

Evans, Clement A., ed. *Confederate Military History*. Vol. 11. Atlanta: Confederate Publishing Co., 1899.

Fulton County Medical Society. *Report of the Delegate of the Fulton County Medical Society*. Atlanta: J. J. Toon, 1871.

Gholson, S. C. "Recollections of My First Six Months in the Confederate Army." *Southern Practitioner* 27 (January 1905): 32–43.

Gross, Albert Haller, and Samuel Weissell Gross, eds. *Autobiography of Samuel David Gross, M. D.* 2 vols. Philadelphia: W. B. Saunders, 1887.

Jones, Joseph. "Roster of the Medical Officers of the Army of Tennessee. During the Civil War Between the Northern and Southern States, 1861–1865. Consolidated from the Original Medical Director's Records." *Southern Historical Society Papers* 22 (1894): 165–280.

Lane, Alex G. "The Winder Hospital, of Richmond, Virginia." *Southern Practitioner* 26 (January 1904): 35–41.

Lane, Miles, ed. *"Dear Mother: Don't Grieve About Me. If I Get Killed, I'll Only Be Dead." Letters from Georgia Soldiers in the Civil War*. Savannah: Beehive Press, 1977.

Langston, Mrs. George. [Obituary] "Mrs. S. H. Stout." *Confederate Veteran* 12 (October 1904): 499.

Lewis, Samuel E. "Samuel Preston Moore, M. D., Surgeon General of the Confederate States." *Southern Practitioner* 23 (August 1901): 380–86.

Medical and Surgical Register of the United States. 2nd ed. Detroit: R. L. Polk & Co., 1890.

Newton, Edwin D. "My Recollections and Reminiscences." *Southern Practitioner* 30 (October 1908): 474–89.

"Obituary." [Ferdinand Eugene Daniel.] *Southern Practitioner* 36 (July 1914): 306–8.

[Obituary] "Dr. E. A. Flewellen." *Confederate Veteran* 20 (January 1912): 33.

"Obituary: Samuel Hollingsworth Stout, A.M., M.D., L.L.D." *Southern Practitioner* 25 (October 1903): 586–87.

[Obituary] "Samuel Hollingsworth Stout." *Confederate Veteran* 11 (November 1903): 518.

"Obituary." [Samuel Hollingsworth Stout] *Journal of the American Medical Association* 41 (1903): 865.

[Obituary] "Thomas Edward Stout." *Confederate Veteran* 28 (November 1920): 429.

Official Register of the United States, Containing a List of the Officers and Employees in the Civil, Military, and Naval Service. Washington: Government Printing Office, 1895.

Osborn, George C., ed. "Civil War Letters of Robert W. Banks: Atlanta Campaign." *Georgia Historical Quarterly* 27 (June 1943): 208–16.

Pember, Phoebe Yates. *A Southern Woman's Story: Life in Confederate Richmond.* Edited by Bell I. Wiley. Atlanta: Mockingbird Books, 1959.

Regulations for the Medical Department of the Confederate States Army. Richmond: Richie & Dunnavant, 1863.

Report of the Committee on Public Schools, to the City Council of Atlanta, Georgia. Atlanta: Economical Book & Job Printing House, 1869.

"The Reunion of Confederate Veterans at Louisville." *Southern Practitioner* 22 (July 1900): 278–79.

"Samuel Hollingsworth Stout, A.M., M.D., LL.D." *Southern Practitioner* 24 (April 1902): 209–12.

Smith, Mrs. S. E. D. *The Soldier's Friend: Being a Thrilling Narrative of Grandma Smith's Four Years Experience and Observation, as Matron, in the Hospitals of the South . . .* Memphis: Bulletin Publishing Co., 1867.

Stout, Margaret J. "Correspondence." *Southern Practitioner* 32 (September 1910): 461–63.

Tebault, C. H. "History of the 'Association of Medical Officers of the Army and Navy of the Confederacy.'" *Southern Practitioner* 32 (August 1910): 397–406.

———. "Hospitals of the Confederacy." *Southern Practitioner* 24 (September 1902): 499–509.

Thomas, J. *A Comprehensive Medical Dictionary.* Philadelphia: J. B. Lippincott & Co., 1872.

The Trial of Henry Wirz. 40th Congress, 2nd Session, House Executive Document 23. Washington, D. C., 1868.

The War of the Rebellion: A Compilation of the Official Records of the Union and Confederate Armies. Washington, D. C., 1880–1901.

Watkins, Sam R. *"Co. Aytch," Maury Grays, First Tennessee Regiment: or, A Side Show of the Big Show.* New York: Macmillan Publishing Co./Collier Books, 1962.

Whitman, Walt. *Memoranda During the War.* 1875. Reprint. Boston: Applewood Books, 1990.

CENSUS RECORDS

1850 Census. Population Schedules: Tennessee. Giles County, roll 879.

———. Population Schedules: Tennessee. Davidson County, roll 875.

———. Slave Schedules. Fayette-Hardeman Counties, roll 903.

———. Slave Schedules. Davidson County, roll 902.

1860 Census. Population Schedules: Tennessee. Giles County, roll 1251.
————. Slave Schedules. Fayette-Hawkins Counties, roll 1282.
1870 Census. Population Schedules: Georgia. Fulton County, roll 151.
1880 Census. Population Schedules: Georgia. Cobb-Coweta (part) Counties, roll 9.
1900 Census. Population Schedules: Georgia. Fulton County, roll 198.
————. Population Schedules: Texas. Dallas (cont.), roll 1625.
1910 Census. Population Schedules: Texas. Dawson-Duval Counties, roll 1546.

PUBLISHED SECONDARY SOURCES

Adams, George W. *Doctors in Blue: The Medical History of the Union Army in the Civil War.* New York: Schuman, 1952. Reprint. Dayton: Morningside, 1985.
Ash, Stephen V. *Middle Tennessee Society Transformed, 1860–1870: War and Peace in the Upper South.* Baton Rouge: Louisiana State University Press, 1988.
Baird, Nancy D. *David Wendel Yandell: Physician of Old Louisville.* Lexington: University Press of Kentucky, 1978.
Barns, Florence Elberta. *Texas Writers of Today.* Dallas: Tardy Publishing Co., 1935.
Black, Robert C. "The Railroads of Georgia in the Confederate War Effort." *Journal of Southern History* 13 (November 1947): 510–34.
Boatner, Mark Mayo, III. *The Civil War Dictionary.* New York: David McKay Co., 1959.
Bragg, William Harris. "Charles C. Jones, Jr., and the Mystery of Lee's Lost Dispatches." *Georgia Historical Quarterly* 72 (Fall 1988): 429–62.
Breeden, James O. *Joseph Jones, M.D.: Scientist of the Old South.* Lexington: University Press of Kentucky, 1975.
————. "A Medical History of the Later Stages of the Atlanta Campaign." *Journal of Southern History* 35 (February 1969): 31–59.
Burnham, W. Dean. *Presidential Ballots, 1836–1892.* Baltimore: Johns Hopkins Press, 1955.
Calhoun, F. Phinizy. "The Founding and the Early History of the Atlanta Medical College." *Georgia Historical Quarterly* 9 (March 1925): 35–54.
Cemetery Records of Giles County, Tennessee. Pulaski, Tenn.: Giles County Historical Society, 1986.
Connelly, Thomas Lawrence. *Army of the Heartland: The Army of Tennessee, 1861–1862.* Baton Rouge: Louisiana State University Press, 1967.
————. *Autumn of Glory: The Army of Tennessee, 1862–1865.* Baton Rouge: Louisiana State University Press, 1971.
Cooling, Benjamin Franklin. *Forts Henry and Donelson: The Key to the Confederate Heartland.* Knoxville: University of Tennessee Press, 1987.

Corner, George Washington. *Two Centuries of Medicine: A History of the School of Medicine, University of Pennsylvania.* Philadelphia: Lippincott, 1965.

Coulter, E. Merton. *College Life in the Old South.* Athens: University of Georgia Press, 1928, 1951. Cox, Edwin T. *History of Eastland County, Texas.* San Antonio: The Naylor Co., 1950.

Crew, H. W. *History of Nashville, Tenn.* . . . Nashville: Publishing House of the Methodist Episcopal Church, South, 1890.

Crocker, Geraldine. "Homer Virgil Milton Miller: A Great Roman." *Georgia Life* 3 (Spring 1977): 40–41.

Cunningham, Horace H. *Doctors in Gray: The Confederate Medical Service.* Baton Rouge: Louisiana State University Press, 1958. Reprint. Gloucester, Mass.: Peter Smith, 1970.

Daniel, Larry J. *Soldiering in the Army of Tennessee: A Portrait of Life in a Confederate Army.* Chapel Hill: University of North Carolina Press, 1991.

Daniels, George H. *American Science in the Age of Jackson.* New York: Columbia University Press, 1968.

Davenport, Francis Garvin. *Cultural Life in Nashville on the Eve of the Civil War.* Chapel Hill: University of North Carolina Press, 1941.

Davis Stephen. "A Confederate Hospital." *Journal of the Medical Association of Georgia* 75 (January 1986): 14–24.

Dew, Charles B. *Ironmaker to the Confederacy: Joseph R. Anderson and the Tredegar Iron Works.* New Haven: Yale University Press, 1966.

Donald, W. J. "Alabama Confederate Hospitals." *Alabama Review* 15 (October 1962): 271–81; 16 (January 1963): 64–78.

Dorland's Illustrated Medical Dictionary. 26th ed. Philadelphia: W. B. Saunders, 1981.

Duffy, John. *The Healers: The Rise of the Medical Establishment.* New York: McGraw-Hill, 1976.

Durham, Walter T. *Nashville: The Occupied City.* Nashville: Tennessee Historical Society, 1985.

Eastwood, Bruce S. "Confederate Medical Problems in the Atlanta Campaign." *Georgia Historical Quarterly* 47 (Fall 1963): 276–92.

Emmons, Julia. "The Medical Career of Samuel H. Stout." *Journal of the Medical Association of Georgia* 69 (November 1980): 904–10; 70 (March 1981): 169–77.

Faust, Patricia L., ed. *Historical Times Illustrated Encyclopedia of the Civil War.* New York: Harper & Row, 1986.

Foster, Gaines M. *Ghosts of the Confederacy: Defeat, the Lost Cause, and the Emergence of the New South, 1865–1913.* New York: Oxford University Press, 1987.

Futch, Ovid L. *History of Andersonville Prison.* Gainesville: University of Florida Press, 1968.

Garrett, Franklin M. *Atlanta and Environs.* 2 vols. [Atlanta?]: Lewis Historical Publishing Co., 1954. Reprint. Athens: University of Georgia Press, 1969.

————. "Historic Oakland Cemetery A Tangible Link to Atlanta's Past." *Atlanta History* 32 (Spring 1988): 42–61.

Ghormley, Ruby Pearl. *Eastland County, Texas, A Historical and Biographical Survey.* Austin: Rupegy Publishing Co., 1969.

Goff, Richard D. *Confederate Supply.* Durham: Duke University Press, 1969.

Govan, Gilbert E., and James W. Livingood. *A Different Valor: The Story of General Joseph E. Johnston, C. S. A.* Indianapolis: Bobbs-Merrill Co., Inc., 1956.

Hallock, Judith Lee. *Braxton Bragg and Confederate Defeat, vol.* 2. Tuscaloosa: University of Alabama Press, 1991.

Hamer, Philip M. *The Centennial History of the Tennessee State Medical Association, 1830–1930.* Nashville: Tennessee State Medical Association, 1930.

Horsman, Reginald. *Josiah Nott of Mobile: Southerner, Physician, and Racial Theorist.* Baton Rouge: Louisiana State University Press, 1987.

Lash, Jeffrey N. *Destroyer of the Iron Horse: General Joseph E. Johnston and Confederate Rail Transport, 1861–1865.* Kent, Ohio: Kent State University Press, 1991.

Long, E. B., with Barbara Long. *The Civil War Day by Day: An Almanac, 1861–1865.* Garden City, N.Y.: Doubleday, 1971. Reprint. New York: DaCapo Press, 1985.

McDonough, James Lee. *Chattanooga—A Death Grip on the Confederacy.* Knoxville: University of Tennessee Press, 1984.

————. *Stones River—Bloody Winter in Tennessee.* Knoxville: University of Tennessee Press, 1980.

McMurry, Richard M. *John Bell Hood and the War for Southern Independence.* Lexington: University Press of Kentucky, 1982.

————. *Two Great Rebel Armies: An Essay in Confederate Military History.* Chapel Hill: University of North Carolina Press, 1989.

McPherson, James M. *Ordeal by Fire: The Civil War and Reconstruction.* New York: Alfred A. Knopf, 1982.

McWhiney, Grady. *Braxton Bragg and Confederate Defeat, vol. 1: Field Command.* New York: Columbia University Press, 1969.

Maher, Sister Mary Denis. *To Bind Up the Wounds: Catholic Sister Nurses in the U.S. Civil War.* Westport, Conn.: Greenwood Press, 1989.

Mohr, Clarence L. *On the Threshold of Freedom: Masters and Slaves in Civil War Georgia.* Athens: University of Georgia Press, 1986.

Moore, Mrs. John Trotwood. "The Tennessee Historical Society, 1849–1918." *Tennessee Historical Quarterly* 3 (September 1944): 195–225.

Moursund, Walter H. *A History of Baylor University College of Medicine.* Houston: Gulf Printing Co., 1956.

Murphy, Gregory. "The Controversy Between Dr. T. S. Powell and the Faculty of Atlanta Medical College." *Georgia Historical Quarterly* 24 (September 1940): 236–52.

National Cyclopedia of American Biography. 63 vols. New York: James T. White & Co., Publishers, 1893–1984.

Nixon, Pat I. *A History of the Texas Medical Association.* Austin: n.p., 1953.

Noll, Arthur Howard, ed. *Doctor Quintard: Chaplain C.S.A. and Second Bishop of Tennessee.* Sewanee, Tenn.: University Press of Sewanee, 1905.

Numbers, Ronald L., ed. *The Education of American Physicians: Historical Essays.* Berkeley and Los Angeles: University of California Press, 1980.

Orr, Dorothy. *A History of Education in Georgia.* Chapel Hill: University of North Carolina Press, 1950.

Peters, Thomas J., and Robert H. Waterman, Jr. *In Search of Excellence: Lessons from America's Best-Run Companies.* New York: Harper & Row, 1982.

Rosenberg, Charles E. *The Care of Strangers: The Rise of America's Hospital System.* New York: Basic Books, 1987.

Rothstein, William G. *American Medical Schools and the Practice of Medicine: A History.* New York: Oxford University Press, 1987.

Simkins, Francis B., and James W. Patton. "The Work of Southern Women Among the Sick and Wounded of the Confederate Armies." *Journal of Southern History* 1 (November 1935): 475-96.

Sklar, Kathryn Kish. "Women, Education of: History." *The Encyclopedia of Education.* New York: The Macmillan Company and The Free Press, 1971, 9:557–62.

Standard, Diffee William. *Columbus, Georgia in the Confederacy.* New York: William-Frederick Press, 1954.

Steiner, Paul E. *Diseases in the Civil War: Natural Biological Warfare in 1861–1865.* Springfield, Ill.: C. C. Thomas, 1968.

Sunseri, Alvin Raymond. "The Organization and Administration of the Medical Department of the Confederate Army of Tennessee." *Journal of the Tennessee State Medical Association* 53 Parts 1–5 (January–July 1960).

Thomas, Emory M. *The Confederate Nation.* New York: Harper & Row, 1979.

Thompson, John D., and Grace Goldin. *The Hospital: A Social and Architectural History.* New Haven: Yale University Press, 1975.

Trelease, Allen W. *White Terror: The Ku Klux Klan Conspiracy and Southern Reconstruction.* New York: Harper & Row, 1971.

Vandiver, Frank E. *Ploughshares Into Swords: Josiah Gorgas and Confederate Ordnance.* Austin: University of Texas Press, 1952.

———. *Rebel Brass: The Confederate Command System.* New York: Greenwood Press, 1956.

Warner, Ezra J., and W. Buck Yearns. *Biographical Register of the Confederate Congress.* Baton Rouge: Louisiana State University Press, 1975.

Warner, John Harley. "Power, Conflict, and Identity in Mid-Nineteenth Century American Medicine: Therapeutic Change at the Commercial Hospital in Cincinnati." *Journal of American History* 73 (March 1987): 934–56.

————. *The Therapeutic Perspective: Medical Practice, Knowledge, and Identity in America, 1820–1885.* Cambridge: Harvard University Press, 1986.

Wiley, Bell Irvin. *The Road to Appomattox.* Memphis: Memphis State College Press, 1956.

Wilson, Charles William, Jr. *State Geological Surveys and State Geologists of Tennessee: A History of the Development of the Division of Geology, Department of Conservation.* Tennessee Division of Geology *Bulletin* no. 81 (1981).

UNPUBLISHED THESES

Gassman, Wade Banister. "A History of Rome and Floyd County, Georgia in the Civil War." M. A. thesis, Emory University, 1966.

Jordan, Mildred. "Georgia's Confederate Hospitals." M. A. thesis, Emory University, 1942.

Sunseri, Alvin Raymond. "The Organization and Administration of the Medical Department of the Confederate Army of Tennessee." M. A. thesis, Louisiana State University and Agricultural and Mechanical College, 1955.

INDEX

All departments, hospitals, organizations, regiments, etc. are Confederate unless otherwise indicated.

Surgeon, of post. *See* Post surgeon
Surgeon general (or his office), 65,
   66, 68, 74, 79, 93, 112, 173;
   Union, 163. *See also* Moore,
   Samuel Preston
Surgeon in charge of a hospital, 69,
   83; duties of, 71
Surgeon in charge of hospitals. *See*
   Post surgeon
Surgeons, 50, 63–64, 69, 70,
   73, 82; acting assistant, 70
   (*see also* Surgeons, contract);
   administrative incompetence of,
   91–92; assignment of to posts, 80,
   82–86, 118, 132; assistant, 69,
   70, 73; contract, 50, 54, 55, 70,
   118; duties of, 70, 73; economic
   concerns of, 85; family concerns
   of, 85–86; field service of, 69,
   132; furlough requests of, 85–86;
   health problems of, 69, 83–85,
   90; incompetence of, 91–92,
   93; leisure activities of, 73–74;
   overworked, 63–64; transfer
   between field and hospital, 83–84
Surgery, 31–32, 38
Surrender, 147, 148
Swamps, 97
Sweet, Forrest, 183, 185

Taliaferro, Dr., 84
Tannehill, Josiah (grandfather), 25
Tannehill, Margaret Wilkins
   (grandmother), 25
Tannehill, Wilkins (uncle), 25
Tennessee: surgeons from, 92; Union
   occupation of, 86, 87
Tennessee campaign (1864), 140,
   145, 146
Tennessee Historical Society, 36,
   163, 171, 172, 185
Tennessee Medical Association, 36
Tennessee River, 145

Tennessee State Library and Archives,
   Nashville, Stout papers at, 20,
   185
Tents used by hosptials. *See* Hospital
   buildings, tents
Terrell State Hospital for the Insane
   (Tex.), 17
Terry, Carlisle, 85, 115n
Texas Central Railroad, 165–66
Texas Courier—Record of Medicine,
   169
Texas Pacific Railroad, 165–66
Theft in hospitals. *See* Hospitals,
   theft in
Third Tennessee Regiment, 17,
   41–45, 49, 50, 52, 54
Thomas, W. E., 183, 185
Thomaston, Ga., hospitals in, 138
Thompson, James L., 97, 99, 100
Thomsen, J. M., 105
Thornton, Francis, 64, 93–94;
   biography, 194–95
"Toast and water," 113
Tooth extraction, 84
Transactions, 169
Transportation: deficiencies of, 126,
   127, 129, 140–41, 143–44, 145,
   147, 148; water route, 143. *See
   also* Patients, transportation of;
   Wagon transportation
Treatments (of diseases), 32–33, 42,
   111, 164–65
Troops: depredations by (either side),
   87, 103, 106, 136, 149; Union,
   122, 124, 133, 135, 138, 146,
   152
Tullahoma, Tenn., 122
Tunnel Hill, Ga., 96, 97; hospitals in,
   60, 63, 115, 124–25, 126
Tupelo, Miss., 56
Tuscumbia, Ala., 141, 143
Tuskegee, Ala., hospitals in, 99–100
Tyler, John, 25